CW00405666

Beyond the
Self-Managing S

Student Outcomes and the Reform of Education

General Editor: Professor Brian J. Caldwell, Dean of Education, University of Melbourne, Australia

Student Outcomes and the Reform of Education is concerned with the reform of public education and its impact on outcomes for students. The reform agenda has gripped the attention of policy-makers, practitioners, researchers and scholars for much of the 1990s, with every indication of more to come with the approach of the new millennium. This series reports research and describes strategies that deal with the outcomes of reform. Without sacrificing a critical perspective the intention is to provide a guide to good practice and strong scholarship within the new arrangements that are likely to provide the framework for public education in the foreseeable future.

**School Effectiveness and School-based Management:**
**A mechanism for development**
*Yin Cheong Cheng*

**Transforming Schools Through Collaborative Leadership**
*Helen Telford*

**The Inner Principal**
*David Loader*

**The Future of School: Lessons from the Reform of Public Education**
*Brian J. Caldwell and Donald K. Hayward*

**Beyond the Self-Managing School**
*Brian J. Caldwell and Jim M. Spinks*

# Beyond the
# Self-Managing School

Brian J. Caldwell
and
Jim M. Spinks

FALMER PRESS

Taylor & Francis Group

UK      Falmer Press, 1 Gunpowder Square, London, EC4A 3DE
USA    Falmer Press, Taylor & Francis Inc., 325 Chestnut Street, 8th Floor,
          Philadelphia, PA 19106

First published in 1998

**A catalogue record for this book is available from the British Library**

ISBN 0 7507 0447 0 cased
ISBN 0 7507 0448 9 paper

**Library of Congress Cataloging-in-Publication Data are available
on request**

Jacket design by Caroline Archer

Typeset in 10/12 pt Times by
Graphicraft Ltd., Hong Kong

*Printed in Great Britain by Biddles Ltd., Guildford and King's Lynn on
paper which has a specified pH value on final paper manufacture of not
less than 7.5 and is therefore 'acid free'.*

*Every effort has been made to contact copyright holders for their
permission to reprint material in this book. The publishers would be
grateful to hear from any copyright holder who is not here acknowledged
and will undertake to rectify any errors or omissions in future editions of
this book.*

# Contents

# List of Figures

# Preface

The self-managing school is now a reality in many systems of public education around the world. This has been achieved in less than a decade and our three books on the topic span these years.

Our first book *The Self-Managing School* was published in 1988, coinciding with the Education Reform Act in Britain. The local management of schools was one of four major initiatives of the Conservative Government that drew fierce criticism from across the political and academic spectrum, invariably labelled by its critics as a market-oriented, ideologically-driven thrust of the New Right. Our third book *Beyond the Self-Managing School* is published in 1998, coinciding with a range of initiatives of the Labour Government, one of which is the extension of local management, now known as devolved funding, that significantly increases the level of financial delegation. Such was the acceptance of local management that each of the major political parties in Britain vowed to retain it in the campaign lead-up to the 1997 election. The self-managing school is a pillar of the education-oriented, standards-driven thrust of New Labour. The same settlement is likely to occur in other nations, including Australia where we have done much of our work.

We have had the opportunity to be involved in the movement to self-managing schools, including design and implementation of the approach at the school level; formulation of policy advice to governments and education authorities; training of principals, teachers and parents; and researching the processes and outcomes. We learned much along the way and shared some of this in 1992 in *Leading the Self-Managing School*. Our focus on that occasion was leadership, but we adapted our original model for self-management to take account of escalating change and increasing complexity. We do the same as the decade draws to a close and the major features of schooling in the early years of the third millennium start to take shape.

The title of this book is not intended to convey the view that the design of the self-managing school is settled. There are many issues to be resolved and many schools and school systems in nations where this book may be read are only now starting the journey. We address these issues and identify the driving and constraining forces on further developments in policy and practice.

We sense that there are three 'tracks' for change in school education, with schools and nations varying in the speed and extent of their journeys. Building systems of self-managing schools is just one track; the others concern the unrelenting focus on learning outcomes and the creation of schools for the knowledge society. The first is primarily a structural reform; the others shift attention to learning and teaching and the nature of school education in the twenty-first century. In one sense, this takes us full circle, because the central feature of the model for self-management in our first book was the organization of school management around programs for learning and teaching and the support of learning and teaching.

The first two books were intended to serve as guides to good practice in self-management. The first described and illustrated an approach to goal-setting, policy-making, planning, budgeting, implementing, and evaluating, organized around learning and teaching, with important and over-lapping roles for policy groups and program teams. The second was organized around four dimensions of leadership, namely, strategic leadership, cultural leadership, educational leadership and responsive leadership. A concern for practice also underpins the approach in our third book. We suggest a range of 'strategic intentions' that might form the starting point for more detailed planning at the school level. Each chapter concludes with 10 strategic intentions on a theme, making a total of 100 for the book.

We extend our appreciation to those who provided the opportunity for us to learn more about the self-managing school. Don Hayward, Minister for Education in Victoria from 1992 to 1996 invited involvement in aspects of the design and implementation of Schools of the Future that allowed take-up of approaches outlined in our second book. The Cooperative Research Project, initiated by principals and chaired by Fay Thomas, resulted in a unique partnership of the Education Department, Victorian Association of State Secondary Principals, Victorian Primary Principals Association and the University of Melbourne, in a five-year longitudinal study of the processes and outcomes of Schools of the Future, findings of which are included in Chapter 3. Two projects commissioned by the Department of Employment, Education, Training and Youth Affairs in Australia provided the opportunity to gather more information about outcomes, especially the impact on student learning, and on administrative and regulatory mechanisms that drive and constrain further developments in self-management. Findings from the reports of these projects have been incorporated in Chapters 3 and 4.

Professor Michael Barber helped us gain an understanding of the new agenda in school education, giving generously of his time, first in 1996 while serving as Dean of Innovations at the Institute of Education in London, and then in 1997, following the election of New Labour, after he took up the post of head of the Standards and Effectiveness Unit in the Department for Education and Employment. Professor Peter Hill, University of Melbourne, showed us the possibilities for learning through his landmark research on classroom effectiveness, especially in the field of literacy. Principal Janice Szmal and her literacy team at Mackellar Primary School provided the case study reported in Chapter 3. Our ideas on schooling for the knowledge society owe much to the insights of Emeritus Professor Hedley Beare, University of Melbourne; David Loader, Principal of Wesley College and former Principal, Methodist Ladies College in Melbourne; and author, broadcaster, researcher and teacher, Dale Spender. Andrew Bunting and John Wood of the Sainsbery Reed Group in Melbourne, contributed text and school designs for Chapter 8.

We are especially appreciative of the encouragement and support of our senior colleagues at the University of Melbourne and the Department of Education, Community and Cultural Development in Tasmania, especially Professor Kwong Lee Dow, who models the art of strategic conversation described in Chapter 10.

We sense that the means are at hand to create and sustain a system of world-class schools, being self-managing and well-suited to the needs of all students in the knowledge society. We hope this book helps fit the pieces together and keeps the focus on learning.

Brian J. Caldwell
Jim M. Spinks

# Acknowledgments

The authors and publisher wish to thank Elsevier Science for their kind permission to reproduce Figure 3.5 Integrated model of school effectiveness reprinted from J. Scheerens and R. Bosker, (1997), p. 46.

# *Tracks for Change in a New Era for Schools*

# Chapter 1

# Tracks for Change in a New Era for Schools

The last two decades have seen continuous change in schools around the world. Teachers are wondering if it will ever stop. Citizens are wondering if government and the profession will ever get it right.

The premise of this book is that the means are at hand to create a system of public schools that will provide a high quality of education for all students and that will be professionally rewarding for teachers and other professionals. The challenge is how to put the pieces together.

The spirit of this book is one of optimism because these things can be done and a new era for schools is about to unfold. The challenge is how to energize those whose commitment and capacities are required to make it happen.

The book is titled *Beyond the Self-Managing School* for two reasons. First, because recent efforts to improve the quality of education have involved the shifting of a significant amount of authority, responsibility, and accountability to schools, that is, schools have become more self-managing. This essentially structural reform has now settled in several countries and the question arises, at least in structural terms: 'What lies beyond the self-managing school?'

The second reason for *Beyond the Self-Managing School* is that we have already written two books on the topic, the first a decade ago when the movement to self-management was gathering momentum. For the authors and those who have followed our work, the question may be posed: 'What do we envisage in a new era of school education?'

## Completing the Trilogy

In the opening lines of *The Self-Managing School* (Caldwell and Spinks, 1988), we suggested that the title would most likely be greeted with incredulity because the view that schools in systems of public education could manage themselves would be foreign to most readers. Such practice was to become a reality within months of publication because the 1988 Education Reform Act in Britain provided for the local management of schools, or local financial management as it was initially known.

In the years to follow, *The Self-Managing School* was to become a helpful guide for school leaders in Britain, and soon after in New Zealand. We were personally involved in a range of in-service programs in both nations as well as our own, for the seminal ideas for the book came from a nationally funded research project on effective schools in Australia in 1983, with immediate take-up over three years in Victoria from 1984 to 1986, where a limited initiative in self-management was under way.

Our work in different countries following publication of *The Self-Managing School* allowed us to learn more about expectations for leadership in self-managing schools. It was also apparent in the late 1980s and early 1990s that the model for collaborative school management in *The Self-Managing School* was not robust enough to cope with the complexity of school operations. The model was based on an annual planning cycle but the rate of change and escalating expectations meant that a multi-year time-frame was required. We refined the model and outlined four dimensions of leadership. We also proposed a school charter to serve as a stabilizing mechanism to manage system and local expectations. The outcome was *Leading the Self-Managing School* (Caldwell and Spinks, 1992).

Since 1992 our interests have spanned the domains of policy, practice and research in the manner described in Chapter 2. We come to 1998, exactly a decade after the publication of *The Self-Managing School*, to find that the phenomenon about which we wrote in 1988 has now settled in several countries to the point that it is essentially irreversible, at least in the foreseeable future. This is especially the case in Britain with the election in May 1997 of a Labour Government that has maintained the framework for the local management of schools. Indeed, the 1997 election campaign was astonishing in the manner in which this and other key elements in the framework provided by the 1988 Education Reform Act had been accepted. This was a far cry from the time of publication of *The Self-Managing School*, where most of these elements were opposed by significant interests in the political, educational and academic domains. There is now a settlement on the local management of schools; indeed, it seemed that the three major parties in Britain were competing in the lead up to the 1997 election in their promises on what proportion of the total available budget should be decentralized to schools.

These observations should not be construed as an indication that all is well with public education and that local management is sufficient in itself to make a lasting contribution to school reform, or that there are not unresolved issues to be addressed. In the short term, what ought to be done to ensure that the self-managing school works efficiently and effectively as one element of reform that contributes to the achievement of a high quality of education for all students? Taking a strategic view, what ought to be done now to prepare for possible and preferred futures in public education? What guidelines can be gleaned from recent experience for those who have roles to play? These are the questions we seek to explore in *Beyond the Self-Managing School*.

### Revisiting the Concept of Self-Management

A self-managing school is a school in a system of education to which there has been decentralized a significant amount of authority and responsibility to make decisions related to the allocation of resources within a centrally determined framework of goals, policies, standards and accountabilities. Resources are defined broadly to include knowledge, technology, power, material, people, time, assessment, information and finance (Caldwell and Spinks, 1988, p. 5; Bullock and Thomas, 1997, pp. 1–2).

A self-managing school is not an autonomous school nor is it a self-governing school, for each of these kinds of schools involve a degree of independence that is not provided in a centrally determined framework. The existence of a centrally determined framework implies that a self-managing school is part of a system of schools, so the concept applies most readily to systems of government or public schools, or to systems of non-government or private schools where there has been decentralization, such as in some systems of Catholic schools. Truly independent, non-systemic schools would ordinarily be considered self-governing schools.

Systems of self-managing public schools differ in important ways as far as ownership of schools is concerned. In Australia, all schools in systems of public education are owned by the government. Australians are often astonished to find that schools that are owned privately, or by trusts, or by churches have been integrated into the system of public education, as with aided schools in Britain (Halls, 1994, p. 6518). Similarly in New Zealand where the Private Schools Conditional Integration Act of 1975 allowed the voluntary integration of private schools and the state system (Barrington, 1994, p. 4106). In The Netherlands, there is an almost seamless integration of all kinds of schools, for the Constitution guarantees the financial equality of public authority and private schools (Vuyk, 1994). (See Caldwell and Hayward, 1998, for a policy framework for the integration of public and private schools.)

It is not intended in this concept of self-managing school that authority be decentralized for its own sake, without consideration of what the school does with that authority. The attachment of responsibility and accountability to the concept implies that this authority is concerned with determining the particular ways in which the school goes about its affairs in addressing the goals, policies, standards and accountabilities that have been centrally determined for all schools in the system as well, of course, in addressing these same matters as they may be unique in the local setting.

Self-management is an appropriate generic term to describe the practice. It is manifested in several ways in these places, most notably in Britain, where it is known as the local management of schools. School self-management is not synonymous with school-based management, or site-based management, as these terms are used in the United States, for while they apply to schools in systems of public education, too often the practices to which they refer are not tightly connected to the centrally determined framework that is an important element in the definition. Expressed another way, school-based management has been implemented in some places almost as an end in itself, to simply empower particular individuals and groups at the local level, which may of course be a worthy intention in its own right, but it does not go far enough in this manifestation to warrant designation as school self-management as defined above.

## What has been Accomplished

It is helpful at the outset to provide some brief descriptions of the concept in practice. These are presented, in order, from Britain, Australia, New Zealand, Canada, the United States and China (Hong Kong) (see Whitty, Power and Halpin, 1998 for an account of developments in Australia, England and Wales, New Zealand, Sweden and the United States). May 1, 1998 is selected as the end point, for this marked the completion of twelve months of government by New Labour in Britain. It is sufficient time to judge the manner in which electoral intentions have been translated into legislative priorities and actions, putting a stamp on the kind of schools that will characterize the new era in Britain.

*Britain*

The most extensive practice as far as the main readership of this book is concerned is in Britain, in England and Wales, where there are about 24,000 self-managed schools in 104 local education authorities. Known as the local management of schools, its chief features involve the decentralization to the school level of at least 85 per cent of the available local education authority budget, the only exceptions being for certain support and capital expenses that are deemed appropriate for the authority to manage. In some instances, the amount decentralized exceeds 90 per cent, and it is the broad intention that all schools enjoy at least this level of self-management, with a preference closer to 95 per cent now widely embraced, without sacrificing the role of the local education authority.

Consistent with the definition of self-management offered above, there is a centrally determined framework in the form of a national curriculum, prepared in the early 1990s but extensively revised after wide dissatisfaction. This framework sets out expectations in learning areas in four key stages of schooling. There is also provision for testing of students in some of these key learning areas, with tests at two stages of primary (elementary) and one stage at secondary, with publication of results on a school-by-school basis in what are known as 'league tables'. Completing the accountability framework are school inspections conducted under the auspices of the Office for Standards in Education (OFSTED), in which teams of inspectors from the public and private sectors are contracted to conduct inspections of schools, with summary reports made available to all parents.

A key feature of the 1988 Education Reform Act was the provision for schools to opt out of control by their local education authorities and become 'grant maintained', thus securing additional resources which are notionally equivalent to the value of services previously provided by the authority. Ownership of the school shifted from the authority to the governing body, as did the contracts of teachers who were employed by the schools. Public funds to grant maintained schools were dispersed by a national organization, the Funding Agency for Schools. While the Labour Party committed itself to maintaining the broad features of grant maintained schools, it became clear in the early months of the new government that the nature of these schools would change in important ways.

Clearly, locally managed schools are self-managing schools. Grant maintained schools were often presented as self-governing schools and they were, to the extent that ownership has shifted from the authority to the board of governors. In general, however, they may be considered further along a continuum of self-managed schools since they still worked within the nationally determined frameworks of the National Curriculum, the testing program with listing in the 'league tables', and accountability through the inspection process and, for funding, to the Funding Agency for Schools.

Whilst initially contentious, there was agreement among the three major political parties that local management was one of the 'success stories' of the Education Reform Act of 1988, and it is clear that this manifestation of the self-managing school is here to stay. Indeed, a significant increase in the level of financial delegation, to be known as Devolved Funding, to take effect from April 1999, was proposed in a Consultation Paper in mid-1998 (Department for Education and Employment, 1998).

After just a few months in power, Labour made clear its intention to focus on standards, not structures and to balance pressure and support in the pursuit of that end (Secretary of State for Education and Employment, 1997). A Standards and Effectiveness Unit was established and special education zones were created, with a role for private bodies in helping raise the level of achievement in these areas where it was lower than it ought to be. All local education authorities must set targets for improvement in student learning.

Grant maintained schools have been returned to control by local education authorities, with most opting for 'foundation' status in a new scheme for the classification of schools, but maintaining a higher degree of autonomy than authority owned 'community' schools. The Funding Agency for Schools has been abolished. The achievements of grant maintained schools are considerable, even though the total never exceeded about 5 per cent. Whether viewed as an opportunity or a threat, they helped challenge the local authority to be more responsive to schools, and this is a good starting point for a culture that heightens the value placed on standards and support.

*Australia*

There has been a steady shift to self-management in Australia over the last 25 years, with the Australian Capital Territory and South Australia making the first moves, followed by Tasmania. A major thrust was made in Victoria in the 1980s, with significant development in the Northern Territory. Momentum in Victoria stalled toward the end of the decade and New South Wales moved ahead until the early 1990s when resistance to further change was evident. Victoria then achieved dramatic change from 1993 to 1996 with its Schools of the Future program, described in more detail below. By 1998, Queensland and Tasmania had taken significant steps through programs titled, respectively, Leading Schools and Directions in Education. Modest developments were evident in Western Australia throughout this period.

After Britain, perhaps the most noteworthy manifestation of self-managing schools is in Victoria. In 1983, the Labor Government gave school councils the authority to determine the education policy of the school, within guidelines provided by the Minister for Education, and to approve the budget. A recommendation in 1986 for a more expansive form of self-management was rejected after powerful opposition from the teacher unions, parent organizations and elements of the bureaucracy and little happened in this domain until late 1992, with the defeat of the Labor Government and the election of a Liberal National Coalition Government that had the immediate task of addressing an unacceptable level of state debt and a precarious budget situation. At the same time, it determined to proceed with a package of reforms that included self-management on a scale that approximates that achieved in Britain for the local management of schools.

In Victoria there is now a curriculum and standards framework that covers all years of primary and secondary schooling, the capacity for schools to select their own staff, the decentralization of more than 90 per cent of the state education budget to schools, and an accountability framework that provides annual reports to the Education Department and community, and a triennial review that provides for external validation. A mechanism that gives a high measure of coherence to the whole arrangement is the school charter, a document of about 20 pages that sets out the distinctive nature of the school and the manner in which it addresses system and local priorities. The charter has a life of three years, and the triennial review is intended to guide the review of the school charter.

The second term of the Liberal National Coalition from 1996 has seen a consolidation of Schools of the Future, with a modest initiative under the banner of Schools of the Third Millennium in which some schools may seek a higher level of autonomy. As in Britain under New Labour, attention is turning to standards rather than structures, with the reports emanating from the triennial reviews providing a starting point.

### New Zealand

After Britain and Victoria, the most comprehensive reforms with a high level of self-management may be found in New Zealand. They followed soon after those in Britain and were a response to a review of the administration of the public school system in New Zealand (Task Force to Review Educational Administration, 1988). Implemented under the umbrella of *Tomorrow's Schools*, a high level of self-management was intended, with a scaled down Education Department and a national curriculum and accountability framework. The roles of school boards and committees were strengthened. Most of these reforms were implemented but they stopped short of what occurred in Britain and Victoria in respect to budgeting for staff. To date, only a small number of schools are budgeting for all staff with full flexibility.

*Canada*

In North America, the most notable initiative in self-management until recently was in Canada, in the urban Edmonton Public School District in the province of Alberta. This commenced as a small-scale seven school pilot project in school-based budgeting in the late 1970s (see Brown, 1990; Caldwell, 1977) but expanded to include all of more than 200 schools in the district from the early 1980s. The program was refined and institutionalized under the leadership of long-serving school superintendent Michael Strembitsky.

It is now intended that all school districts in Alberta develop the same capacity in self-management and the Edmonton approach has served as a model for similar developments in British Columbia, notably in Langley, whose superintendent Emery Dosdall returned to Edmonton to succeed Strembitsky as superintendent in the mid-1990s.

While the early focus in Edmonton was on school-based budgeting, the system had a well-defined framework of district priorities and accountability mechanisms, with a key role for assessment against standards and opinion surveys. In these respects, it has served as a model for self-management from the time of its inception.

*United States*

There have been many initiatives in school-based management in the United States over nearly thirty years, but they have taken so many forms and have been implemented with so many purposes that it is difficult to generalize. In the early stages, developments in New York attracted attention, but they were limited to decentralization to the sub-district level. There were significant developments in California and Florida in the 1970s, and more in Florida, notably in Dade County, in the 1980s. The Chicago reforms of the 1990s have been notable, especially in respect to the empowerment of school councils. Only rarely did these developments involve a centrally determined framework of the kind that emerged in Britain and Victoria.

A notable development in the mid-1990s was the inclusion of proposals for school-based management in most of the school and school system designs in the initiative known as New American Schools (see accounts in Stringfield, Ross and Smith, 1996). Indeed, it is hard to find a proposal for reform that does not include such an element, increasingly with provision for a tight linkage with a centrally determined framework, the main feature of which is a curriculum and standards framework. An interesting link with pioneering practice elsewhere was the appointment of Michael Strembitsky from Edmonton to the National Alliance for Restructuring Education in the United States. The Alliance works with some of the largest states and school districts to generate designs for standards based reforms, with a significant place for school-based management. An example of comprehensive reform that integrates a high level of decentralized decision-making within a centrally determined framework may be found in Seattle Public Schools, where funds have been decentralized to the school level. Seattle provides a model for transparency, since the funding mechanism is fully accessible on the internet, so schools anywhere can model their resource entitlements under the scheme in operation in that city. The self-managing school is thus starting to emerge in the United States.

The most important manifestation of the self-managing school in the United States is the charter school movement. These are a kind of US counterpart to the grant maintained schools in Britain but, in important ways, they go further. About half of the states have adopted legislation that allows an organization to assume control of or start up a school that is fully funded from the public purse and receives a charter from the state. It is free of many of the constraints that bind schools that remain in school districts. They must accept all students that apply, up to their capacity, with the range of clientele determined in the main by the special programs that are offered in this distinctive collection of schools. There are relatively few charter schools but the movement captured national attention, including that of President Clinton, who proposed in his 1997 budget that federal support for their initiation double to about US$100 million. Even though there are still less than 1,000 charter schools in the United States, about 1 per cent of the total, they must be considered a significant development in the movement to self-managing schools.

### China (Hong Kong)

There have also been important developments in the self-managing school in Hong Kong, where the concept helped shape the School Management Initiative (SMI) that got under way in the early 1990s following a review of the public sector. Only 8 per cent of Hong Kong's approximately 1,200 schools are government schools, the rest are in the so-called aided sector, owned by a range of foundations, trusts, churches and private organizations. All receive substantial funding from government. There are very few truly private schools. Under the SMI, a larger proportion of government grants was to be decentralized to the school level for local decision-making, with schools to involve the community and their teachers more in decision-making and to adopt new accountability mechanisms. By 1998, just over 200 schools had volunteered to join the scheme, including most government schools.

### Summary

In general, one is hard pressed to find any system of education in any country that has not endeavoured to decentralize some measure of authority, responsibility and accountability to the school level in recent years, at the same time that centrally determined frameworks have been maintained if not strengthened. In respect to the latter, one can equally observe a trend to establish curriculum and standards frameworks with a range of accountability measures where these have not existed before.

There is thus the paradox of simultaneous centralization and decentralization. An issue has been the linkage between these frameworks and capacities at the school level that come with self-management on the one hand, and learning outcomes for students on the other. Evidence of such linkage is described in Chapter 3.

### Beyond the Self-Managing School

It was observed at the start of Chapter 1 that it is now a decade since *The Self-Managing School* was published. In 1988 it seemed that the idea of the self-managing school was radical if not unrealistic, and it was certainly contentious since, as the opening pages of the book pointed out, it was a key feature of reforms under the 1988 Education Reform Act in the UK, initiated by the market-oriented Conservative Government led by Margaret Thatcher. Now, ten years later, *Beyond the Self-Managing School* is published at a time when the self-managing school is an accepted and widely applauded feature of the educational scene in Britain to the point that none of the three major political parties intend to retreat from it, and the Labour Government is moving beyond the self-managing school to address important unresolved issues in an effort to achieve lasting school reform.

This book is concerned with the outcomes of the self-managing school, paying particular attention to problems of implementation, unintended consequences, and unfulfilled expectations. Matters raised by the critics of the self-managing are addressed, but the intention is to move beyond the structural rearrangements that have been a feature of the introduction of self-managing schools, shifting the focus to improving the quality of learning and teaching, increasing performance and achieving the best possible outcomes for all students. At the same time, it is noted that technology, in particular, is changing the nature of learning and teaching. Indeed an epic transformation of society is under way as it speeds into the information age and the knowledge society. The challenges to the school are profound and how the self-managing school should respond is an important issue to address.

### Tracking Change in School Education

A review of developments around the world suggests that there are three different movements under way. The image of a 'track' rather than 'stage' seems appropriate, because the three movements are occurring at the same time in most places: schools, school systems and nations vary in the distance they have moved down each track.

- Track 1: Building systems of self-managing schools

- Track 2: Unrelenting focus on learning outcomes

- Track 3: Creating schools for the knowledge society

*Track 1: Building Systems of Self-Managing Schools*

The shifting of significant responsibility, authority and accountability to the school level within a curriculum and standards framework, with new alignments of personnel and other resource functions, will likely become the norm for the management of schools in the public sector. On the evidence available, no system that has moved in this direction is likely to return to arrangements that provided good service over much of the last century but are now obsolete.

Information technology is critically important for change on Track 1. Indeed, much of what has occurred in the self-management and accountability components of local management could not have been achieved without the still-expanding capacities in this area.

*Track 2: Unrelenting Focus on Learning Outcomes*

Restructuring on one track alone will not, by itself, have an enduring impact on the quality of schooling. New responsibilities, authorities and accountabilities must be used to improve learning and teaching. Evidence of how this has been accomplished is now emerging. Really significant change now depends on schools taking up and applying knowledge about school and classroom effectiveness and improvement, and this body of knowledge is richer and deeper than ever. There are some imperatives around which consensus is building, including early literacy, adoption of approaches that smooth the transition from primary to secondary, and managing increasingly complex arrangements in programs at senior secondary. 'Unrelenting' is an appropriate word to describe the commitment that will be required to ensure that all students learn well.

Much change on Track 2 is energized by advances in technology, not least in respect to the liberation of teachers and learners who have access to the lessons of the world's best teachers and whose learning may be customized without reference to dog-eared lesson plans and worksheets that still constrain many classrooms.

*Track 3: Creating Schools for the Knowledge Society*

The third track for change in school education cannot be described in detail but may be presented as a vision, illustrated in a *gestalt* in Figure 1.1: a perceived organized whole that is more than the sum of its parts.

It is schooling for the knowledge society, because those who manage information to solve problems, provide service or create new products form the largest group in the workforce, displacing industrial workers, who formed the largest group following the industrial revolution and who, in turn, displaced agricultural and domestic workers who dominated in pre-industrial times.

In this *gestalt* for schooling in the third millennium:

*Figure 1.1   A vision for schooling in the knowledge society illustrated in a* gestalt

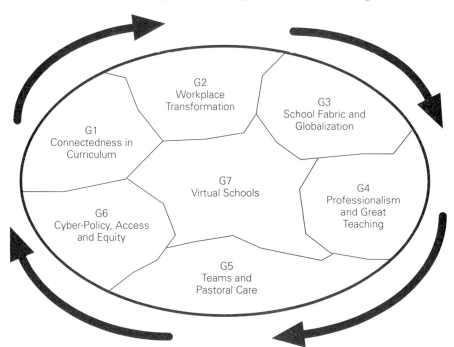

- Dramatic change in approaches to learning and teaching is in store as electronic networking allows 'cutting across and so challenging the very idea of subject boundaries' and 'changing the emphasis from impersonal curriculum to excited live exploration', to use the words of Seymour Papert in *The Children's Machine* (Papert, 1993). At risk is the balkanized curriculum that has done much to alienate children from schooling, especially in the middle years of the transition from primary to secondary (g1 Connectedness in curriculum).

- Schools as workplaces are transformed in every dimension, including the scheduling of time for learning and approaches to human resource management, rendering obsolete most approaches that derive from an industrial age, including the concept of 'industrial relations' (g2 Workplace transformation).

- The fabric of schooling is similarly rendered obsolete by electronic networking. Everything from building design to the size, shape, alignment, and furnishing of space for the 'knowledge worker' in the school is transformed. In one sense, of course, the school has no walls, for there are global learning networks. Much of the learning that previously called for the student to be located at school occurs in many places, at home, and at the upper years of secondary schooling and for lifelong learning, at the work place (g3 School fabric and globalization).

• A wide range of professionals and para-professionals support learning in an educational parallel to the diversity of support that may be found in modern health care. The role of teacher is elevated, for it demands wisdom, judgment, and a facility to manage learning in modes more complex and varied than ever. While the matter of intellectual capital must be resolved, the teacher is freed from the impossible task of designing from their own resources learning experiences to challenge every student: the resources of the world's great teachers will be at hand (g4 Professionalism and great teaching).

• A capacity to work in teams is more evident in approaches to learning, given the primacy of the work team in every formulation of the workplace in the knowledge society. This, of course, will confound those who see electronic networking in an outdated stereotype of the loner with the laptop. The concept of 'pastoral care' of students is as important as ever for learning in this mode, and in schools that quite literally have no boundaries ( g5 Teams and pastoral care).

• Dale Spender's challenge in *Nattering on the Net* (Spender, 1995) to formulate 'cyber-policy of the future' is a priority. The issues of access and equity will drive public debate until such time as prices fall to make electronic networks as common as the telephone or radio, and that may soon be a reality, given trends in networked computers (g6 Cyber-policy, access and equity).

• The concept of the virtual organization or the learning network organization is a reality in the knowledge society. Schools take on many of the characteristics of such organizations, given that learning occurs in so many modes and from so many sources, all networked electronically (g7 Virtual schools).

*Horizons of Change*

It is helpful to have some sense of time and distance in this view of change in education. How far down each track have different systems moved? How long will it take to progress down each track?

On the basis of the review presented in this chapter, it seems that Britain has largely completed reform on Track 1. Since that reform began on a national scale in 1988, a period of about 10 years seems an appropriate indicator for the amount of time it takes to move a nation. Some local authorities moved earlier, notably Cambridgeshire, and some authorities and schools within authorities were able to move quickly, once the framework for reform had been established. For participants, the decade it took to transform the nation to self-management was not long enough, or too long, depending on how one valued and experienced what occurred, for it was traumatic for many, especially when so many other changes were occurring at the same time.

The same time-frame is suggested by experience in New Zealand, where momentum for reform was at its peak in the late 1980s. Experience in Australia, as illustrated in Victoria, was a little different, for it occurred in two parts. The first began in the late 1970s, with the creation of school councils, reaching a peak in the period under Labor from 1983 to 1986, when the movement stalled. The second part took place under the Liberal National Coalition and this occurred from 1993 to 1996. Taken together, a period of 10 years is suggested for the transformation of the system.

These are the experiences of nations that have largely completed their journey down Track 1. What of Track 2? For Britain, momentum is now building for the journey down this track, and on the basis of the evidence, at least the full period of the first term of New Labour is indicated. This is not to say that there was no movement down this track in the decade of movement down Track 1. There was, because key elements in the 1988 Education Reform Act were concerned with the raising of standards. As will be clear in Chapter 3, however, there is little evidence that approaches to learning and teaching changed in a fundamental way during this time. The same may be said of Victoria, Australia, despite initiatives in fields such as early literacy where there is powerful evidence of a change in practice and increases in levels of student achievement. As reported in Chapter 3, the majority of principals believe there has been an improvement in outcomes for students. It took until 1998, after a bi-furcated journey down Track 1, for momentum to build for unrelenting attention to learning and teaching. To complete the journey, based on progress and intentions in both countries, a period of 5 to 10 years is indicated for the transformation of the system.

A similar analysis may be offered for movement on Track 3 where developments have been under way for some time. Some schools are already well down the track. Interestingly, momentum for movement down Tracks 2 and 3 is building at the same time for a variety of reasons, not least of which is realization that information and communications technology can make a contribution in the effort to improve learning. Moreover, it can help complete a successful journey down Track 1. A pre-condition for self-management is a capacity for the management of information. In a sense, the journey on Track 3 will not be completed, since developments are increasing at an exponential rate. It is likely that a decade will be required for all schools to reach what is currently viewed as 'best practice'.

Taken together, allowing for overlapping developments on the three tracks, it is likely that at least two decades will have elapsed since the decision to restructure systems of public education to the time when there is general consensus that all students are receiving a high quality education and are learning well, with this learning and the efforts of teachers and other professionals supported by state-of-the-art technology. Some nations have barely started, but it is likely that their journey may be completed in shorter time, if there is the will to make that journey and lessons are learned from experience in other places.

For all nations, however, the future is now, since every element in the *gestalt* is evident somewhere. The detail will be clearer as the years advance, as opportunities are sensed and seized, as new factors come in to play, and as exemplars emerge. What an exciting era for education!

### Mapping the Terrain

It is the purpose of this book to map some of the terrain to be covered in moving down the three tracks 'beyond the self-managing school'. In Chapter 1, the concept of 'tracks' in accounting for change in schools was introduced. Chapters 2 to 4 deal with Track 1. Chapter 2 contains an assessment of progress in the creation of systems of self-managing schools and the take up of what was proposed in *The Self-Managing School* (Caldwell and Spinks, 1988) and *Leading the Self-Managing School* (Caldwell and Spinks, 1992). Matters raised by critics are addressed. In Chapter 3, evidence of the impact that self-management has made thus far on learning outcomes for students is assessed. Promising links between self-management and outcomes are explored. In Chapter 4, driving and constraining forces that appear to affect progress down Track 1 are identified and ways for changing the balance to help complete the journey are suggested. The focus in Chapter 4 is Australia, with illustrations from other nations.

Chapters 5 and 6 are concerned with Track 2, namely, an unrelenting focus on learning outcomes. The starting point in Chapter 5 is the new agenda in school reform as illustrated in the actions taken thus far by New Labour in Britain. It is self-evident that improvement in outcomes can only be secured if there is improvement in approaches to learning and teaching. This is the central concern in Chapter 6, where knowledge and skills for teaching are identified. The new era is characterized by a 'new professionalism' and its major dimensions are explored in this chapter.

Chapters 7 to 10 provide a glimpse of the terrain for the journey along Track 3 that sees the creation of schools for the knowledge society. One cannot be specific beyond the next few years because many breathtaking, unknowable possibilities surely lie ahead. Chapter 7 describes the new environment for schools, and reference is made to the concept of 'the knowledge society' and 'the civil society', drawing on the work of Peter Drucker (1993, 1995), William Bridges (1995), Dale Spender (1995, 1997) and Jeremy Rifkin (1996) to help build a framework to guide the effort in schools. Chapter 8 provides illustrations of approaches to learning and teaching in this era. The *gestalt* in Figure 1.1 provides the framework for this chapter (g1–g3 in Figure 1.1). In Chapter 9 the *gestalt* is completed (g4–g7 in Figure 1.1), with further consideration of the 'new professionalism' considered in Chapter 6. Chapter 10 explores requirements for leadership and management for schools in the third millennium. A model for strategic management is provided to extend the work in the first two books in the trilogy. *The Self-Managing School* (Caldwell and Spinks, 1988) had a focus on year-to-year operational planning. *Leading the Self-Managing School* (Caldwell and Spinks, 1992) added a strategic dimension as a guide to managing continuous and often turbulent change. Operational planning and strategic planning are as important as ever, but the new era for schools demands a higher level of flexibility, and the concepts of 'strategic thinking' and 'strategic intention' are added to the repertoire. The art of 'strategic conversation', based on the work of Hirschhorn (1997) and van der Heijden (1997), is added to the requirements for leadership. Leadership in a new era for schools is viewed as the heroic quest in learning.

The first two books were intended to be guides to practice for leaders and managers in schools as well as explorations of the theme of self-management on the basis of research and experience. The balance in *Beyond the Self-Managing School* shifts to the latter, but guides to practice are still central to the purpose. These guides are presented as a set of 10 'strategic intentions for schools' at the conclusion of each chapter. The outcome is 100 strategic intentions that are brought together in Chapter 11. It is hoped that they will make a contribution to a successful journey 'beyond the self-managing school'.

## Strategic Intentions for Schools
## Tracks for Change

1  Centrally determined frameworks of goals, policies, priorities, curriculum, standards and accountabilities will be strengthened.

2  More authority, responsibility and accountability will be decentralized to schools.

3  There will be unrelenting pressure to achieve high levels of learning outcomes for all students.

4  Schools will play an important role in the knowledge society and advances in technology will be central to this effort.

5  There will be a high level of coherence across areas of the curriculum, schools as workplaces will be transformed, the existing fabric of schools will be rendered obsolete, and globalization will be evident in learning and teaching.

6  A new concept of professionalism will emerge, based around necessary and unprecedentedly high levels of knowledge and skill.

7  A capacity to work in teams will be required in virtually every facet of professional practice.

8  Policies to address issues of access and equity will be required for the successful utilization of information and communications technology.

9  Virtual schooling will be a reality in every setting, but there will always be a place called school.

10  A continually updated 10-year time horizon will be necessary for every school to plan the journey along these tracks for change.

# *Building Systems of Self-Managing Schools*

# Chapter 2

# Models for Self-Management

While much progress has been made on Track 1, namely the creation of systems of self-managing schools, it is helpful to assess the value of models for self-management to determine their applicability as that journey continues. In respect to the models outlined in *The Self-Managing School* (Caldwell and Spinks, 1988) and *Leading the Self-Managing School* (Caldwell and Spinks, 1992), which elements proved helpful? What aspects were not taken up? What did the critics say? How did we respond? We address these questions in this chapter in what is a personal account of our work as much as it is a report on events in the journeys of others.

### Model for Management in *The Self-Managing School*

The model for self-management in *The Self-Managing School* (Caldwell and Spinks, 1988), as illustrated in Figure 2.1 (p. 239), had its origins in research in Australia in 1983 that was funded as a Project of National Significance by the Commonwealth Schools Commission. The school effectiveness movement was gathering momentum at this time, as was interest in how schools were allocating resources in their budgets, for it was in the 1970s that education authorities in Australia, like their counterparts in other nations, made funds available for schools to address the needs of particular groups of students. Reflecting these developments, Brian Caldwell, then at the University of Tasmania, secured a grant for research under the title of the Effective Resource Allocation in Schools Project.

The research was conducted in Tasmania and South Australia, the two states that had decentralized more resources for school operations than any other (see accounts in Caldwell, 1986; Curtis, 1986; Misko, 1986a, 1986b; Smith, 1986). Panels of knowledgable people nominated two groups of schools: those considered highly effective in a general sense, and those considered highly effective in the manner in which they allocated resources. Panels were provided with two sets of characteristics to guide their nomination, the first drawn from a comprehensive review of the literature on school effectiveness that was in existence at the time, the second from a review of literature on exemplary approaches to resource allocation, generally and in schools. A feature of the second list was a demonstrated capacity to link the use of resources to the central purpose of the organization which, in the case of schools, is learning. Many nominations were secured from public (government) and private (non-government) schools, and those that were nominated most frequently in each category were selected for study.

The school that was nominated most frequently in Tasmania was Rosebery District High School, a K–10 school on the remote west coast of the state. Jim Spinks was Principal at Rosebery. Research revealed that, more than any other school, Rosebery had all of the characteristics of effective resource allocation, and all in the school community who participated in the study were able to articulate the approach that had been adopted. It was understandable that this approach featured in the recommendations of the Effective Resource Allocation in Schools Project.

The findings from the project were the focus of a summer conference held at the University of Tasmania in January 1984 attended by system and school personnel from South Australia, Tasmania and Victoria. There was immediate take up of the findings and recommendations in Victoria where the Labor Government led by John Cain was making major changes in school education through the Minister for Education, Robert Fordham. Changes to the Education Act in 1983 had given school councils the power to set educational policy for the school, within guidelines provided by the Minister, and to approve the school budget. At the same time, the Government had introduced a form of program budgeting to all public sector services and sought a training program for schools to develop the requisite knowledge and skills for principals and other school leaders as well as for school councils. The model identified in the Effective Resource Allocation in Schools Project was selected for this purpose, with Brian Caldwell and Jim Spinks invited to serve as consultant trainers.

We set about the preparation of a two-day training package based on the approach at Rosebery which, with slight adaptation, is illustrated in Figure 2.1. In summary, this involved a cycle of management that called for a school to determine goals, formulate policies, make annual plans, allocate resources, implement plans through programs of learning and teaching, and evaluate outcomes. Noteworthy features were that plans were based on programs, defined by normal patterns of work in the school, most of which were areas of curriculum. There were clearly defined roles for different groups. The 'policy group', being the school council at Rosebery and in Victoria, set goals, formulated policies, approved budgets and shared in the conduct of program evaluations. Program teams, formed mostly of teachers, were involved in each of these activities but were mainly responsible for preparing program plans and program budgets. Programs were implemented in the normal day-to-day work of the school. Program teams had major responsibility for the design and implementation of program evaluation.

Special aspects that had considerable appeal were the guidelines for carrying out these tasks, including the view that no policy should exceed one page, no program plan and budget should exceed two pages, no minor evaluation should exceed one page, and no major evaluation should exceed two pages. The distinction between minor and major evaluations was important, with the former carried out annually by members of program teams and the latter carried out on a five-year cycle, with members of program teams joined by others, from the school council or outside the school where special expertise may be found.

We draw attention to two particular features of the approach which are significant in the light of issues raised in Chapters 3 on learning outcomes and of the focus

*Figure 2.1   The model for self-management*

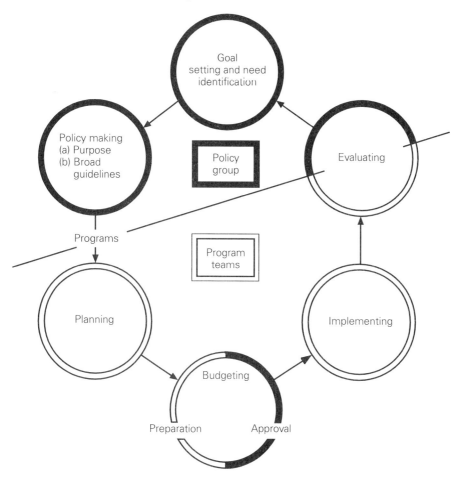

*Source:* Caldwell and Spinks, 1988

of change on Track 2. First, the relatively tight connection between the planning and budgeting process and activities related to learning and teaching. This was not self-management as an end in itself but self-management that was linked to what occurred in the classroom. This was in an era where there were no curriculum and standards frameworks and no expectation that schools engage in program evaluation in such a systematic fashion. The second noteworthy feature was the emphasis on teachers working in teams, which had all of the characteristics of high-performing teams, that is, they went beyond work groups or committees to address important tasks based on targets and outcomes. The concept of the high-performing team is, of course, endemic in the management literature in the 1990s.

Rosebery furnished an example of a standards-based high-performing team effort in the early 1980s that would be exemplary in the contemporary setting. The school received a grant under the Priority Projects scheme, known in some states as the School Improvement Program or the Disadvantaged Schools Program. This was money from the Commonwealth (national) Government channelled through the Education Department. Tasmania, which more than any other state at the time, ensured that almost all of this money was decentralized to the school level. Under the terms of the scheme, each school had to consult staff and the community in establishing its plans to meet particular needs or redress disadvantage. Unlike most schools in the state, Rosebery had chosen to establish a school council for this purpose, and its functions were generalized to cover all programs in the school.

Tasmania was also a pioneering state in adopting state-wide student achievement tests, in this instance the 10N and 10R, and 14N and 14R, being tests for 10- and 14-year-old students, respectively, in numeracy and literacy. These tests were designed by the Australian Council for Educational Research. Literacy levels were relatively low at Rosebery and the school obtained a Priority Project grant to address the issue. Using the distinctive team approach to policy, planning, budgeting and evaluation, funds were targeted at particular activities, with the result that literacy scores improved to the extent that the school disqualified itself from receiving further funds from this source. This is a relatively rare phenomenon, then and now. It is precisely this capacity that is sought in all schools as efforts are made to introduce standards-based approaches to school reform and to connect school-based management to purposeful efforts to improve learning.

We introduced this approach to schools in Victoria under the umbrella of School-based Program Budgeting, with the model for management formally styled by the Collaborative School Management Cycle. We conducted more than 50 training programs, each of two days, for about 5,000 school councillors, principals, teachers and in some instances, students, from about 1,200 schools. These were held in almost every part of the state in every setting, urban and rural, large and small, highly advantaged and highly disadvantaged communities. The Education Department of Tasmania published the workshop program, with its foundation in research, in a book titled *Policy Making and Planning for School Effectiveness* (Caldwell and Spinks, 1986) with an accompanying workshop package. The model was intended as a guide but every conceivable adaptation was soon evident. The programs were received well and the rate of take up of program budgeting, with adaptations of the model, was relatively high.

One limitation of the context was that relatively few resources were decentralized to the school level in Victoria, unlike Tasmania, which at that time led the nation in this regard. Toward the end of our consultancy work in Victoria, there was an expectation that more funds would be decentralized, especially with the release of the report *Taking Schools into the 1990s*. However, the opposition of teacher unions, parent organizations and some bureaucrats led to formal rejection by the government (see Government of Victoria, 1986).

Soon after this rejection, it became apparent that governments in two countries would proceed with a relatively high level of decentralization, within a centrally determined framework, in a manner consistent with our definition, and these events were recounted in Chapter 1 for Britain and New Zealand. Falmer Press acknowledged the 'fit' between the approach described in our book published by the Education Department in Tasmania and the capacities that would be required of schools for the implementation of local management of schools in Britain with the passing of the Education Reform Act in 1988. The Education Department in Tasmania released its right to the book which was re-published in 1988 with little amendment as *The Self-Managing School* (Caldwell and Spinks, 1988).

It was only at this stage that the concept of 'the self-managing school' was adopted, this being suggested by David Reynolds, now Professor of Education at the University of Newcastle-upon-Tyne, who served as Series Editor for Falmer Press at the time. Reynolds is eminent in the field of school effectiveness and a key adviser to the Labour Government in Britain, serving as the Chair of the Numeracy Task Force.

The book formed the basis of extensive involvement in training, with most conducted by Jim Spinks in Britain and New Zealand. He visited Britain on three occasions from 1988 to 1990, for a total of nearly 12 months of training programs for officers, governors, principals and teachers in more than one-third of the local education authorities. He also worked with about 10,000 parents, principals and teachers in an extended consultancy in New Zealand in 1989. Brian Caldwell undertook a study of emerging patterns in the management of education for OECD and completed several consultancies at the system and school levels in Australia and New Zealand. Both studied at first hand related developments in other countries, notably Canada and the United States.

We recounted the origins of our work for three reasons. First, because the model is still helpful as a guide to annual planning where there is an intention to empower different members of the school community in appropriate ways that secure a link between school-based management and learning. Second, to demonstrate that the model, which first came to international attention through its application in Britain, had its origins in efforts to empower the school to improve learning, and not in some approach to management that was inspired by a market orientation such as characterized the Thatcher Government's view of school reform. Events have subsequently demonstrated that, while some elements of a market orientation unrelated to our work have their pitfalls, the broad features of the 1988 Education Reform Act, especially the local management of schools, are eminently sensible and have drawn wide support. The third reason is to show the development of our experience and our thinking about the concept of the self-managing school, to help place in perspective the way in which we believe policy-makers and practitioners ought now move 'beyond the self-managing school'.

### Refining the Model in *Leading the Self-Managing School*

During our work with *The Self-Managing School*, it became apparent that the model should be refined in important ways for effective self-management in the 1990s. We accomplished this in *Leading the Self-Managing School* (Caldwell and Spinks, 1992) .

We acknowledged that the model, as it was initially devised at Rosebery, should not be implemented in the same manner in all settings. We had encouraged adaptations in our training programs and observed them in practice. We made the point in *Leading the Self-Managing School*. More important, however, was the need to take account of the dramatic change in the external environment for schools. Strong links were being made in the corporate community between knowledge and skills required for success in a global economy in the post-industrial age and the programs being offered by schools. More and more was expected of schools, and any expectation that there would be a period of consolidation following the changes of the 1980s were soon dashed.

We believed that three responses were required. The first was to describe the new environment and we did this by suggesting that what was happening could be accommodated in ten megatrends in school education, adapting to schools the concept of megatrend as coined by John Naisbitt in 1982, a decade before the publication of our second book (Naisbitt, 1982; see also Naisbitt and Aburdene, 1990). We feel that these megatrends are still evident and thus list them again as a helpful account of the current context for school education:

1 There will be a powerful but sharply focused role for central authorities, especially in respect to formulating goals, setting priorities, and building frameworks for accountability.

2 National and global considerations will become increasingly important, especially in respect to curriculum and an education system that is responsive to national needs within a global economy.

3 Within centrally determined frameworks, government [public] schools will become largely self-managing, and distinctions between government and non-government [private] schools will narrow.

4 There will be unparalleled concern for the provision of a quality education for each individual.

5 There will be a dispersion of the educative function, with telecommunications and computer technology ensuring that much learning that currently occurs in schools or in institutions of higher education will occur at home and in the workplace.

6 The basics of education will be expanded to include problem-solving, creativity and a capacity for lifelong learning and re-learning.

7 There will be an expanded role for the arts and spirituality, defined broadly in each instance; there will be a high level of 'connectedness' in the curriculum.

8 Women will claim their place among the ranks of leaders in education, including those at the most senior levels.

9    The parent and community role in education will be claimed or reclaimed.

10   There will be unparalleled concern for service by those who are required
     or have the opportunity to support the work of schools.

(Caldwell and Spinks, 1992, pp. 7–8)

We also refined the model for self-management in the manner illustrated in
Figure 2.2 (p. 29). Schools needed a capacity to manage continuing change and set
priorities rather than continue to 'add on' to existing programs. Systems were
making substantial demands on schools but schools were also expected to respond
to local needs and priorities. We proposed two mechanisms for dealing with this
situation. First was the concept of the school charter. We had been impressed by the
potential of the school charter from our work in New Zealand but were concerned
about the length and complexity of these documents. We wondered if there would
indeed be an ongoing link between the charter and programs for learning and
teaching. We therefore proposed a school charter, but one that would be relatively
short and simple, perhaps no longer than 20 pages, that would set out the nature of
the school and its current and expected profile in respect to students and programs.
It would then set out in general terms how it would address central and local
priorities. Whilst the original model for self-management encouraged schools to set
priorities and have a multi-year time-frame, we believed this ought to be made
more explicit, hence our proposal for schools to have a 3–5 year management plan,
that may also be described as a school development plan or a strategic plan. The
annual cycle of self-management remained the same, except for some changes in
terminology to reinforce the focus on learning and teaching.

The second response was in many ways the most important, for we believed
it was important to make clear what ought to be expected of leaders in the
self-managing school. We had introduced the theme in *The Self-Managing School*,
drawing on emerging concepts in leadership, but we wanted to take it up more
comprehensively in the sequel. Further, we did not wish to focus exclusively on the
principal, even though the principal had a key role to play. The principal and other
leaders need a capacity for transformational leadership, to adopt a powerful concept
that has emerged in recent years (based on the pioneering writing of James McGregor
Burns, 1978), working with others to change the way the school was managed
but also, more importantly, to make a significant impact on the quality of learning
and teaching.

We proposed four dimensions of transformational leadership: strategic, cultural,
educational and responsive. Strategic leadership calls for a capacity to see 'the big
picture', to discern the megatrends, to see the implications for the school, to build
a capacity for others in the school to do the same in their areas of interest, and to
establish structures and processes to deal with the implications in the school setting.
We sensed from our work that principals and other school leaders were not generally aware of the momentous changes affecting society in the late twentieth century
and that they ought to take the lead to ensure that all in the school community
gained an understanding of what was happening and why, with appropriate responses

*27*

at the school level. The management counterpart to strategic leadership is associated with the development of the school charter and the longer term management plan.

Cultural leadership is concerned with changing in a fundamental sense 'the way things are done around here'. First, of lesser importance, is to lead the change in culture from dependence on the centre to a culture of self-management. Of greater importance is to help change a culture to one that focuses all energies on improving the quality of learning and teaching. It is a culture that accepts the need to measure and monitor achievement, to set targets and priorities, and prepare and implement plans to address these. We shared our own view of a culture of excellence, choosing to express it in the form of an equation, based on earlier work by Fantini (1986):

$$\text{Excellence} = \text{Quality} + \text{Effectiveness} + \text{Equity} + \text{Efficiency}$$

We demonstrated how concepts that appeared initially foreign to those in school education, such as marketing, can be adapted to suit a culture that has, at its core, a concern for excellence.

Educational leadership is a broad concept but we chose to focus on the notion of 'building a learning community', which was the sub-title of the chapter that dealt with this dimension of transformational leadership. We outlined some strategies for building the capacity of teachers and others in the school community to provide programs in teaching and learning of the highest quality. The focus was very much on professional development. A concern for educational leadership was evident in our view of the self-managing school, which was not the adoption of a new approach to management borrowed from the corporate sector, but a framework at the school level for action to improve learning and teaching. As made clear in Chapter 3, this linkage has not been made in most settings. It is part of the effort that must be made to go 'beyond the self-managing school', energizing the journey along Track 2.

The fourth dimension is responsive leadership, the nature of which is evident in the sub-title of the chapter, namely, 'coming to terms with accountability'. Our case was built on the 'right to know' about the achievements of the school that was held by many individuals, groups and institutions in society, not just teachers and parents on receipt of a report of their child's progress. We endorsed the approach to minor and major program evaluations that were a feature of *The Self-Managing School* and accepted that a wider range of achievement tests was likely to be the order of the day in the new environment for school education. We supported these developments, based on our premise of the 'right to know' but took a strong stand against unethical or fraudulent use of 'league tables' derived from raw scores on system-wide tests.

Compared to what followed after *The Self-Managing School*, we had only limited involvement in training programs based on *Leading the Self-Managing School* because the nature of our work changed and, in any event, the book was less of a training manual than its predecessor. Our work did, however, afford ample opportunity to shape practice in accordance with its recommendations. Jim Spinks was appointed Superintendent of School Self-Management for Tasmania and led the effort that resulted in all schools having a charter along the lines we proposed. He then returned to the principalship, this time at Sheffield District High School.

*Figure 2.2   The refined model for self-management*

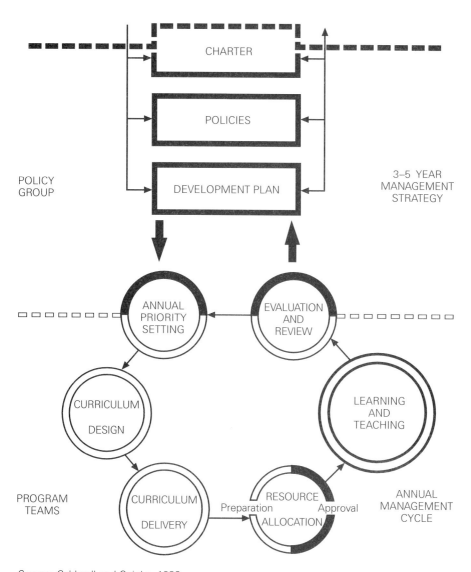

CENTRAL FRAMEWORK

CHARTER

POLICIES

DEVELOPMENT PLAN

POLICY
GROUP

3–5 YEAR
MANAGEMENT
STRATEGY

ANNUAL
PRIORITY
SETTING

EVALUATION
AND
REVIEW

CURRICULUM

DESIGN

LEARNING
AND
TEACHING

PROGRAM
TEAMS

CURRICULUM

DELIVERY

Preparation

RESOURCE

ALLOCATION

Approval

ANNUAL
MANAGEMENT
CYCLE

*Source:* Caldwell and Spinks, 1992

There was a change in government in Victoria within months of the release of *Leading the Self-Managing School* and Brian Caldwell had the opportunity to apply the recommendations of the book in that state when he was invited to serve as a member of the Task Force that helped design the Schools of the Future program (see design in Hayward, 1993). In one sense, the Liberal National Coalition led by

Jeffrey Kennett, with Don Hayward as Minister for Education, took up the stalled agenda that followed the rejection of recommendations in the *Taking Schools into the 1990s* report of 1986. However, Schools of the Future is a more comprehensive reform than envisaged in 1986, for it has a clearly defined curriculum and standards framework and an approach to accountability that institutionalizes the approach to minor and major evaluations, with the Annual Report and Triennial Report, each of which utilizes a repertoire of performance indicators. A detailed account of the design and implementation of Schools of the Future is given by Don Hayward in the book he co-authored with Brian Caldwell titled *The Future of Schools: Lessons from the Reform of Public Education* (Caldwell and Hayward, 1998).

The four dimensions of transformational leadership were reflected in several recommendations of a national project that defined the emerging role of the principal in Australia (see Evans, 1993) and they helped shape a major training program over three years for more than 1,000 principals of Schools of the Future conducted by Brian Caldwell and the late Max Sawatzki.

### Critiques

We turn now to scholarly critiques of the concept of the self-managing school, including the initial model and the manner in which we applied it in the context of schooling that emerged in the late 1980s and early 1990s. We briefly summarize the early critiques up to about 1990 before turning to the critical theorists, market perspectives and the anti-management position in academic writing that spanned a five-year period from 1993 to 1997. We conclude with our own appraisal of the model and its refinement, highlighting what needs to be accomplished if intentions are to be realized.

#### *Early critiques of the model*

In *Leading the Self-Managing School* (Caldwell and Spinks, 1992, pp. 43–6), we addressed scholarly critiques of the model for self-management as presented in *The Self-Managing School* (Caldwell and Spinks, 1988).

The critique of Marsh (1988), who broadly commended the model and continues to do so (Marsh, 1997), referred to several shortcomings to do with its primarily technical orientation, with insufficient attention being given to political and cultural orientations; an undue separation of policy groups and program teams (see Figure 2.1); a lack of detailed attention to the role of parents; an apparent reliance on a strong principal; overemphasis on the financial aspects of planning; its demanding nature; and the apparent dismissal of spontaneities. Brown (1990) noted its basis in a single school case study and felt that we tended to oversell its benefits, a point also made by Glatter (1990) in his review of *The Self-Managing School*. Corson (1990) questioned whether our approach to policy-making, which called for a search for at least three options in response to contentious issues, offered any advance over a common-sense approach.

We responded to these critiques by citing Dye's view of a model as 'a simplified representation of some aspect of the real world' and his six criteria for appraising the utility of a model, namely, capacity to order and simplify, identification of significant features, congruence with reality, communicative power, explanation of a total process, and a basis for inquiry and research (Dye, 1975, p. 21). The model for self-management (Figure 2.1) and its refinement (Figure 2.2) generally satisfy these criteria.

Difficulties arise when findings from research — in this case, case studies of effective schools — are synthesized and presented as or perceived as 'theory', for faithful implementation in every setting. This was not claimed or intended and, indeed, was rarely taken up as such, for every conceivable adaptation of the model in practice has emerged over the last decade in a range of settings as diverse as bustling, urban Hong Kong and remote rural locations in inland Australia. We support Sergiovanni and Starratt's view that models 'are not true with respect to telling the professional what to do but are useful for informing the professional's judgement, guiding the decision-making process, and making professional practice more rational' (Sergiovanni and Starratt, 1988, p. 41).

*New Right Associations*

These early critiques of the model were minor compared to the those that greeted the wide dissemination of *The Self-Managing School* and the extensive training programs in Britain and New Zealand in the late 1980s and early 1990s. Our support for the concept of self-management, especially in the context of the 1988 Education Reform Act and the initiatives of the Conservative Government in Britain, led to the association of our work with the agenda of the New Right and associated market-oriented policies in school education. These criticisms, mostly by academics writing with a critical theory orientation, rarely noted the foundation of our work in research on highly effective schools and the extensive developmental work in Victoria from 1984 to 1986 as part of the implementation of the education policies of a moderate left of centre Labor Government to which a New Right label could never be pinned. It was claimed that:

> . . . their [Caldwell and Spinks] account is politically coy rather than naive. They acknowledge, briefly, that the policies being pursued by the Conservatives in Britain will lead to self-managing schools and that 'What is proposed in Britain is potentially the most far-reaching development in any of the countries considered' (p. 9); but they have nothing to say about the politics of the New Right or about the extensive criticism of right-wing education policy in Britain. (Demaine, 1993, p. 40)

We were, of course, making an obvious comment about the potential of developments in Britain, but were not writing a book about education policy in Britain except to note that the model for self-management was likely to be helpful for those with responsibility for the implementation of local management, as it proved to be. Critics should now read or re-read beyond the opening pages in *The Self-Managing School* and *Leading the Self-Managing School* and note how much of what is described, illustrated and advocated is central to the reform agenda of New Labour, as illustrated further in Chapter 5 of this book. They should also read what series editor David Reynolds, who was appointed Chair of the Numeracy Task Force in 1997, had to say in his Foreword to *The Self-Managing School*:

> Experience of past top–down change programs or improvement schemes was one of dismal failure and it is therefore easy to see why the self-managing school is currently such a popular concept. The school effectiveness literature also shows that the more effective schools in all countries have staff groups who 'own' their school because they as a staff are responsible for its management and general well-being. It is also clear from the various school improvement programs that commitment to personal and institutional change is greatest where the individual school is in charge of its own schemes. (Reynolds, 1988, p. vi)

The shrillness of the critique reached its peak in the writing of John Smyth, who edited the book that contained the contribution from Demaine cited above (Smyth, 1993). Smyth had made important scholarly contributions in the field of teaching and had edited a valuable collection of papers on leadership (Smyth, 1989) before turning his attention to self-management, judging it time to 'call in the evidence'. The objectivity of his effort may be judged from the following intemperate comments on the initiative in self-management in Victoria that dramatically extended what had been accomplished in the 1980s.

> Since this book was completed, many of the predictions about what was envisaged as likely to happen under a conservative government in Victoria have come to pass . . . It is interesting that perpetrators of policies like those behind that of *The Self-Managing School* are so arrogantly self-assured of the 'rightness' of what they are doing and the efficacy of their own narrow minded ideas that they are prepared to go to the extreme of closing off public debate by steamrolling them in without proper public discussion. Could it be that those who deem to 'know best' in respect of these matters understand that were their ideas allowed to be put under the light of careful debate and scrutiny, they would in all likelihood be exposed for the fraud that they are? What other explanations are there for governments who stoop to pushing through controversial measures like this in the dark of night? Far from actions like this being a sign of courage and leadership, they are a shameful and shallow reminder of what is coming to pass as 'democracy' in Western capitalist countries. (Smyth, 1993, pp. 8–9)

Smyth was referring to the initiative in self-management in Victoria known as Schools of the Future. The reality is that the main elements of Schools of the Future had been widely canvassed in the public arena prior to the election campaign of 1992, were spelt out in the election policy of the then Opposition in the weeks leading up to the poll, and were the focus of a ministerial statement in early 1993 (Hayward, 1993) that was the subject of wide consultation before the final form of implementation was determined. Implementation was more expansive than originally proposed because the number of schools seeking to enter the program was well above expectations. Implementation occurred largely by ministerial action, since little change to the existing Act set up by the previous Labor Government was required. This sequence can hardly be described as 'a shameful and shallow reminder of what is coming to pass as "democracy" . . .' The actions in the 'dark of night' described by Smyth were late night debates in parliament on matters other than Schools of the Future.

Many of the key elements of Schools of the Future were developed in the months and years following the events described by Smyth, including the Curriculum and Standards Frameworks, that were the focus of extensive consultation in 1993 and 1994, in contrast to the initially aborted British experience that involved relatively little consultation. Similarly for the development of a funding mechanism for decentralizing resources to schools, that came about in an orderly manner, shaped by recommendations of the Education Committee of the School Budget Research Project chaired by Brian Caldwell that met from early 1994 to the end of December 1996 (see Education Committee, 1994, 1995, 1996, for accounts of the processes, consultations and recommendations arising from this work). The accountability framework was also developed in a methodical manner, with the approach to triennial reviews being trialed before full implementation in 1997, carefully balancing local responsibility with external validation (see Chapters 2 and 3 in Caldwell and Hayward, 1998, for a detailed account of the design and implementation of Schools of the Future).

The substance of the critique by other writers in the collection edited by Smyth is one that we do not share. Many of the matters they raised are concerned with quite fundamental issues that are shaping public education and the profession of teaching, triggered in the main by the social transformation that is sweeping much of the world, but affected by the budget crises that are impacting the public school in many, mainly western nations. The irony in terms of a democratic tradition is that the concept of self-management or local management was embraced by all political parties in Britain in the election campaign of 1997, reflecting its broad acceptance, by the profession as well as by the public.

A more rigorous critique of our work and of self-management in general was provided by Geoff Whitty, Sally Power and David Halpin (Whitty, Power and Halpin, 1998) in their account of developments in Australia (Victoria), Britain (England and Wales), New Zealand, Sweden and the United States. They write 'from the perspective of sociologists of education with a particular interest in the relationship between education and equity' and:

> While not denying that school autonomy can bring benefits to individual schools and students, and even have their progressive moments, we surely also need to consider the implications of this for schools that are less disadvantaged through the new found 'freedoms'. (Whitty, Power and Halpin, 1998, p. 11)

Their account of our work is generally accurate and balanced but it is astray in two respects. They question our claim (Caldwell and Spinks, 1988, p. 8) that the case for self-management can be argued on the basis of findings from studies of school effectiveness, despite the foundation of the model for self-management in research on school effectiveness in Australia, funded in 1983 as a Project of National Significance. They take us to task for exhorting schools to engage in goal-setting, policy-making, planning, financial budgeting, implementing and evaluating performance, functions that are 'more reminiscent of business than that previously associated with educational institutions' (Whitty, Power and Halpin, 1998, p. 53). It is astonishing that the need for such functions in schools is questioned, especially if they apply to programs of learning and teaching and the support of learning and teaching, as is the case with the models for self-management that were proposed.

The most serious shortcoming is their selective use of research in appraising the Schools of the Future reforms in Victoria that drew to some extent on designs in both books, especially *Leading the Self-Managing School*. They rely heavily on just one study (Blackmore, Bigum, Hodgens and Laskey, 1996) and generalize the findings when, in fact, the research was conducted in just 4 of 1700 schools, relatively early in the reform. They make no reference to the extensive research programs and findings of the five-year Cooperative Research Project, with its 7 representative state-wide surveys and 17 focused investigations completed or under way by 1998 (Cooperative Research Project, 1994, 1995a, 1995b, 1996, 1997, 1998, as referred to in Chapter 3). There is no mention of the three-year School Global Budget Research Project that drew on data from a large representative sample of schools to guide the development of a scheme for needs-based formula-funding of schools, with equity considerations to provide additional resources for students with special educational needs (see Education Committee, 1994, 1995, 1996).

We agree with their assessment that there is little evidence of a direct link between self-management and learning outcomes, and we address this matter in Chapter 3. In general, while we disagree with much of its thrust, it is a valuable book, offering a coherent and comprehensive critique of self-management from a sociological perspective.

## *Market Perspectives*

One of the forces shaping the transformation of public education is a faith in the market as a mechanism to induce the achievement of higher quality schooling. This was clearly on the agenda of the New Right as reflected in policies of conservative governments, and critics such as those cited above quite properly pointed this out. In Britain, these policies were implemented by de-zoning school attendance, tying financial allocations to the numbers of students attending schools, furnishing parents with data on student achievement in 'league tables', and encouraging schools to 'opt out' of control by their local education authorities.

In some respects, this market or parent choice approach was not exclusively the intention of the New Right. The practice of 'de-zoning' to allow students to attend the school of choice rather than the local school is now widespread, being implemented by governments of every persuasion. In the final analysis, however, nothing like a pure market ever eventuated, given that self-managing schools are systemic schools, with centrally determined frameworks including those related to curriculum and standards, and with central authorities continuing to exercise a planning role across all schools, although an insufficient one according to recent evidence in Britain, for serious inefficiencies in school places were revealed after a decade of local management.

A major shortcoming of the market critique is that it was virtually the only perspective adopted by many writers, who assumed that all governments taking the path of self-management were doing so exclusively because of their commitment to ideologically driven market approaches. In reality, governments everywhere responded to a set of forces that led them to re-structure public schooling in similar ways.

It is refreshing to read the account of Michael Barber in this respect (Barber, 1996). Barber is former research officer with the National Union of Teachers in Britain. He was Professor of Education at Keele University and at the Institute of Education at the University of London, where he also served as Dean of Innovations, before being appointed on the first day of the new Labour administration as head of the Standards and Effectiveness Unit. He recalled a public meeting during the 1987 election campaign in which he stood as Labour candidate in Henley-on-Thames against sitting Conservative Michael Heseltine:

> Though we won easy applause at the local meeting, the Liberal and I had missed two fundamental points . . . Firstly, we offered no credible alternative to what was perceived by the public at large, if not in that public meeting, to be an inadequate existing state of affairs. Secondly, we had completely failed to identify a series of underlying social changes which would sooner or later have forced a radical shift in education policy, whether we liked it or not. It was these changes that caused the crisis, not the market reforms which the Thatcher government drove through. In short, we lacked both a vision of the future and an understanding of the past. (Barber, 1996, p. 37)

While Barber is unrelentingly critical of aspects of the Conservative reforms, his work in the Standards and Effectiveness Unit and his influence on the directions of New Labour reflect a deep appreciation of the scale of societal transformation and the importance of leadership and will in extending the agenda for reform, with most of the action on Track 2 as set out in Chapter 5.

### The Anti-Management Position

Apart from the fundamental design of the reform, the success of local management is a tribute to the leadership and management skills of heads and other school leaders, and the commitment and capability of teachers who have worked under conditions that are for the most part incompatible with teaching and learning for the knowledge society. While many leaders have thrived under local management with knowledge, skills and attitudes nurtured long before 1988, a tribute should be paid to the timeliness and effectiveness of management development over the last decade. It was therefore disappointing to read Helen Gunter's denigration of efforts in this field (Gunter, 1997).

While we hold no brief for 'management by ring binder', an approach derided by Gunter, a comment on her reference to our own work is appropriate. It is hard to believe she has read the work she criticizes. She asserts that the strategy in *The Self-Managing School* is 'rooted in the work of Peters and Waterman' (Gunter, 1997, p. 29) when in fact it was based on studies of effective schools in the government and non-government sectors in two states of Australia as part of a Project of National Significance in 1983 as described earlier in Chapter 2. She takes up one of Smyth's several misrepresentations of the work as 'this kind of derelict model that failed so demonstrably as evidenced in the corporate excesses of the 1980s' (Smyth, 1993, p. 7 cited by Gunter, 1997, p. 4). In fact, the model in *The Self-Managing School* is the antithesis of what Smyth asserts, with its emphasis on management focused on the core work of the school, namely, learning and teaching; an ahead-of-its-time advocacy of teams; and a publicly transparent approach to annual and triennial review by internal teams with external validation. The 'corporate excesses' of the 1980s were characterized by 'corporate cowboys' who rarely took teams into their confidence, whose operations were opaque rather than transparent, and where there was little or no accountability to stakeholders.

The opening pages of *The Self-Managing School* made the obvious connection between what we had learned about management of effective schools in Australia under conditions of decentralization and capacities that would be required by heads and other leaders for local management following the 1988 Education Reform Act. Our subsequent work in Britain, especially that by Spinks from 1988 to 1990, was undertaken at the invitation of and in partnership with Cambridge Education Associates, whose directors were outstanding and highly respected leaders in the pioneering scheme of local financial management in Cambridgeshire that commenced in 1982.

### Reflections and Refinements

In retrospect, the models were useful and continue to be so, as schools and school systems continue the journey on Track 1, but they must be utilized in the spirit of modelling described by Sergiovanni and Starratt: 'informing the professional's judgement, guiding the decision-making process, and making professional practice more rational' (Sergiovanni and Starratt, 1988, p. 41). Especially valuable is their emphasis on teams based around areas of learning and teaching, and the support of learning and teaching; an approach to program evaluation and external accountability that calls for building the capacity of people in schools to gather data and form their own judgments, with opportunities for validation by others outside the school; the notion of 'nurturing a learning community'; and ensuring a capacity for strategic leadership is deeply embedded in the school.

The models may be helpful in these matters, but they are not sufficient. A much deeper capacity is required to transform approaches to learning and teaching, for achievements in this respect have been modest, as described in Chapter 3.

We share common ground with the critics in regretting that many initiatives in self-management were taken during difficult times in some places, notably in the midst of a budget and debt crisis in Victoria. But the critique has been utterly superficial to the extent that it ignored the need for restructuring public sector services under conditions that prevail at the end of the twentieth century. Nations that failed to act have found themselves in dire straits.

In similar vein, we reject the extravagant claims that have been made for adopting a pure market approach in school education, and we resent the rhetoric of those who have denigrated the efforts of teachers and their leaders who are battling against the odds in some settings. On the other hand, along with many in the profession, we are disappointed in the stance of teacher unions in some places, the leaders of which failed to see or ignored the implications of the societal transformation that has been under way for decades and have trenchantly opposed virtually every aspect of the reform agenda. We share with critics a concern at the lack of resources, but a mindless mantra of more from the public purse for schools, with little more than a whiff of private effort, is disempowering the profession and steadily reducing the chances of long-term survival for the public school. This need not be the case, for we have seen unions and their leaders as partners in the process in some places, as is the case in most of the significant developments in the United States.

### Strategic Intentions for Schools
### Models for Self-Management

1   Learning and teaching, and the support of learning and teaching, will be the starting point and the sole and continuing focus of effort in school leadership and management.

2   Schools will continue to need a basic model for self-management that shapes an annual cycle of goal-setting, policy-making, planning, budgeting, implementation (learning and teaching, and the support of learning and teaching), and program evaluation, with clearly defined roles for policy groups and program teams.

3   A basic model for self-management may be necessary but it is not sufficient, for success in times of continuing complexity and change will require a capacity for strategic management that includes priority setting and developmental planning within a multi-year time-frame.

4   Capacities for strategic leadership, cultural leadership, educational leadership and reflective leadership will be deeply embedded in the school.

5   The core task in strategic leadership will be to help build an understanding in the school community of the scale of social transformation now under way and its impact on the school.

6   The core task in cultural leadership will be to help build a school culture based around a commitment to excellence that values quality, effectiveness, equity and efficiency, and that recognizes and accepts the interdependence of these four elements.

7   The core task in educational leadership will be to help build the school as a learning community, in the fullest sense of that term, for all involved in learning and teaching, and the support of learning and teaching.

8   The core tasks in responsive leadership will be to build recognition that the 'right to know' about performance should be deeply embedded in the school and its community, and to develop a capacity to respond to needs and aspirations that arise from that knowledge.

9   Strategies based on a narrow reading of the need for school reform will be prone to failure.

10  There will be no 'one best way' as far as models for self-management are concerned; each school must design its own, based on situational factors that include mission and vision.

*Chapter 3*

# Self-Managing Schools and Learning Outcomes

The central issue in any consideration of recent reform, especially that part that has entailed the introduction of the self-managing school in the public sector, is the relationship between reform and outcomes. Is there a direct cause-and-effect relationship between self-management and learning outcomes for students? Expressed simply, has there been an impact on learning for schools and schools systems that have embarked on a journey along Track 1, the building of systems of self-managing schools?

The evidence is examined in this chapter, but first it is helpful to look at the reasons why self-management was introduced in the first place. Was there an expectation that it would have an impact on learning?

### Expectations for Recent School Reform

A superficial reading of forces that underpinned recent reforms in some places, notably Australia, Britain and New Zealand, is that it was an attempt to improve quality through the introduction of markets in school education. Indeed, many of the critiques have been based almost entirely on the market perspective (see various contributions in Smyth, 1993) and it has been pointed out that few educational outcomes can be tied to the effects of markets and movements of students among schools.

The limitations of this view of the cause of reform have been raised by Michael Barber. In *The Learning Game* (Barber, 1996), he recounts his embrace of the market critique, cited in Chapter 2, when he stood unsuccessfully as a Labour candidate in the 1987 election. In reflecting on the experience, he states that:

> ... we had completely failed to identify a series of underlying social changes which would sooner or later have forced a radical shift in education policy, whether we liked it or not. It was these changes that caused the crisis, not the market reforms which the Thatcher government drove through. (Barber, 1996, p. 37)

Barber now takes a much broader view of the forces that shaped the 'cultural revolution' in school education: growing social diversity; growing dissatisfaction with the output of the education service ('it failed too many young people too much of the time'); growing dissatisfaction with the performance of the British economy in comparison with that of competitor countries; the economic crisis of the mid-1970s and a need to control public spending; a consequent need for accountability in public expenditure (with associated impact on professional autonomy); and decision-making that was painfully slow: 'far too slow for a world in which social, cultural, economic and technological changes were gathering pace and would continue to do so' (Barber, 1996, pp. 44–9). He concluded:

> For all these reasons, therefore, it is a mistake to see Thatcherism as the cause of the educational crisis of the late 1980s. A crisis was coming anyway. Thatcherism's contribution was to shape decisively the solutions that have been attempted. From the range of possibilities available for dealing with the problems . . . the Thatcher government chose solutions based on a radical combination of market forces and centralization. Historians writing twenty years from now will be able to tell if they worked. (Barber, 1996, p. 49)

Pressure for reform in the United States prompted several American scholars to make comparisons between developments in Britain and the United States (see contributions in Beare and Boyd, 1993; also Cooper, 1990; Guthrie and Pierce, 1990; and Wirt, 1991). The commentary of political scientist Frederick Wirt is cited here and taken up later in the chapter because of his insightful assessment of links between self-management and learning outcomes.

Wirt explained developments from an economic and a political perspective. Drawing on the work of Douglas Mitchell, he recalled the accepted view in the middle of the twentieth century that national governments should stimulate the economy through educational development. He suggested that 'acceptance had unravelled by the 1970s due to inequalities in service provision and to lowering student achievement, and consequently political leaders stepped in again to change school programs and organizations' (Wirt, 1991, p. 35). This continued in the 1980s. From a political view, he drew from dissatisfaction theory:

> . . . there was a common triggering event, namely, the growing reports of lowered student achievement in both nations that were perceived as disasters. That event was independent of any economic explanation of subsequent reform. When parents complain increasingly to school authorities that Johnny can't read, that fact is not economic. . . . Faced by such dissatisfaction, for politicoes to defend the current school system was not a good strategy for survival; on the other hand, 'credit-claiming' for instituting reforms certainly was. They may have used the idea of better schools for a better economy either as rhetoric or as passionate ideological belief. This was an ideology that was compatible with the renewed political strength of business interests in both nations in the 1980s. But note that such ideas were not what first fastened their attention on school problems — it was public discontent. (Wirt, 1991, pp. 37–8)

Brian Caldwell also offered an account of forces that led, in particular, to self-managing schools or school-based management, reviewing developments in six nations: Australia, Canada, China (Hong Kong), New Zealand, United States and the United Kingdom (Caldwell, 1994). Caldwell identified five interrelated concerns, or interests, that were not experienced uniformly across these nations but, taken together, seemed to account for developments: (1) efficiency and effectiveness in the delivery of public services; (2) ideology that embraces a faith in the market mechanism in the public as well as the private sector; (3) equity in the allocation of scarce resources; (4) a broad societal valuing of empowerment of the community; and (5) findings in research on school and classroom improvement.

These perspectives on forces underlying recent efforts to reform school education come from three continents and are consistent. An expectation that the quality of learning or outcomes for students would be enhanced is present in each. It is therefore appropriate and timely to press for evidence on impact.

## Self-managing Schools and Learning Outcomes

The following question was posed in *Leading the Self-Managing School:* 'Where is the evidence that radical decentralization has led, in direct cause-and-effect fashion, to educational benefits, including measurable gains for students?' (Caldwell and Spinks, 1992, p. 116). A review of research at the time suggested that evidence was sparse, although there was a powerful 'theory of action' that a capacity for self-management should be considered a pre-condition for school improvement, and that other actions utilizing this capacity are required if there is to be an impact on learning (see Goodlad, 1984; Miles, 1987; Sizer, 1984 cited by Caldwell and Spinks, 1988, pp. 116–117 and referred to later in this chapter). It is timely to pose the question again, especially as a decade has elapsed since major reforms such as the Education Reform Act of 1988.

Whitty, Power and Halpin reviewed evidence in Australia, England and Wales, New Zealand, Sweden and the United States. Their general conclusion was that 'there were insufficient grounds to claim that self-managing schools are currently enhancing student attainment' (Whitty, Power and Halpin, 1998, p. 111).

Evidence from four countries is reviewed in the pages that follow, namely, Australia (Victoria), Britain (England and Wales), China (Hong Kong) and the United States. Much of the research from the United States consists of studies of school-based management and, until recently, the findings have been discouraging. The British research deals with a more comprehensive program of reform, not limited to local management. While some effects are discernible, there is little to illuminate the links between elements of reform and outcomes for students. Research from China (Hong Kong) is, in several respects, the most interesting because of the rich conceptualization and sophisticated analysis. Evidence from Australia (Victoria), while not explicitly based on measures of student achievement, is promising in respect to confirming a 'theory of action'.

This section lays the foundation for an exploration of what needs to be done to make the links between self-management and learning more explicit and effective.

### United States

Research from the United States of greatest interest is on school-based management (SBM) or school-site management. There is now more than 20 years' of experience with school-based management and the literature in the late 1990s contains several meta-analyses or syntheses of different investigations over the years. Meta-analysis of developments in the 1980s revealed little if any impact (Malen, Ogawa and Kranz, 1990).

More recent meta-analysis by Summers and Johnson (1996) confirmed the generally held view that school-based management has so many different meanings and has been practised in so many different ways that it is difficult to generalize from experience, the only common element being the delegation of authority to the school (Summers and Johnson, 1996, p. 77).

Summers and Johnson located 70 studies that purported to be evaluations of school-based management, but only 20 of these employed a systematic approach and just 7 included a measure of student outcomes. They conclude that 'there is little evidence to support the notion that SBM is effective in increasing student performance. There are very few quantitative studies, the studies are not statistically rigorous, and the evidence of positive results is either weak or non-existent' (p. 80). Apart from the 'overwhelming obstacles' in the way of assessing the impact of SBM, Summers and Johnson drew attention to the fact that few initiatives 'identify student achievement as a major objective. The focus is on organizational processes, with virtually no attention to how process changes may affect student performance' (Summers and Johnson, 1996, pp. 92–3).

For Eric Hanushek, the findings are not surprising because of the absence of a purposeful link between SBM and student performance. He notes the review of Summers and Johnson and observes that 'Decentralization of decisionmaking has little general appeal without such linkage and, indeed, could yield worse results with decentralized management pursuing its own objectives not necessarily related closely to student performance' (Hanushek, 1996, p. 45). In an update of research on the effects of school resources on student achievement, Hanushek (1997, p. 156) drew attention to the finding 'that simply decentralizing decision-making is unlikely to work effectively unless there exist clear objectives and unless there is direct accountability'.

Marshall Smith, Under Secretary, US Department of Education, in commenting on the reform agenda of the Clinton Administration (Smith, Scoll and Link, 1996) stressed the importance of linkage by referring to the findings of an OECD study that paralleled those of Summers and Johnson (OECD, 1994):

> The OECD report goes on to suggest, however, that to the degree that a reorganization effort is conducted with a clarity of purpose to improve classroom teaching and learning, positive outcomes may accrue. In other words, to improve student learning, the content and instruction delivered to students must change as well as the organizational structure of the school. They complement each other. . . . This is not rocket science. (Smith, Scoll and Link, 1996, p. 21)

Evidence to support these contentions comes from four recent studies of developments in the United States, one with negative conclusions, two with cautiously optimistic conclusions. The first, funded by the Annie E. Casey Foundation, was a study by a research team from four universities (Washington, Chicago, Colorado in Denver, and Pomona College, California) of six decentralization efforts in Charlotte-Mecklenburg (North Carolina), Chicago, Cincinnati, Denver, Los Angeles, and Seattle. The conclusion was that none of the cities had achieved noteworthy improvement in student achievement, most had failed to provide schools with any significant freedom or accountability, and 'all of them floundered when it came to implementation' (Olson, 1997, p. 29). While some gains had been made in achievement at the primary level in Chicago and Charlotte-Mecklenburg — schools had become more responsive to communities and the role of principals had changed — the work lives of teachers had remained largely untouched. At best 'decentralization creates the conditions that allow schools to improve one at a time' (Olson, 1997, p. 30). In general, it is apparent that the linkages identified by Smith, Scoll and Link cited above have not been made in these six high-profile decentralization initiatives.

More promising but contested evidence on impact was found in Chicago (Lawton, 1997b, p. 3). Reading scores in 1990, before the reforms, were compared with those achieved in 1997. Nearly half of the schools included in the study posted impressive gains, with Donald R. Moore, Executive Director of Designs for Change that conducted the study reporting 'strong evidence that the schools that have taken the greatest advantage of that decisionmaking opportunity [under decentralization] are improving student achievement', with the most improved schools having higher ratings of a school council focus on improvement, principals, teacher influence, teacher–parent relationships, safety, cooperative teacher effort and learning. While the researchers included controls on student backgrounds in their analysis, other researchers not involved in the study questioned whether sufficient account had been taken of change in student demographics on a school-by-school basis.

The most powerful evidence of a linkage between self-management and learning outcomes in Chicago, indeed in any jurisdiction, has emerged in the longitudinal research of the Consortium on Chicago School Research, presented at the 1998 Annual Meeting of the American Educational Research Association (Bryk, 1998). Value-added measures of student achievement over a number of years were included in the design of an innovative productivity index. A model of direct and indirect effects, including a capacity for self-management, was presented.

Other positive evidence was reported in Philadelphia following three years of sweeping reform under the leadership of Superintendent David Hornbeck. Local decision-making was encouraged by the creation of 22 clusters of schools based on K–12 feeder patterns, each of which dealt with articulation and transition issues, the design and sharing of support services, and the delivery of professional development opportunities. Large schools were reorganized into schools-within-schools of no more than 400 students. Cluster-based Teaching and Learning Networks and Family Resource Networks were created. Schools councils of principal, parents and teachers were formed, with teachers comprising the majority, and these have the authority to make decisions on the selection of the principal, staffing patterns and learning environment, including curriculum and approaches to learning and teaching. Some areas of decision-making were constrained by the collective agreement. A system of rewards, assistance and consequences was established for schools, based on their success in realizing improvement in student performance as measured on tests administered system-wide at years 2, 4, 6, 8, and 11. Results in the second year of testing revealed significant overall improvement, especially in primary schools, in reading, mathematics and science, when compared to results in the first year and when compared to achievement on the same tests across the nation (Stanford Achievement Test 9). These developments were planned and implemented with substantial support from the corporate and foundations sector in an initiative known as the Children Achieving Challenge (this account of the reform and its outcomes was provided by Vicki Phillips, Director of Children Achieving Challenge, Phillips, 1997).

It is important to note that the Philadelphia reform was much contested, in the courts, within the school board and by the Philadelphia Federation of Teachers, which opposed the introduction of the standards-based achievement tests and ensured that local decision-making was constrained. The PFT challenged the conclusions drawn from the test results on the basis of the number of students who did not sit the tests in the first and the second years of their administration (see Hendrie, 1997, p. 9 for an account of the results and the PFT reaction).

It is evident, however, that the program of reform in Philadelphia involved a relatively high level of decentralization within a curriculum and standards framework, and that changes penetrated the classroom, especially through the initiatives of the cluster-based networks described by Phillips. In this respect, Philadelphia is an example of the kinds of linkages that need to be made if school-based management is to have an impact on learning.

### Britain

There is a growing research base on the impact of local management in Britain. Levacic (1995, p. 190) found that, of four criteria associated with intentions for the local management of schools (effectiveness, efficiency, equity and choice), 'cost-efficiency is the one for which there is most evidence that local management has achieved the aims set for it by government,' especially through the opportunity it provides for schools to purchase at a lower cost for a given quality or quantity than in the past, and by allowing resource mixes that were not possible or readily attainable under previous more centralized arrangements. She found evidence for effectiveness to be more tenuous, although the presumed link is through efficiency, making resources available to meet needs not able to be addressed previously.

In Britain, as elsewhere, there has been no research to determine the cause-and-effect relationship between local management and discretionary use of resources, on the one hand, and improved learning outcomes for students on the other, although there is opinion to the effect that gains have been made. Bullock and

Thomas (1994, pp. 134–5) reported that an increasing number of principals believed there are benefits for student learning from local management (LM). In responding to the statement that 'Children's learning is benefiting from LM', the number of agreements among primary principals increased from 30 per cent in 1991 to 44 per cent in 1992 to 47 per cent in 1993. A similar pattern was evident among principals of secondary schools, increasing from 34 per cent in 1991 to 46 per cent in 1992 to 50 per cent in 1993. Among both primary and secondary principals, those in larger schools were more positive than those in smaller schools.

Bullock and Thomas updated their research on local management in Britain in a comprehensive account of decentralization (Bullock and Thomas, 1997). Drawing predominantly on evidence from Britain (England and Wales) but referring also to outcomes elsewhere, they concluded that:

> It may be that the most convincing evidence of the impact of local management is on the opportunities which it has provided for managing the environment and resources for learning, both factors that can act to support the quality of learning in schools. What remains elusive, however, is clear-cut evidence of these leading through to direct benefits on learning, an essential component if we are to conclude that it is contributing to higher levels of efficiency. (Bullock and Thomas, 1997, p. 217)

Bullock and Thomas then go to the heart of the issue:

> If learning is at the heart of education, it must be central to our final discussion of decentralization. It means asking whether, in their variety of guises, the changes characterized by decentralization have washed over and around children in classrooms, leaving their day-to-day experiences largely untouched. In asking this question, we must begin by recognizing that structural changes in governance, management and finance may leave largely untouched the daily interaction of pupils and teachers. (Bullock and Thomas, 1997, p. 219)

Their final conclusion offers little advance on findings earlier and elsewhere:

> If the standard and quality of learning is to be at the centre of education — and it is surely the key test of decentralization — it is not apparent that the policies and practices of decentralization we have discussed in this book are adequately geared to its achievement. (Bullock and Thomas, 1997, p. 222)

The choice of the word 'gearing' is important here, because it refers to the manner in which changes at national, state, regional, and school levels connect to drive and impact on change at another level (classroom and student). Hanushek (1996), cited earlier, made the same point in his commentary on the lack of impact reported in the United States. He used the word 'linkage' to describe what was necessary. Gearing and linkage are central to some outstanding conceptual work and subsequent research in China (Hong Kong).

*China (Hong Kong)*

Research on school-based management in Hong Kong, led by Cheng and Cheung, is arguably at the forefront, not only conceptually and methodologically, but also in the manner in which it is beginning to illuminate the links between the practice of school-based management or self-management and outcomes for students.

The conceptual framework shown in Figure 3.1 (Cheng, 1996, p. 78) suggests that three levels of self-management must link in a coherent way: school, group and individual. If one seeks an impact on learning, it is not sufficient simply to decentralize authority and responsibility to the school; it must penetrate the classroom. It suggests that a similar cycle of self-management ought to be evident at each of these levels. Each individual and group ought to be engaged in and empowered in the same processes that make up the cycle of self-management at the school level, shown as the perimeter in Figure 3.1, namely, environmental analysis, planning and structuring, staffing and directing, implementing, monitoring and evaluating.

Figure 3.2 (p. 48) illustrates the links between actors at each of these levels (Cheng, 1996, p. 89; Cheung and Cheng, 1996). Activities illustrated in Figure 3.1 at different levels cannot be random or unconnected; they must be 'geared', foreshadowing an image that shapes analysis in the next section of this chapter. Figure 3.2, which may be viewed as three geared wheels, illustrates how congruent, coherent and comprehensive must be the field for self-management, extending across affective, behavioural and cognitive domains for administrators, teachers and students. Confirmation of the model was secured through research by Cheung (1996, reported in Cheung and Cheng, 1997). He used student achievement data in determining impact.

The schools in which Cheung conducted his research were participating in the School Management Initiative (SMI) established by the Education Department of Hong Kong in the early 1990s following a review of management in Hong Kong schools. The SMI called for schools to volunteer their participation in an approach involving higher levels of local participation in decision-making, more resource flexibility, a deeper planning capacity and more accountability. By 1997, almost all government schools and a small fraction of schools in the aided sector had joined (in Hong Kong, only about 8 per cent of schools are government schools, with most of the others being aided schools that are privately or corporately owned but receiving grants from government to meet a major part of their recurrent costs).

The Education Commission in Hong Kong, established in 1984 to make recommendation on education policy, called for full implementation of the SMI approach in all schools by 2000, referring to it more generically as school-based management but, significantly, proposing that it be integrated with a range of practices in pursuit of quality schooling for all. The linkages that emerge as so important in the review of research on school-based management are intended for Hong Kong. The Education Commission observed that:

> With the implementation of the School Management Initiative in 1991, the Education Department has introduced certain arrangements which provide School Management Initiative schools with a more accountable framework for school-based

*Figure 3.1   Three levels of self-management at the school level*

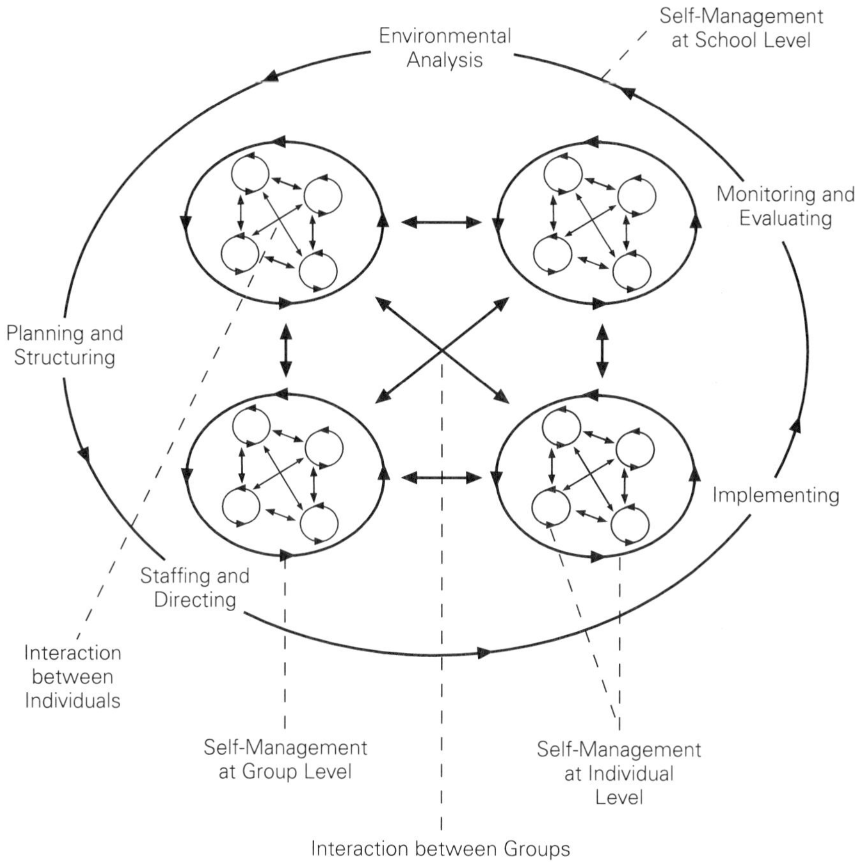

*Source:* Cheng, 1996, p. 78

management with teacher, parent and student participation. After several years of implementation, the experience from School Management Initiative schools suggests that such management is helpful in achieving school goals and in formulating long-term plans to meet student needs. The Commission therefore recommends that all schools should by the year 2000 practise school-based management in the spirit of School Management Initiative so that they can develop quality education according to the needs of their students. (Education Commission, 1996, p. xi)

In general, across the three nations considered thus far, it is apparent that many approaches to self-management have been adopted for reasons that may be worthwhile but, in their practice, do not involve strategies that call for different approaches to learning and teaching. Where they have, it appears that few research studies have employed approaches to analysis that are likely to reveal the linkages between self-management, a range of practices that penetrate the classroom, and learning outcomes. The Cheung and Cheng studies are a notable exception.

Figure 3.2   Actors in levels of self-management in schools

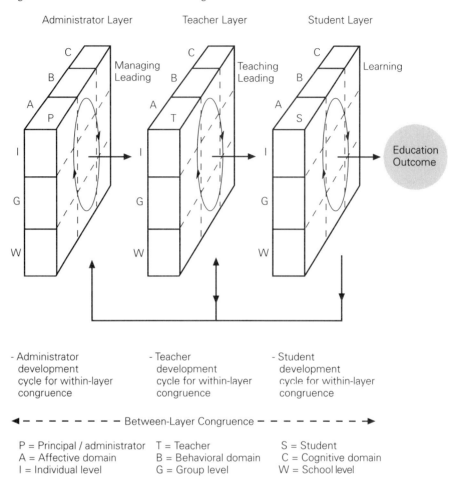

- Administrator
  development
  cycle for within-layer
  congruence

- Teacher
  development
  cycle for within-layer
  congruence

- Student
  development
  cycle for within-layer
  congruence

◄ – – – – – – – – Between-Layer Congruence – – – – – – – – ►

P = Principal / administrator   T = Teacher              S = Student
A = Affective domain            B = Behavioral domain     C = Cognitive domain
I = Individual level            G = Group level           W = School level

*Source:* adapted from Cheng, 1996, p. 89

### Australia (Victoria)

The Schools of the Future program in Victoria, implemented since 1993, calls for a high level of self-management within a curriculum and standards framework. Indeed, with about 1700 schools, it is the largest system anywhere to have decentralized as much as 90 per cent of its resources for school-level decision-making. Expectations for an impact on learning are clear in the objectives and purposes of the program (adapted from Hayward, 1993):

- encourage the continuing improvement in the quality of educational programs and practices in Victorian schools to enhance student learning outcomes;

- actively foster the attributes of good schools in terms of leadership, school ethos, goals, planning and accountability process;

- build on a state-wide framework of quality curriculum, programs and practices;

- encourage parents to participate directly in decisions that affect their child's education;

- recognize teachers as true professionals, able to determine their own careers and with the freedom to exercise their professional skills and judgments in the classroom;

- allow principals to become true leaders in their school with the ability to build and lead their teaching teams;

- enable communities, through the school charter, to determine the destiny of the school, its character and ethos;

- within guidelines, enable schools to develop their own programs to meet the individual needs of students; and

- be accountable to the community for the progress of the school and the achievements of its students.

In Victoria, Schools of the Future was the focus of a major investigation known as the Cooperative Research Project, established in early 1993 as a joint endeavour of the Department of Education, Victorian Association of State Secondary Principals, the Victorian Primary Principals Association and the University of Melbourne. Its purpose was to monitor the processes and outcomes of Schools of the Future as perceived by principals. Annual surveys of principals were conducted (see reports in Cooperative Research Project, 1994, 1995a, 1995b, 1996, 1997, 1998. The findings below are from Cooperative Research Project (1998)).

A key component in each survey was an invitation to principals to rate their confidence that the objectives and purposes will be attained in their schools. A confidence scale from 1 ('low') to 5 ('high') was provided. The two items concerned with outcomes and good schools have received the highest mean ratings in each of the seven surveys:

- Schools of the Future are accountable to the community for the progress of the school and the achievements of its students (mean of 3.6 in 1997).

- Schools of the Future actively foster the attributes of good schools in terms of leadership, school ethos, goals, planning and accountability (mean of 3.6 in 1997).

Principals in the base-line study in 1993 were invited to list the benefits they expected from their schools being Schools of the Future. Twenty-five benefits were classified in four areas: curriculum and learning, planning and resource allocation, personnel and professional, and school and community. These expected benefits were included in subsequent surveys, with principals asked to rate on the 5-point scale the extent to which each had been realized in their schools. Noteworthy as far as outcomes are concerned are responses in 1997 for items related to curriculum and learning: more responsive and relevant curriculum (mean of 3.3), improved learning outcomes for students (mean of 3.3), and opportunity to innovate (mean of 3.3). For the second of these, improved learning outcomes for students, 84 per cent of principals provided a rating of 3 or more on the 5-point scale in 1997. Assuming this is a considered response, it is an important finding worthy of closer examination.

It is possible to undertake analysis of responses in the survey to determine the direct and indirect effects of selected factors on learning. The approach known as structural equation modelling was employed, using LISREL 8 (Jöreskog and Sörbom, 1993). This approach allows the analysis of ordinal-scaled variables such as those utilized in the items of this survey.

The 45 items in the questionnaire that related to objectives and expected benefits were reduced to 7 variables or 'constructs' by grouping in related areas. Those that carried the highest weight in the formation of each construct were those that form part of an intuitive explanation of which capacities ought to impact on curriculum and learning in Schools of the Future. These include greater financial and administrative flexibility, higher community profile, planning the provision of curriculum, advice to teachers in support of the curriculum and standards framework, and confidence in the objectives of the program to encourage continuing improvement to enhance learning outcomes.

Structural equation modelling resulted in the model shown in Figure 3.3 which illustrates the direct and indirect effects among six constructs and their influence on the seventh construct, curriculum and learning benefits. This seventh construct is of major interest and it includes perceptions of improved learning outcomes. The model in Figure 3.3 is powerful in an explanatory sense for it has a Goodness of Fit Index of 0.969, indicating that 96.9 per cent of the variances and co-variances in the data are accounted for in the model.

The numbers in Figure 3.3 are standardized path coefficients and may be explained in this way. The coefficient for the path from Personnel and Professional Benefits to Curriculum and Learning Benefits is 0.299. This means that an increase of 1 standard deviation in principals' ratings of Personnel and Professional Benefits is associated with an increase of 0.299 of a standard deviation in ratings of Curriculum and Learning Benefits. In terms of direct effects, the model indicates that principals who gave high ratings on the achievement of Personnel and Professional Benefits and who report Curriculum Improvement due to the Curriculum and Standards Framework, as well as having confidence in Attainment of the Objectives of Schools of the Future, tend to be those who also give high ratings to the achievement of Curriculum and Learning Benefits. Among the indirect effects, the most interesting is for Planning and Resource Allocation Benefits. The effect on Curriculum and Learning Benefits is indirect, mediated through Personnel and Professional Benefits and confidence in Attainment of SOF Objectives.

*Figure 3.3 Explanatory model of direct and indirect effects among factors influencing principals' perceptions of Curriculum and Learning Benefits in Schools of the Future, Victoria, showing standardized path coefficients*

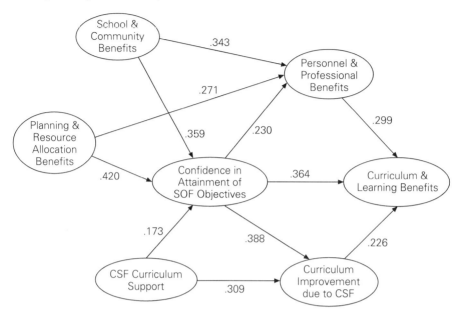

*Source:* Cooperative Research Project, 1998

The explanatory model is confirmation of what research elsewhere has shown, namely, that decentralization of decision-making in planning and resource allocation does not, of and in itself, result in improved learning for students. There is no direct cause-and-effect link between the two. What the model does suggest, however, is that if the linkages are made in an appropriate way, then an indirect effect is realized through action in the personnel and professional domain and also confidence in the efficacy of the reform.

The limitations of the research are acknowledged, since it is based on perceptions of principals. However, the application of a powerful analytical tool to the large body of data has yielded a consistent pattern for ratings in three surveys completed after several years experience in Schools of the Future, pointing to linkages that should be made in the self-managing school if this aspect of a reform program is to have an effect on learning outcomes for students. The final stage of the Cooperative Research Project was to undertake studies in particular schools to illuminate these linkages and to utilize student achievement data that are now available. Five such projects were in progress at the time of writing, with three being studies of linkages in primary and secondary schools that have reported gains in student achievement, and two concerned with initiatives in the Personnel and Professional domain that was found to be so important in the modelling illustrated in Figure 3.3: Full Staffing Flexibility and Professional Recognition.

## *International Comparisons*

When international comparisons are made, the conclusions about the achievements of systems of self-managing schools can be stated no more bluntly than the following:

> At the macrolevel, there is no evidence whatsoever that national educational systems where there is more autonomy for schools perform better in the area of basic competencies. (Meurat and Scheerens, 1995, cited by Scheerens and Bosker, 1997, p. 279)

The most recent evidence in support of this conclusion is furnished in the findings of the Third International Mathematics and Science Study in which relatively centralized nations of the East and Eastern Europe outperformed relatively decentralized nations in the West (see Lokan, Ford and Greenwood, 1996 and 1997).

Green (1997) provided a comprehensive account of international comparisons that is illuminating. He acknowledged that broad brush comparisons and hypotheses 'cannot be tested empirically since we have insufficient data currently to do this' (p. 107) but documented the manner in which relatively centralized nations such as France, Germany, Japan, Sweden and, more recently, Singapore, have higher 'aggregate attainments' than relatively decentralized nations such as the UK and the USA. He was not prepared to state that this conclusion would apply to 'average educational results' (p. 116). In seeking explanations he noted that, apart from time on task, 'many of the factors which appear to dominate debates about standards, like school organization, class size and levels of finance, seem to have little explanatory power in relation to the causes of differences in national standards, at least among countries at similar levels of development' (pp. 116–117). In particular, he cited the work of Lynn (1988), who found that there was no statistically significant relationship between levels of expenditure and educational attainment, with the former being relatively low in Singapore and Japan, each of which has high attainment, and relatively high in the USA, which has relatively low attainment (p. 117). Taking all things into account, he concluded that the high performing nations appear to have one thing in common:

> . . . as nations they place great emphasis on educational achievement, engendering high educational aspirations amongst individual learners. They tend to have a 'learning culture' in which parents and teachers have high expectations of their children's educational achievements, where the education systems are designed to provide opportunities and motivation for learners of all abilities, and where the labour market, and society in general, rewards those who do well in education. (Green, 1997, pp. 117–118)

The effects of this 'cultural priority' for education results in a willingness to stay on in education and, in the case of Japan, to invest additional resources in private tuition (juku). For nations such as the UK and the USA, the lower cultural priority seems to explain why they have been relatively unsuccessful in meeting the needs of all students: 'They have both been consistently successful in educating their elites to the highest international standards, but have failed to generalize the high aspirations of their elites to the generality of their populations' (Green, 1997, p. 120).

## Self-Governing Schools and Learning Outcomes

Evidence on the impact of a higher level of autonomy on learning outcomes is sparse. Considered here are findings from grant-maintained schools in the UK, private schools in an international perspective, and charter schools and voucher plans in the USA.

### Grant Maintained Schools

Some interesting and contentious data have emerged from comparisons of outcomes in locally managed schools (self-managing schools) and grant maintained schools (self-governing schools) in Britain. The latter used the 'opt out' mechanism provided in the 1988 Education Reform Act to leave their local education authorities. In a speech in Birmingham in February 1997 (GMSAC, 1997), reported also in the House of Commons, Michael Tomlinson, former Director of Inspections, Office for Standards in Education (OFSTED), offered a heavily qualified comparison of student achievement in the two types of schools using scores for the GCSE (General Certificate of Secondary Education). In classifying schools, he used the standard criterion for Britain for socio-economic condition, namely eligibility of students for free school meals. Five categories were established along these lines: grant maintained schools had higher scores than locally managed schools in all classifications. There were similar results when comparisons were made on other indicators: standards, efficiency, ethos, quality of education, overall.

Grant maintained schools have been resourced at a higher level than locally managed schools — initially through special grants to encourage opting out — because they get extra money roughly equivalent to the cost of services formerly provided by the local education authority. When asked why he thought differences in outcomes had been achieved, experienced grant maintained head Michael Bell referred to the very powerful commitment that staff in grant maintained schools had to their ongoing success. Other 'pre-existing' differences between the two types of schools are not likely to account for the apparent gap in performance of the two sectors (Bell, 1997).

On the other hand, independent research on differences between levels of achievement in locally managed and grant maintained schools suggests that a different conclusion should be reached, at least as far as examination results are concerned. Rosalind Levacic from the Open University surveyed 319 secondary schools in 89 areas, one-third of which were grant-maintained. Using the same criterion as OFSTED (percentage of students achieving five good results in examinations for the GCSE), but over a five-year period, Levacic found that grant maintained schools did indeed show an above average rate of improvement, but if the effects of the changing composition of their intakes were taken into account, there was no difference in levels of achievement between the two classifications of schools (Doe, 1998, p. 1; Levacic, Hardman and Woods, 1998).

One hesitates to draw conclusions on the basis of the foregoing, given that there are many factors that distinguish grant maintained from locally managed schools, and that the comparisons were based on student achievement data at one level only. The OFSTED conclusion is compelling because differences were found across a range of indicators, not just achievement, but the Levacic study, while not examining the impact of different intakes on other indicators, certainly suggests the need for caution in drawing implications for policy on these matters.

### Private Schools

Private schools are the most clear-cut form of self-governing schools and the evidence of impact on learning outcomes is mixed when comparisons are made with public schools. Scheerens and Bosker (1997) adopted an international perspective and concluded that:

> Generally, in developed countries, private schools appear to be more effective, even in countries where both private and public schools are financed by the state, as is the case in The Netherlands. (p. 278)

Explanations for this superiority include the view that 'parents who send their children to these schools are more active educational consumers and make specific demands on the educational philosophy of schools' (Scheerens and Bosker, 1997, p. 279). This view echoes that of Coleman and Hoffer (1987) whose studies of schools in the US revealed that, all other factors being equal, schools with a high level of what they termed 'social capital' seemed to do better than others, with social capital considered to be the strength of mutually supporting relationships among principal, teachers, parents, students, and others in the school community, including the church where the school was a church school.

### The Effects of Competition

A variant of research on public and private schools was carried out in Texas where data on student achievement in school districts were analyzed according to the degree of penetration of private schools. There was no evidence that achievement was associated with penetration, suggesting that competition engendered by private schools had no impact on level of achievement in public schools (Grosskopf, Hayes, Tayfor and Weber, 1995, cited by Levin, 1997, p. 309).

Research in Britain also suggests that claims that increased competition will drive up standards should be treated with caution. Studies by Rosalind Levacic

(Levacic, Hardman and Woods, 1998) were cited earlier in respect to the differences in student achievement at the level of the GCSE between locally managed and grant maintained schools. She also compared levels of achievement in areas that differed according to levels of competition among schools. She took account of the extent to which parents exercised choice where such choice was available. She found that schools with little or no competition showed a slight improvement over a five-year period compared to a slight decline in schools where competition was strongest. Levacic's conclusion was explicit: 'Improvement was worse in areas of high competition. There was no evidence to confirm the claim that competition improves schools' (cited by Doe, 1998, p. 1).

### Charter Schools and Voucher Plans

The charter school movement in the United States, while still small, is gathering momentum, with more than 800 across the nation at the time of writing. Tests of student achievement in Michigan indicated levels of proficiency in the state's 106 charter schools were generally lower than in public and private schools in science and writing (Schnaiberg, 1997, p. 5). These early findings do not warrant a judgment at this time for several reasons. First, charter schools in Michigan tend to draw children with a history of academic failure, and also a higher proportion of minority students (53 per cent compared to 22 per cent for the state as a whole). Second, many charter schools whose students were tested had just commenced operations under their new status. Third, it is clear that attention thus far has focused on structural, governance and financial arrangements, with little opportunity to develop the linkages and gearing to classroom practice of the kind illustrated earlier in this chapter.

There are few instances of voucher plans wherein resources are given to parents who then deploy them after making a choice of school for their children. Witte and his colleagues provided an analysis of relative achievement after four years of experience in the Milwaukee Parental Choice Program for students from low income families. Voucher students attending private schools performed no better than their counterparts in public schools (Witte, Thorn, Pritchard and Claubouern, 1994, cited by Levin, 1997, p. 309).

### From Adult Games to Children Games

Taking school reform and associated research as a whole, it is understandable that few clear indications emerge of how outcomes for students have been impacted. Self-management has been one of a complex array of changes in most settings under consideration. Giving additional authority to a school has, for example, been associated with empowerment, as in the changes that followed the Karmel Report in Australia in the early 1970s, or with a determination to limit power, illustrated with intentions in respect to local education authorities in Britain following the

1988 Education Reform Act. There has been no attempt to systematically gather data on student achievement before and after change in a way that will enable conclusions to be drawn. In most instances, there have been no means of gathering such data, since it is only in very recent times that systems have developed schemes for assessing student achievement at different levels across all schools, and those that have a 'value added' dimension or intention are still in the formative stages.

Against this backdrop there is evidence, based on professional opinion, that key players tend to report improved outcomes, as in the case of principals in surveys in Britain and Victoria. Other key players, notably teachers and parents, are less inclined to report so positively, except where they refer to actions in which they have played a part (as illustrated in Townsend, 1996).

If the conceptual models of Cheng, the critique of Hanushek and the findings from Victoria are taken as a guide, it is apparent that attention in research and practice should now focus on the linkages between systemic reform and school reform, and between school reform and classroom reform. An example of the first link is a school using its capacity for self-management to select and provide professional development for staff to address a key priority such as improving literacy levels in a primary school. An example of the second link is for teachers so selected or developed to teach differently or construct learning experiences for students differently, consistent with what is now known about the most effective approaches to literacy, to monitor student achievement on a continuous basis and be able to report the outcomes of their efforts.

Political scientist Frederick Wirt used game imagery to describe what is needed: it is time to move from 'adult games' to 'children games'. He argued that 'much of this reform turbulence seems like an "adult game" that appears regularly in democratic policy context', being mainly a political game 'because it is a struggle for power to decide dominant symbols, to secure resources, to employ facilitative structures, and to express historical influences' (Wirt, 1991, pp. 39–40). Such struggles should be distinguished from the 'children game':

> The essence of this game in not overtly centred on power, hence it is not overtly political, but rather focuses on leading children to learn; hence it is primarily educational. This kind of game:
>
> 1  centres on the curriculum and instructional aspects of the education profession; and
>
> 2  commences, operates, and concludes with an evaluation mode to determine whether these efforts actually do increase learning.
>
> I suggest that the evaluation component of the children game is central to how it is played, thereby distinguishing it from the adult game of policy making. . . Any reform effort arising out of the adult game must also be judged for how the learning environment is altered and how that produces, in turn, improved achievement. (Wirt, 1991, p. 40)

In his international comparative review of the reform effort to 1991, Wirt concluded that 'The cold truth is that there is no convincing evidence that these UK and US reforms have played the children game successfully' (Wirt, 1991, p. 40). It is interesting that Michael Barber, head of the Standards and Effectiveness Unit in the UK, cited earlier, has also used game imagery to describe what is now needed. His 1996 book, which foreshadowed the substance of the White Paper of the Labour Government in 1997, had the title *The Learning Game* (Barber, 1996).

A variant of the adult game is the academic game in which critics of the self-managing school cite the lack of direct cause-and-effect evidence of a link between decentralization and student outcomes as reason to oppose the movement. It is, of course, a fair statement on the evidence but, as implied above, if an academic variant of the children game is played, one is led to consider the matter of linkages and a 'theory of action' that underpins the case for self-management. That theory derives from more than a decade of research on school and classroom effectiveness and improvement.

### Gearing Self-Management to Learning

The 'theory of action' for a children or learning game about self-management emerged in the early to mid-1980s, before landmark legislation such as the 1988 Education Reform Act in Britain. The work of respected scholars Theodore Sizer (1984) and John Goodlad (1984) is striking in this regard and was cited in *The Self-Managing School* (Caldwell and Spinks, 1988). In each instance, they found in their extended studies of schools in the US that tight, centralized controls on schools placed constraints on teachers, limiting the extent to which they could address the range of student needs with available resources. Sizer concluded that 'one imperative for better schools' was to give teachers and students room to take full advantage of the variety among them, a situation which 'implies that there must be substantial authority for each school. For most public and diocesan Catholic school systems, this means the decentralization of power from headquarters to individual schools' (Sizer, 1984, p. 214). Goodlad concluded that there was a need for 'genuine decentralization of authority and responsibility to the local school within a framework designed to assure school-to-school equity and a measure of accountability' (Goodlad, 1984, p. 275).

A compelling 'theory of action' emerged from studies by Matthew Miles and his colleagues in urban secondary schools in the US (reported by Miles, 1987). Case studies were completed following a nationwide survey of schools which had shown major educational gains in the wake of system- and school-initiated improvement projects. They identified 16 factors that contributed in a cause-and-effect manner to school improvement. Four of these were preconditions to the extent that a system-wide policy was required to set them in place. These were the appointment of strong educational leaders; a relatively high level of school autonomy, especially in relation to resources; appointment of staff to help ensure a high level of staff cohesiveness; and the decentralization of decision-making to the extent that the principal and staff have the opportunity to adapt the program of the school to meet the needs and interests of students and community. The remaining 12 factors were matters for the attention of the school, including the empowerment of staff, the provision of rewards for staff, vision, the exercise of control over staffing, the exercise of control over resources, staff willingness and initiative in the management of change, evolutionary program development, the building of external networks, evidence of 'deep' rather than 'shallow' coping in addressing problems, good strategies in the implementation of change and the institutionalization of change, and change in organizational structures and processes.

Three observations may be made about findings on school improvement reported by Miles. First, that a capacity for self-management is a pre-condition. Second, that system policy on self-management is linked or geared to a school's willingness and capacity to take up the opportunities afforded by self-management. Third, that these findings and the earlier research by Sizer and Goodlad pre-date the reforms of the late 1980s and early 1990s that have been concerned with massive system-wide change. This change has achieved system-wide scale-up of the pre-conditions described by Miles but not, generally speaking, of the linkage or gearing at the school level. It has been an adult game in design and implementation as well as in political and academic debate. Returning to these earlier landmark studies helps shift attention to the children game.

### Linking Self-Management to Learning and Teaching

While the studies and strategies reported above make clear the kind of linkages that are needed, none really focus on what occurs in the classroom. The findings of recent research help complete the picture in this regard. One of the most detailed studies was undertaken by Elmore, Peterson and McCarthey (1996) in three schools in the US where school restructuring had occurred. Their starting point was that restructuring at the school level, by itself, was insufficient if there was to be improvement in outcomes for students. By restructuring, they were referring to how students were grouped, how teachers relate to students and to each other, and how content is allocated to time over the school day. They cite Fred Newmann, Centre on Restructuring Schools, University of Wisconsin, Madison, who argued that 'new organizational structures alone are unlikely to improve education' in the absence of new commitments and competencies (cited by Elmore, Peterson and McCarthey, 1996, p. 7). On larger restructuring efforts, including school-based management, they take a similar stance to Wirt in arguing that structural change 'is often undertaken for political or symbolic reasons, many of which are unrelated to the improvement of teaching and learning' (the 'adult game' rather than the 'children game'). They draw four conclusions about efforts to change learning and teaching:

- the relationship between changes in the formal structure and changes in teaching practice is necessarily weak, problematic and indirect; attention to structural change often distracts from the more fundamental problem of changing teaching practice.

- there probably is no single set of structural changes that schools can make that will lead predictably to a particular kind of teaching practice.

- it is just as plausible for changes in practice to lead to changes in structure as vice versa.

- the transformation of teaching practice is fundamentally a problem of enhancing individual knowledge and skill, not a problem of organizational structure; getting the structure right depends on first understanding that problem of knowledge and skill.

(Elmore, Peterson and McCarthey, 1996, pp. 237–41)

The final conclusion is the most important, for it leads to their single recommendation for educational practitioners, namely: 'providing access to new knowledge and skill for teachers should supersede attention to the problem of how to restructure schools' (Elmore, Peterson and McCarthey, 1996, pp. 241–2). If this is indeed the most important implication, then the process of 'backward mapping' makes clear the linkages with structural reforms such as the creation of systems of self-managing schools. Providing access to new knowledge and skill calls for professional development programs for teachers in a particular school that will be shaped by needs and priorities at that school. Having a capacity to determine the kind of professional development, select a provider and resource the involvement of teachers is a capacity that is afforded by self-management. This linkage, determined by backward mapping, was affirmed in the structural equation modelling in the recent research in Victoria (see Figure 3.3, p. 51, based on Cooperative Research Project, 1998). Continuing the process, ensuring that teachers have required knowledge and skill can also be accomplished by the school having a capacity to select teachers whose knowledge and skill is up to date and a match with needs and priorities at the school level. Mapping further, one is led into a different policy domain, namely the preparation of teachers in pre-service programs, or to another, namely, strategies that should be in place to direct and support schools that fail to make these linkages.

### Backward Mapping

The technique of 'backward mapping' is advocated by Elmore, Peterson and McCarthey (1996, p. 243), who contend that 'we would rather map backward from an understanding of teaching practice to an understanding of what a good school structure might be — recognising that the solution to that problem will vary from school to school — than we would map forward from structural changes in schools to changes in teaching practice'. Dimmock (1995, p. 280) draws on Elmore's earlier advocacy of backward mapping (Elmore, 1979–80) to propose five layers, illustrated in the model in Figure 3.4, commencing the process with consideration of student outcomes, working back through learning styles and processes; teaching strategies; school organization and structure; and leadership, management, resources, culture, and climate. He contends that the model 'provides an overarching framework and strategy by which all schools and their communities can address the challenge of providing school leadership and management for quality teaching and

*Figure 3.4   Backward mapping from student outcomes: An illustration*

*Source:* adapted from Dimmock, 1995, p. 280

learning in the 1990s and into the twenty-first century' (Dimmock, 1995, p. 281). In an environment in which each school has a unique mix of learning needs among students and where such high expectations are now set for the achievement of all students, the capacities that are available to the self-managing school can assist at several levels.

### Linkages Illustrated in the Early Literacy Research Project

An impressive illustration of how linkages can made at the school and class-room level in a system of self-managing schools is furnished in the Early Literacy Research Project in Victoria, initiated in late 1995 as a partnership of the Department of Education and the University of Melbourne. Its purpose was to design, implement and evaluate a program to raise levels of literacy of 'at risk' students in the early years of schooling. It stemmed from an interest in what resources were required to deliver a program of this kind (along the lines recommended in the report of the Education Committee, 1995) and from the state initiative to improve literacy standards. A coherent strategy of 7 elements was implemented in 25 schools selected from more than 400 expressing an interest, with criteria for inclusion being a low score on the system's index of educational disadvantage, a clear need in the literacy area, and a commitment to participate in the project that called for intensive professional development. A matched sample of 25 schools was selected as a control. Preliminary results in the first year indicated significant and large effects of the program across ten measures of literacy, with shortcomings of existing approaches revealed in graphic fashion and a clear indication of how the professional development program can be made effective, as evidenced in the trial schools (see Crevola and Hill, 1997, for a detailed account of the program and its outcomes in the first year of operation).

*Case Study of System–School–Classroom Links in Schools of the Future*

Linkages are illustrated in a case study of the experience of one school in the Early Literacy Research Project, with the commentary indicating the manner in which the authorities of self-management in the Schools of the Future program were utilized. The school is Mackellar Primary School. It was built in 1991 in an outer suburban area of Melbourne. It now has more than 500 students. It is multicultural in every sense of the word, with more than 40 languages spoken by children who attend and more than half not speaking English at home. Staff include classroom teachers, integration aides, and school support officers, with several on contract appointment. Mackellar was included in Intake 4 of Schools of the Future and has full staff flexibility.

The current principal, Janice Szmal, was appointed in 1994 to find low levels of morale and a still growing school. Many teachers joined the staff as over-entitlement from other schools. The principal immediately established a leadership team consisting of the principal, assistant principal, and three leading teachers. Professional development in the early stages of the principal's appointment included much team-building.

The charter development process in 1995 readily confirmed what many staff and parents were aware of, namely, that many students had difficulties in literacy, and addressing these needs became a priority for the school, along with the introduction of information technology, Languages Other Than English (LOTE) and some curriculum development intended to build a higher level of coherence and connectedness in the face of pressures to fragment the curriculum as the key learning areas of the Curriculum and Standards Framework (CSF) took hold.

The capacity of the School Global Budget and full staffing flexibility was used to advertise and select a person to serve as coordinator of a team of teachers to tackle the issue of literacy, and for several new appointments to replace teachers who retired or took up appointments elsewhere. Only those teachers who were committed to a strategy to dramatically lift literacy levels were appointed to teach in Prep and Year 1. Trade-offs were made in budget and staffing to secure smaller classes in the early years and larger classes in the higher years.

The literacy team had 12 members and generally met weekly since it commenced operations in late 1995. Teachers in the early years are members along with associated integration aides and school support officers. The principal was not a member but played a key role at the outset and on a continuing basis, much along the lines of an 'educational strategist', discussed later in this chapter. The principal was knowledgeable about strategies that work in literacy, having attended seminars and other professional development activities on the theme and continued to read digests of research findings as these came to hand in the growing state network on literacy.

The team proceeded with clear strategic intentions, with plans established for a full-time coordinator of literacy, one-to-one tutoring in the form of Reading Recovery, at least 90 minutes per day on structured reading, and parental involvement along the lines of Parents as Tutors. A sense of team was rapidly built through the regular meetings and personal and team professional development. Each member had a personal professional development plan, as is now generally required, but for the team, this has meant acquiring state-of-the-art knowledge in the field.

One of the key characteristics of a high performing team was built in from the outset with the pre-testing and continual monitoring of student achievement in reading. Marie Clay's Observation Survey (New Zealand), the Woodcock Language Proficiency Battery (USA) and Record of Oral Language were utilized. Students were matched to books according to their levels, with groupings of students rotated through tasks appropriate to their level. There was not agreement among all at the outset, or even now, with discussions and debates similar to those that rage around the world about the relative merits of phonics and whole language, and whole class instruction and group work. The literacy team provided a constructive and vibrant environment for managing these encounters.

The characteristics of a high-performing team were also built as the weeks and months passed, with different people quickly bringing to bear their capacity for acquiring information outside the school, or monitoring the progress of the team, or taking responsibility for chairing or facilitating meetings, or maintaining the morale of the group, or feeding a stream of creative ideas for discussion, or generally making sure that 'things happen around here'. While the importance of incentives and rewards was recognized by the coordinator and principal, few funds were available, so these largely came in the form of clear expectations that were linked to charter priorities; coherence in the work of the team, personal professional development and other aspects of performance management; an exciting atmosphere in team meetings as creative ideas were shared, strategies were formulated, and results were secured; and parties and other occasions for celebration were organized. The increased opportunity for networking was also a form of reward and recognition, electronically on the web, personally through professional development, and team visits to several schools as the possibilities for benchmarking performance against those in similar kinds of communities and with similar high expectations were explored.

The results were positive and highly rewarding for all concerned. There was clear evidence of improved literacy, beyond expectations and beyond that achieved prior to the formation of the team. Parental satisfaction was evident along with improved staff morale in the early years, with focused teaching linked to professional development, and a greater sense of collegiality through mentoring and coaching. There was an air of expectation among teachers in Years 2 and 3 because they sensed that many of the problems of the past that derive from low levels of literacy would be alleviated when children who had benefitted from the literacy initiative reached their classes. Opportunities to achieve at higher levels in other areas of the curriculum started to emerge.

The principal is passionate about what occurred, and acknowledged the importance of key elements of the strategy: the focus that the charter provided from the
outset; the flexibility made possible by the School Global Budget and new staffing
arrangements; the capacity to build a team; the importance of gathering information
to manage performance; and the general coherence of the program, including professional development, teaching and outcomes. There was acknowledgment by the
principal that trade-offs had to be made, in resources, in class size and in balance in
the curriculum to secure the key elements of the literacy strategy.

The experiences of Mackellar Primary School and the findings to date in the
Early Literacy Research Project are consistent with contemporary models of school
effectiveness such as that developed by Scheerens (Scheerens and Bosker, 1997,
p. 46) as shown in Figure 3.5.

Most elements of the model have been 'tapped', including Context (achievement stimulants from higher administrative levels, development of educational con-
sumerism); Inputs (teacher experience, per pupil expenditure, parent support); Process
at School Level (degree of achievement-oriented policy, educational leadership,
consensus, cooperative planning of teachers, quality of school curricula in terms of
content covered and formal structure, orderly atmosphere, evaluative potential);
Process at the Classroom Level (time on task, structured teaching, opportunity to
learn, high expectations of pupils' progress, degree of evaluation and monitoring of
pupils' progress, reinforcement); and Outputs (student achievement).

A key issue is the extent to which what was accomplished would have
occurred without the capacity for self-management at the school level. Clearly, if
inputs and processes at the outset were optimal, a capacity for self-management
would be unnecessary. However, it is evident that a contribution was made to the
extent that the school was responsive to its community, utilized its flexibility in
staffing to make appropriate selection of teachers, and provided targeted professional development with resources from its school global budget. Overall, this is a
compelling illustration of the kind of linkage or gearing that must be made if the
'theory of action' that underpins the self-managing school is to have effects on
outcomes for students.

### Principals and Other School Leaders

Just as an enhanced capacity for self-management appears in most prescriptions for
school reform in many nations, so too does a heightened expectation for the principal. The appointment and subsequent leadership of the principal were important
in the case study of Mackellar. Research by Matthew Miles and his colleagues cited
earlier (Miles, 1987) found that the appointment of strong educational leaders to the
principalship was a 'pre-condition' for school improvement.

A meta-analysis of research on the relationship between the role of the principal and school effectiveness was carried out by Hallinger and Heck, with their work
spanning the period from 1980 to 1995, the years in which the school effectiveness

Figure 3.5   *Integrated model of school effectiveness*

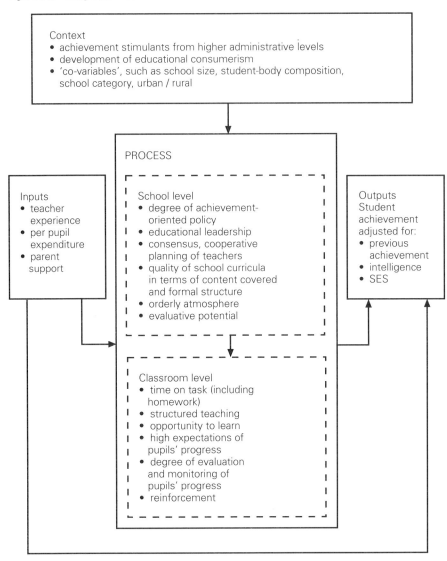

and school improvement movement gathered momentum. They found surprisingly little evidence of a direct relationship, but consistent evidence of an indirect effect in their testing of models which suggest that:

> . . . principal leadership that makes a difference is aimed toward influencing internal school processes that are directly linked to student learning. These internal processes range from school policies and norms (e.g., academic expectations, school mission, student opportunity to learn, instructional organization, academic learning

time) to the practices of teachers. Studies based on a mediated-effects model frequently uncovered statistically significant indirect effects of principal leadership on student achievement via such variables. (Hallinger and Heck, 1996, p. 38)

Gurr conducted a study of secondary principals in Victoria's Schools of the Future. He identified 17 themes in the role and 10 of these had emerged since the reform was initiated in 1993. Three powerful themes were that leadership which focused on learning and teaching was important, but less direct than was practised or advocated in the past; that transformational leadership was evident, marked by a future orientation, with cultural and symbolic dimensions; and that a capacity for accountability and responsiveness was needed in self-managing schools (Gurr, 1996a, 1996b, 1996c).

Johnston conducted case studies of three secondary schools in Victoria identified by knowledgeable people as having the characteristics of a learning organization (Johnston, 1997). Her doctoral research addressed the question 'What are the characteristics of schools and principals which are perceived to be successful learning organizations?'. She found that four key elements were instrumental in the development of a learning organization in these schools: inclusive collaborative structures, effective communication channels, integrated and inclusive professional development programs, and learning focussed leadership.

Johnston's concept of 'learning focussed leadership' appears critical if the linkages described in this chapter are to be made effective. It is a rich concept but it is strategic and empowering more than it is heroic or 'hands on'. She described the principal of the exemplar among the three schools in the following terms:

> The principal was clearly influential but, at the same time, was regarded as a team player. She was particularly adept at demonstrating what the current reality was while exposing the school to a vision of what could be. She articulated the creative tension gap and indicated the way forward. In the process the school was infused with an energy and optimism not often seen in schools at this time. The idea that all within the school should be leaders captures the notion of leadership of teams. . . (Johnston, 1997, p. 282)

The research findings of Hallinger and Heck, generally, and Gurr and Johnston, in Victoria, resonate with those on self-management, where the consistent conclusion is that there is no direct cause-and-effect link. They are also consistent with the findings from the Cooperative Research Project in Victoria cited earlier. It is the principal and other school leaders who, for example, will set in train the processes for the selection of staff; the professional development of teachers; the focusing of curriculum to the particular learning needs of students; and the management of a planning and resource allocation system that ensures that data on need and performance are analyzed, priorities are set and action proceeds. In other words, the linkages and gearing illustrated earlier must be made effective and this calls for leadership and management (see conceptualization in Figure 3.1, p. 47, and Figure 3.2, p. 48). Consistent with general contemporary writing on leadership, the whole enterprise will be shaped by a shared vision of what can be accomplished.

### When Linkages Are Not Made: Supporting
### the Self-Managing School

A key issue, now at centre stage in public policy in several nations, is the manner in which schools shall be supported when there is clear evidence that the linkages have not been made or, for any other reason, a self-managing school, or any school, is seen to be 'failing' or simply 'cruising'. This stage of reform in Victoria was reached in 1998, with all schools completing Annual Reports and approximately one-third completing a Triennial Review, which integrates Annual Reports with insights from an external validator. All schools are utilizing an unprecedented amount of data in the compilation of these reports.

This issue is important in the next stage of reform in Britain, as illustrated in strategies set out in the White Paper on *Excellence in Schools* (Secretary of State for Education and Employment, 1997) and subsequent legislation and plans. The key appears to be achieving a balance of pressure and support, with the previous government seen to be giving too much attention to the former:

> All the evidence indicates that standards rise fastest where schools themselves take responsibility for their improvement. But schools need the right balance of pressure and support from central and local government. Because the education service has been poorly coordinated in recent years, we have not achieved that balance. The support from central and local agencies has been patchy and inconsistent. Schools have had plenty of pressure, but not always of a kind which raised standards. There has been an excessive concentration on the structure and organization of schools at the expense of improving teaching, learning and leadership. (Secretary of State for Education and Employment, 1997, p. 24)

A range of strategies was canvassed, including the temporary withdrawal of budget delegation where schools are unresponsive, with important roles for schools, local education authorities, the Standards and Effectiveness Unit, OFSTED and the Department for Education and Employment. An important mechanism is the requirement that each local education authority prepare an Education Development Plan setting out how it intends to promote school improvement.

The manner in which these intentions are to be brought to realization warrants close attention and this is done in Chapter 5.

### Summary

There is no doubt that, while factors underpinning the movement to self-managing schools are many and varied, there has always been an expectation that they will make a contribution to improved outcomes for students. There is also no doubt that evidence of a direct cause-and-effect relationship between self-management and improved outcomes is minimal. This is understandable given that few initiatives in self-management have been linked in a systematic way to what occurs in classrooms in a manner that is likely to impact on learning. As Frederick Wirt has opined, it has to date been an adult game rather than a children game. A variant of the adult game is an academic game that limits attention in research to structural and organizational change.

An understanding of how self-management may impact on student outcomes may be gained by examining the linkages or gearing that must be achieved, and early evidence in Victoria is promising. It confirms a 'theory of action' that involves 'backward mapping' from learning outcomes to a range of contextual, input and process factors, several of which are enhanced with a capacity for self-management. These are mainly concerned with the selection, placement and ongoing professional development of teachers as schools develop a capacity to set targets and implement strategies for improvement based on the systematic collection of data about student achievement. The principal plays an important leadership role that, like the capacity for self-management itself, is more indirect than direct in its effects. The focus of all effort is learning and teaching and the support of learning and teaching, all shaped by a shared vision of what is possible, underpinned by state-of-the-art knowledge about school and classroom effectiveness and improvement. A balance of external pressure and support is important if self-managing schools are to be high performing schools.

### Implications for Policy and Practice

These findings are rich in their implications for policy and practice in further work on Track 2. What follows are illustrative and introductory rather than comprehensive.

A shared vision of what is possible has implications for the stance of governments at every level, indeed for all institutions with an interest in education, if account is taken of the high and sustained levels of student achievement in some nations, especially in Europe and the East compared to others in the West, where outcomes for students in some settings are relatively and consistently low. Without drawing implications as far as resources are concerned, there should be a concerted effort to set expectations for high achievement by all. High levels of leadership will be required and must be sustained over time at every level, from national government to local school council to the classroom, if expectations and values in respect to outcomes are to become a part of the culture, as they have in nations against which student achievement is benchmarked. Policies and practices devoted to this effort should apply across the board, regardless of the extent of self-management in schools.

There are implications for a range of organizations and institutions if state-of-the-art knowledge and skill about school and classroom effectiveness and improvement are to permeate every level of schools and school systems. Included here are those concerned with teacher preparation, as well as professional associations and others with a role to play in ongoing development. This knowledge is more comprehensive and robust than it has ever been, as is the skill required to apply it for all students in every setting. There are implications here for the capacity of those who

seek to prepare for a career in the education professions. Cultural change of the kind described above will be important, if not a prerequisite, if the standing of the education professions is to match those in other fields where similar levels of knowledge and skill are required.

A theme running through the findings in Chapter 3 is that linkages must be made at every level, most importantly in schools and classrooms. This means a policy framework that ensures the selection of staff who share the vision and have the capacities to bring it to realization. It means the selection of principals and others who can lead the effort and establish the structures and processes for the selection, placement and ongoing professional development of teachers; manage a system that ensures the setting of targets and the implementation of strategies for improvement based on the collection of data about student achievement; and nurture a learning community where all are committed to the endeavour. It means schools and classrooms designed and resourced so that expectations for teaching and learning can be achieved. Included here are matters related to learning technologies that will transform schools in the new millennium.

Achieving a balance of pressure and support has implications for policy and practice at several levels, with linkage important if the effort is to succeed. Pressure includes the setting of high expectations, specification in curriculum and standards frameworks, and creation of information systems for the collection of information about student progress and achievement. This pressure may be applied at the system level by government, at the local level by school council, and within the school by the principal and others with authority and responsibility. Support is similarly required at these levels. Apart from ongoing professional development and the establishment and maintenance of information and learning systems, this will require measures to identify, assist and, if necessary, replace those who fail or fall short of expectations. This support is also important in a cultural sense to the extent that all organizations with an interest or a stake in the future of schools should be aligned in their support of policies and practices of the kind illustrated here. It is clear that this alignment has not been achieved in many places.

---

### Strategic Intentions for Schools
### Linking Self-Management to Learning Outcomes

1 The primary purpose of self-management is to make a contribution to learning, so schools that aspire to success in this domain will make an unrelenting effort to utilize all of the capacities that accrue with self-management to achieve that end.

2 There will be clear, explicit and planned links, either direct or indirect, between each of the capacities that come with self-management and activities in the school that relate to learning and teaching and the support of learning and teaching.

3   There is a strong association between the mix and capacities of staff and success in addressing needs and priorities in learning, so schools will develop a capacity to optimally select staff, taking account of these needs and priorities.

4   There is a strong association between the knowledge and skills of staff and learning outcomes for students, so schools will employ their capacity for self-management to design, select, implement or utilize professional development programs to help ensure these outcomes.

5   A feature of staff selection and professional development will be the building of high performing teams whose work is needs-based and data-driven, underpinned by a culture that values quality, effectiveness, equity and efficiency.

6   There is a strong association between social capital and learning outcomes, so schools will utilize their capacities for self-management to build an alliance of community interests to support a commitment to high achievement for all students.

7   Self-managing schools will not be distracted by claims and counter-claims for competition and the impact of market forces, but will nonetheless market their programs with integrity, building the strongest possible links between needs and aspirations of the community, program design, program implementation and program outcomes.

8   Schools will have a capacity for 'backward mapping' in the design and implementation of programs for learning, starting from goals, objectives, needs and desired outcomes, and working backwards to determine courses of action that will achieve success, utilizing where possible and appropriate the capacities that accrue with self-management.

9   Incentive, recognition and reward schemes will be designed that make explicit the links between effort and outcomes in the take-up of capacities for self-management and improvement in learning outcomes, acknowledging that as much if not more attention must be given to intrinsic as to extrinsic incentives and rewards.

10  A key task for principals and other school leaders is to help make effective the links between capacities for self-management and learning outcomes, and to ensure that support is available when these links break down or prove ineffective.

# Completing the Journey:
# Driving and Constraining Forces

Chapter 4 deals with what needs to be done to complete the journey on Track 1: building a system of self-managing schools. Some nations are well down that track, notably Australia (in Victoria especially). Britain, New Zealand and some parts of Canada and the United States. Some systems have barely commenced. Particular attention is given to the legal, political and industrial environment that impinges on efforts to decentralize authority, responsibility and accountability to schools in the public sector.

It is not feasible within a single chapter to address these matters in all or even a few countries. The focus is on Australia, with illustrations from other nations.

### Scope

Within Australia, particular attention is paid to states where significant change has occurred recently, or is planned in the near future. For this reason, extensive reference is made to Victoria and its Schools of the Future program, under way since 1993, and developments in two states: Queensland with Leading Schools and Tasmania with Directions in Education. Reference is also made to Western Australia, where proposals for the overhaul of the Education Act include a limited extension of the already constrained level of self-management.

Developments in other states and territories have been noteworthy at one time or another in the past, but current practices are not the subject of attention in this report. South Australia was a pioneer of 'Freedom and Authority in Schools', the title of an energizing and landmark Memorandum to Principals by Director-General of Education, Alby Jones, in 1970 (see Department of Education, South Australia, 1970).The Australian Capital Territory also made progress in the 1970s. The Northern Territory has had a relatively high level of self-management for several years, and is relatively stable in this regard. New South Wales moved sharply in the direction of self-management in the late 1980s and early 1990s, but intentions were thwarted for a variety of reasons and there is some evidence of re-centralization. Constraining forces in New South Wales are identified in several places.

While particular attention is paid to Australia, reference is made to what has occurred in other nations where efforts have been made or intentions have been announced to achieve higher levels of school autonomy. An assessment is made of driving and constraining forces where these have had or are expected to have an impact on autonomy. Reference is made to developments in respect to charter schools in the United States and locally managed and grant maintained schools in the United Kingdom following the election of the Labour Government. Brief reference is also made to New Zealand.

A total of 20 forces have been identified as impinging on efforts to provide greater autonomy for schools in the public sector, of which 8 are driving forces and 12 are constraining forces. The conclusion is that, unless a significant initiative appears on the scene to either add to the driving forces or mitigate the constraining forces, there is unlikely to be a change to current patterns of authority, responsibility and accountability. As far as Australia is concerned the Schools of the Future program in Victoria is likely to be the high water mark in school autonomy for the foreseeable future.

### Victoria as the Benchmark

The level of school autonomy in Victoria increased steadily from the mid-1970s to the early 1990s, with school councils making their appearance early in this period. At about this time some funds were decentralized for local decision-making, especially in the wake of the Report of the Interim Committee of the Australian Schools Commission (1973) (Karmel Report) that established special purpose grants, often with state counterparts, to address particular needs or redress particular disadvantages at the school level.

Impetus was given to these developments in 1983, under the Labor Government elected in 1982, with school councils being given policy powers, within a framework provided in state legislation and policy, and a capacity to approve the budget of the school. Zoning of students to their nearest school was removed and significant local input was introduced in the process of selecting the school principal. The decentralization project stalled in 1986 (see Government of Victoria, 1986), largely in response to the opposition of unions, parent organizations and some bureaucrats.

Schools of the Future was the title given to a package of educational reforms introduced by the Kennett Government in 1993, following its election in late 1992 (see Caldwell and Hayward, 1998, for a detailed account of design and implementation of Schools of the Future). While building to some extent on the existing framework, there were sweeping changes in scope and style, in the manner summarized below.

A capacity for local selection of principals was extended to a limited capacity for the local selection of teachers, within a policy framework known as Full Staffing Flexibility. This capacity is constrained in important ways, as described later in the chapter.

Where only about 6 per cent of state funds were decentralized to schools previously, under Schools of the Future this rose to nearly 90 per cent, which means that some schools have control of several million dollars in the School Global Budget, as it is called, which covers virtually all categories of non-capital expenditure. Schools may allocate their resources across most categories of expense, according to local priorities within a state-wide framework. Autonomy thus lies in two principal areas, namely, staffing and budget.

The state-wide framework has three main components. There is a Curriculum and Standards Framework covering eight Key Learning Areas for all years from Preparatory to Year 10, with requirements for the Victorian Certificate of Education defining expectations for Years 11 and 12. These frameworks are determined by the Board of Studies. There is also a testing regime, with the Learning Assessment Project for testing in several key learning areas at two points in primary schooling. A secondary counterpart is under way. There is also an accountability framework that calls for schools to prepare an Annual Report for transmission to the Education Department and the local community, and a Triennial Review, with provision for external validation. There is a range of indicators upon which all schools must report, and school-determined indicators relevant to local priorities are encouraged.

The integrating mechanism for local autonomy and central frameworks is the School Charter, a relatively concise document that sets out the nature of the school and the manner in which it will address and resource state-wide priorities and local needs. The School Charter is an understanding between the school and the local community on the one hand, and the school and the Education Department on the other. The extent of autonomy and the level of constraint associated with this mechanism is described later in this chapter.

The main features of Schools of the Future were in place by early 1996. The period since the re-election of the Kennett Government in April 1996 has been characterized by consolidation, implementing the Triennial Review and exploring the possibilities of additional but still constrained autonomy in a project called Schools of the Third Millennium. Plans for up to 50 such schools were announced in April 1998, with $11.1 million included in the 1998–99 state budget to support their introduction.

## Driving Forces

Eight driving forces are identified: changes in the role of government in the delivery of public services in the face of concerns about efficiency and effectiveness; the capacity of state governments to deliver more autonomy within current legislative frameworks where there is the will to do so; the preferences of professional associations of school principals; competition policy that challenges the current discriminatory funding arrangements in the use of public funds for private schools; the building of social capital in relation to school education and the burgeoning home school movement; knowledge and skills of staff; technology; and flexibility in workplace arrangements.

### 1 Role of government in the delivery of public services

It is remarkable how quickly roles in government are changing around the world. It was only recently that Osborne and Gaebler (1993) startled many when they wrote of reinventing government: articulating a principle that governments should be in the business of 'steering' rather than 'rowing', referring to a role that sees governments setting direction, providing standards, furnishing resources, and utilizing frameworks for accountability in the delivery of public services, but as far as it was effective and efficient to do so, vacating the arena of actually delivering the service. This principle has passed quickly into the currency of language and practice, although many issues remain to be resolved in some settings, including the extent to which governments should actually engage in the delivery of a service that meets a basic societal need such as school education.

This change in role for government has accounted in part for recent developments in respect to the autonomy of schools but it is a relatively constrained form of autonomy. The new culture of public service has led to the down-sizing of bureaucratic arrangements at the centre of a system of public education, with a parallel shift in authority, responsibility and accountability to the school level. However, what at first sight appears to be a shift from 'rowing' to 'steering' may be simply a transfer of 'rowing' to a fleet of schools. An exception will be the extent to which there has been an out-sourcing of services to individuals, organizations and agencies elsewhere in the public sector or in the private sector.

In general, this change in the culture for the delivery of public services in the interests of efficiency and effectiveness may be seen as a driving force, but the outcome has been a relatively constrained form of autonomy, even in the Schools of the Future program in Victoria, and in international counterparts, including locally managed schools in Britain. Inertia in the schools sector is evident when proposals are made for more autonomy, as illustrated in the modest approach to extending autonomy in Victoria in the Schools of the Third Millennium initiative, or in the difficulties encountered in the early stages of the charter school movement in the United States. There is evidence of a countervailing force for re-centralization in each of these settings, including Britain, where grant maintained schools have been reined in.

## 2   Capacity in current state legislation

Current legislation in the states and territories allows governments to create systems of self-managing schools. Examples of how this is being taken up, or how new legislation may have an impact, are set out below in the instances of Victoria, Queensland, Tasmania and Western Australia.

### Victoria

While what has occurred in Victoria in Schools of the Future appears at first sight to be a revolution, the reality is that most of what has been achieved has been within the Education Act that existed at the time of election of the Kennett Government in October 1992. The key powers of the School Council that involve a capacity for self-management are largely those established under predecessor Labor

Governments, notably in 1983 with provision for the council to 'determine the general educational policy of the school within the guidelines issued by the Minister' (Victoria, Education Act 1958, Section 14, 1, a). The role of the principal is specified in regulations rather than legislation. A new section in 1993 allowed the creation of a special class of schools ('Designated Schools') to ensure that each School of the Future would have a charter, but for virtually all other aspects of the reform, change was achieved through regulatory mechanisms. The constrained nature of the concept of 'charter' is evident in the Education Act, which asserts that 'A school charter (a) does not create any contractual relationship between any persons; (b) does not give rise to any rights or entitlements, or impose any duties, that are capable of being enforced in a legal proceeding' (Victoria, Education Act 1958, Section 15L). For Schools of the Third Millennium and the self-governing option for 50 schools, existing legislation will be amended with the introduction of the Education (Self-Governing Schools) Act 1998.

### Queensland

A relatively high level of self-management may be achieved in other states and territories within existing frameworks, so it is largely the policy intentions of government and political feasibility at the time that is the chief determinant of the capacity of states and territories to act in respect to the introduction or extension of self-management for schools, subject of course to constraining forces in other domains, as set out later in this chapter. Intentions along these lines were evident in Queensland's program for Leading Schools.

Leading Schools was a component of a comprehensive planning and reform effort in Queensland, shaped by a Strategic Plan 1997–2001 entitled *Partners for Excellence* (Department of Education, Queensland, 1997a). Intentions in respect to Leading Schools were announced in February 1997 (Department of Education, Queensland, 1997b), with the Director-General making clear in his introduction to the program that the initiative was to increase the level of school-based management, that was seen to facilitate:

- an improvement of student learning outcomes;

- greater local participation in education, including increased accountability of the school to its community;

- enhanced parent choice in the type of education they want for their children;

- increased flexibility, efficiency and effectiveness in the provision of educational services; and

- service structures that are closer to schools.

(Department of Education, Queensland, 1997b)

Implementation over three years was planned, with 100 volunteer schools involved in a pilot program in the Band 11 to Band 8 range, that is, for larger schools only.

Special schools were not included. Noteworthy was the systematic effort to develop a needs-based, formula-driven approach to the allocation of resources to schools, and the recognition of the importance of achieving linkages between the capacities provided through school-based management and changes in approaches to learning and teaching in order to achieve a positive impact on outcomes for students.

Leading Schools was part of a strategic planning initiative rather than a new legislative framework, illustrating that higher levels of autonomy can indeed be achieved if there is the political and administrative will to take action. The title and future of the program are dependent on the intentions of the new Labor Government elected in June 1998.

### *Tasmania*

Tasmania has had a relatively high level of autonomy in some aspects of school operations since the mid-1970s (see Caldwell, 1991, for a review of developments in Tasmania in the 1970s and 1980s). Until recently, it provided the benchmark for other states in approaches to decentralizing resources to the school level. On the other hand, school councils are a relatively recent development.

Tasmania is another example of a state moving to increase school autonomy within an existing legislative framework. In a coherent program known as Directions in Education, six initiatives are planned:

1  Learning outcomes will be measured, monitored and reported with schools being accountable for improving these outcomes.

2  Schools and their communities, in partnership with the Government, will determine the learning outcomes that schools will deliver, through formal agreement.

3  There will be more opportunities for local decision making and flexibility in school operations and more 'funds through the school gate'.

4  There will be improved school leadership through principal accreditation and performance based contracts.

5  School staff will be better equipped and empowered to do the job required of them, through improved professional development opportunities.

6  Schools will have access to modern information technology to facilitate teaching and learning processes as well as accountability and administrative arrangements.
(Education Planning Branch, Tasmania, 1997, p. 3)

There is much in common with Schools of the Future, especially in respect to accountability for learning outcomes and principal accreditation accompanied by principal performance-based contracts. Several of the six directions may be seen as constraining action at the school level, with the notable exception of more 'funds through the school gate'. In general, however, it is a further impetus to the self-managing school in a state that pioneered the concept (Caldwell and Spinks, 1988). As in Queensland and Victoria, it has been accomplished mainly within the existing framework of legislation.

*Western Australia*

An initiative in the legislative arena in Western Australia is a proposal for a new School Education Bill ( Department of Education Services, Western Australia, 1997). The background notes for the Bill indicated that the current Education Act and regulations had been in place for almost 70 years and assert that 'the education system they oversee in the 1990s bears little resemblance to the 1928 system for which they were originally written'. Two of four key principles reflected in the proposed Bill relate to Choice: 'The right of children and parents to choose the form of education that best suits their needs; whether in a government school, a non-government school or in a home school setting'; and Partnerships: 'The need for schools and parents to work together in partnership for successful schooling', with Councils having an enhanced capacity in planning, finances and review of school perform- ance (the agreement of the Minister will, however, be required for School Council involvement in the selection of the principal). There is also provision for a more flexible approach to schooling, with off-site options possible with the written agree- ment of principal and parent; a loosening of school boundaries while maintaining the right of a child to attend a neighbourhood school; and more powers for prin- cipals on the management of property and school finances.

While developments in Western Australia are noteworthy, given the various proposals for an increase in school autonomy over the last decade, these intentions, if enshrined in legislation, will leave the state well short of what has been achieved in Victoria and what is intended in Queensland and Tasmania.

### 3   Professional preference

Setting aside a likely preference of the Commonwealth, the continued interest of the Kennett Government in Victoria, and modest developments in some other states, notably Queensland and Tasmania, a key question is 'Which stakeholders are sup- portive of recent measures to provide more autonomy for schools and are currently pressing for more?'

It is evident that teacher unions and most organizations purporting to represent the interests of parents are not supportive, with stances ranging from uncompromis- ing opposition to wait-and-see scepticism. These attitudes are considered to be constraining forces and are discussed later in this chapter. The one stakeholder group that is broadly supportive is school principals, although that support is heav- ily qualified. The clearest manifestation of this support has been in Victoria, where the leaders of the Victorian Association of State Secondary Principals and the Victorian Primary Principals Associations have been key players in the design and implementation of Schools of the Future. The majority of their members are clear that they would not wish to return to arrangements prior to Schools of the Future, a view documented in the findings of the five-year longitudinal Cooperative Research Project, with the 1997 survey of a representative sample of principals revealing support at the 89 per cent level (Cooperative Research Project, 1998).

This is consistent with findings in other places, elsewhere in Australia and New Zealand, as reflected in a report by Tony Misich who, while serving as President of the Western Australia Primary Principals Association, received the Australian Primary Principals Association 1995–96 Telstra Research Award to study developments in Australia and New Zealand. He concluded that:

> ... one common variable is that all Principals, having gone down the path of de-volved decision making, do not wish to return to a more centralized system, regard-less of the extra work or responsibility. There is far greater satisfaction in schools being 'in charge' at the local level. (Misich, 1996, p. 3)

This support should be seen in the context of earlier arrangements, especially in the case of Victoria where, for nearly a decade to late 1992, principals had their authority sharply constrained by the requirement that any decision of note had to be referred to a Local Administrative Committee that was usually controlled by school repres-entatives of the teacher union.

The only body directly representative of school-based community interests that has consistently and unambiguously supported greater autonomy for public schools in recent years has been the Association of School Councils in Victoria (ASCIV) which has developed from a small base of secondary schools. The larger parent bodies in the state have resisted the efforts of the Kennett Government in this domain and were opponents of efforts by the predecessor Cain Labor Govern-ment in 1986 to extend school autonomy (Government of Victoria, 1986).

This pattern seems to be the same in Britain. As in Australia and New Zea-land, principals (headteachers) have consistently preferred local management to the previous, more centralized control by local education authorities (see survey findings by Bullock and Thomas, 1994). Teacher unions have consistently opposed a higher level of school autonomy, a situation addressed in more detail as a constraint. This situation prevailed even after the election of New Labour where, at most, a high level of scepticism about government intentions prevails.

### 4  Competition policy and the use of public funds for private schools

The first three driving forces set out above are largely those already evident. A potential driving force may derive from the National Competition Policy (NCP) established by the Council of Australian Governments (COAG) in April 1995. The agreements provide a comprehensive program that includes 'the introduction of com-petitive neutrality so that public businesses do not enjoy unfair advantages when competing with private businesses' (National Competition Council, 1997, p. 1).

A review of action to date reveals that no government has applied the policy to school education in more than a minor way, although the sweeping implications of full application are recognized. The Commonwealth has applied it to Education Services for Overseas Students. A sampling of state and territory responses reveals that New South Wales has not applied it at all. Victoria has classified application to the Education Act 1958 as entailing a 'complex / minor review', meaning that 'cases where the removal of existing legislative restrictions on competition would be technically straightforward, but there are complex public interest issues to be addressed' (National Competition Council, 1997, p. 42). Reviews of Ministerial Orders are under way in respect to the payment of fees by overseas students and distance education centres. Queensland has similarly identified different pieces of legislation, including that related to teacher registration and the formation of grammar schools, but has only moved on programs for overseas students. Notes on intentions by South Australia acknowledge that the Education Act 1972 and Regulations constitute a 'barrier to market entry and restricts market conduct' (National Competition Council, 1997, p. 184). The Tasmanian review in school education does not get under way until 1999.

The full application of National Competition Policy in the field of school education has potential for dramatically affecting the development of more autonomous schools by strengthening the non-government sector. For example, the resources received from public sources, Commonwealth and State, for non-government schools are significantly less than for government schools when expressed on a per capita basis. This may be considered an unfair advantage to the publicly owned enterprise, in this instance, systems of government owned and operated schools, when both sectors of schooling (government and non-government) must operate within the same curriculum and standards frameworks. If capacity to contribute to the cost of schooling is taken into account, it may be argued that the advantage to government owned and operated schools is appropriate. The Australian Bureau of Statistics Census of 1996 reveals that, for primary schools, 25.6 per cent of students come from families with an income less than $26,000 compared to 17.4 per cent of students in Catholic schools and 15.7 per cent in non-government schools (although, for higher categories of income, the profiles of parental income are not dissimilar except for other non-government school students for family income more than $104,000 per year).

The implications of the National Competition Policy have not been tested by organizations representing the interests of non-government schools. It is interesting to speculate on the outcome of a case that addresses costs, prices and capacity of parents to pay. In respect to costs of schooling, Gannicott (1997, p. 35) drew on data from several public and government sources to demonstrate, for example, that per capita recurrent costs of schooling for the non-government sector tend to be lower than for the government sector. In general, the National Competition Policy ought to be considered a driving force for greater autonomy for schools to the extent that it has the potential to test the boundaries between public and private education.

### 5   *Social capital and the home school movement*

The steady trend in enrolments in non-government schools at the expense of government schools is an indicator of a driving force for greater autonomy to the extent that it expresses a preference of parents. This suggests that social capital is building around the non-government sector: parents are prepared to meet the costs of non-government schooling because they value the kinds of education they perceive to be offered in this setting.

Another driving force is the value an increasing number of parents are placing on home education, which may be considered to lie at the end of a continuum of autonomous schooling. One state has recently changed its Education Act to make explicit provision for home schooling (Tasmania), with the number of students in home schooling doubling since 1992 to its current level at about 500. Another state is planning to do so (Western Australia) with a proposal that 'All children of compulsory school age must be enrolled in a schooling program at either a government school, a non-government school or in an approved home school' (Department of Education Services, Western Australia, 1997). Accountability is established in each state through access and inspection of records. The proposed legislation has drawn the opposition of the home schooling movement in Western Australia, which rejects the concept that home education should be considered a formal option in schooling as much as it rejects the intrusive accountability mechanism.

A review of related web sites reveals that the home schooling movement in Australia and other nations is a burgeoning phenomenon. Given the sophistication of information technologies, including distance learning on the web, CD ROM, the range of software programs, and the declining cost of hardware, there is every reason to expect this to continue, drawing a broader spectrum of students than in the past, when home schooling was largely the province of parents with particular religious beliefs and lifestyles. There is also evidence that home schoolers are willing to enter agreements with schools, especially private schools, for particular aspects of learning, notably the arts. There is interest among schools in making such arrangements. In one scenario, a case can be made for full public resourcing on a per capita basis for students whose home schooling is as rich and as comprehensive as these possibilities imply.

### 6 Knowledge and skills of staff

The knowledge and skills of staff are listed as both a driving and a constraining force. Considered here are the capacities of principals, teachers and non-teaching support staff. The stance of principals and their organizations toward self-management cited earlier is an indicator of a self-perception of capacity to take on higher levels of authority, responsibility and accountability. This capacity is likely to be broader and deeper in the years ahead, given the rapid development of principals centres around the country. This development follows the earlier work of the Australian Principals Associations Professional Development Council (APAPDC) funded by Commonwealth and state governments.

The APAPDC work tends to be broad brush, building knowledge and understanding of the emerging role of the principal. The principals centre movement is more focused. While most states and territories now have such organizations, the benchmark appears to be the program of the Australian Principals Centre, which is an incorporated body owned by the Education Department of Victoria, Victorian Association of State Secondary Principals, Victorian Primary Principals Association and the University of Melbourne, located at the Hawthorn Campus of the University of Melbourne. The Australian Principals Centre has a small staff, but scores of programs, all outsourced, and different levels of membership reflecting professional standing have been established.

In general, the unprecedented level of professional development programs for principals around the country; the increasing level of professionalism among organizations representing the interests of principals, as indicated by the increase in full- or part-time staff employed by such organizations; the accreditation programs; and the performance-based incentive and reward schemes suggest that the capacity of principals to take on more authority, responsibility and accountability in the years ahead is likely to increase and, taken together, these can be considered a driving force.

Not so clear cut is whether the capacities of teachers and other professionals are increasing to the extent that they may be considered a driving force. To be sure, there is an increase in the attention given to standards, and teachers are gaining experience in adapting curriculum and standards frameworks to suit the needs of particular students, especially in association with testing programs and adoption of a range of indicators of performance. Several large-scale development programs have been implemented in some states in recent years, notably in the areas of early literacy and the use of information technology. The capacities gained in the former may be considered a potential driving force because it is these capacities that are required to build the link between self-management and improved outcomes for students. Similarly for technology in the manner described below.

In general, increasing the level of professional development for principals and teachers is likely to build a deeper capacity for self-management, so those with an interest in an increase in school autonomy ought to be among the strongest advocates of such programs.


## 7   Technology

Technology is also both a driving and constraining force. In general, however, the rate of development, and depth and breadth of utilization, should be considered powerful driving forces for a higher level of self-management in schools. The first and most obvious capacity requiring the use of technology is the availability of a comprehensive, understandable, and reliable computer-based cost accounting and management information system. If budgets are to be devolved to schools and the personnel management function is to be performed at the school level, all within an accountability framework, then the school system must develop such a capacity, and this is increasingly the case around the country. The imperative becomes even more acute when information needs for the management of student achievement data are considered.

By international standards, what has been accomplished to date has been impressive, especially in Victoria, with its twin systems of CASES (Computerized Administrative Systems Environment in Schools) and KIDMAP, with the latter meeting the needs for a student database. Despite these advances, there is apparently room for improvement. The Cooperative Research Project has monitored the views of principals each year since the Schools of the Future began in Victoria in 1993, and principals have reported problems with both systems. For 1997 (see Cooperative Research Project, 1998), moderate levels of satisfaction were recorded for CASES (mean satisfaction scores on 5-point scales of 3.8 for quality of hardware and software, and 3.4 for support for implementation), but for KIDMAP there was clearly more work to be done (with a mean satisfaction score on the 5-point scale of 1.6).

New tools are now making their appearance as schools are required to monitor levels of student achievement across all learning areas and at each grade level. A battery of indicators is required for school review and reporting, and the need for an effective management information system for school managers and classroom teachers is clearly evident. Developments in Britain are probably the most impressive in this regard (see the first issue of *TES Online Education*, *Times Educational Supplement*, 9 January 1998). The Editor of *TES Online Education* suggests that it is the second wave that is about to break, the first being the adoption of a range of internet and administrative support by a few: 'the second wave should involve all teachers and students, and this time there will be no excuses for not getting schools and colleges afloat' (John, 1998, p. 3).

The emerging interest in value-added measures of student achievement (see Chapter 5) has already led to the creation of software to help British schools manage the information for school-level decision-making. 'Smart card' technology is available to keep track of all information for decision-making at the level of the individual student. This is a notable development, with increasing international interest in needs-driven, formula-based funding that will allow funding to be attached to each student at the learning area level as well as the school level.

## 8   Flexibility in workplace arrangements

Profound changes are occurring in the nature of work and views about what constitutes a 'job'. These changes are occurring in virtually every field of work in the public and private sectors; in business, government and 'third sector' (service) employment; in Australia as in comparable countries; and, increasingly, in education. These changes may be broadly described as having fewer people in permanent, full-time employment with one employer over the course of a life-time, and more people in contract or casual employment, often part-time, with many employers over the course of a lifetime, often in quite different areas of work (see Bridges, 1995; Jones, 1995; and Rifkin, 1996, for an account of these developments). There is movement from an industrial society to a knowledge society, where the largest single group of workers are 'knowledge workers', earning a living by solving problems, managing information, and creating new products and services (see Drucker, 1993, 1995).

It is beyond the scope of this chapter to describe these changes in detail or to identify all of the forces that are responsible for their manifestation. This is a task in Chapter 7. Suffice to say that they are, at least in part, a response to the needs of the enterprise at the end of the twentieth century, no matter what the work or the setting, and they will characterize the workplace in the new millennium, at least in the foreseeable future. Enterprises need flexibility in their employment arrangements. Legislation has changed to reflect these developments, including frameworks in which workplace agreements are determined. The change in terminology from 'industrial' to 'workplace' reflects the profound social transformation now under way. The Workplace Relations Act 1996 is the clearest manifestation of these changes in Australia. Australian Workplace Agreements are possible.

While developments in school education in the public sector are proceeding at a slower pace than in many other settings, they are nonetheless evident, and apparently irreversible. The need for flexibility is apparent if one reflects on needs for work at the school level. If the focus is to be the school and the needs of students, there will likely be a need for a core of continuing full-time appointments in the key learning areas, but otherwise the staffing patterns may be short-term, from a matter of a few months to several years, as schools respond to particular priorities among student learning needs. While Australian Workplace Agreements have not made their appearance at the school or individual level in public schools, the various Teaching Awards recognize the new realities and provide a framework for their management.

The emergence of the self-managing school is in part a reflection of these changes in society and interest in providing a program that responds to the needs of each student. However, as is evident in the second part of this chapter that deals with constraining forces, the absence of a framework that facilitates this flexibility is a constraint on further developments as far as self-managing schools are concerned. Issues that have arisen in Victoria are addressed, for they are important in understanding the limits of school autonomy if the concept of a system of public schools is to be sustained. In general, however, these broad societal changes, the particular way they are manifested in schools, and the new flexibilities in the workplace relations scene may be viewed as driving forces for a higher level of school autonomy.

## Constraining Forces

A total of 12 constraining forces are identified: accountability requirements; inertia at the state level in taking up capacity in existing legislation and tendencies for re-centralization in the implementation of policy on decentralization; selection of staff to meet the needs of a system; curriculum and standards frameworks; registration requirements and the employment of teachers; the stance of teacher unions; the industrial relations framework; Commonwealth–State arrangements and relationships;

funding mechanisms for public and private schools; obligations under international agreements; knowledge and skills of staff; values in public policy and the issue of trust.

### 1 Accountability requirements

A review of state legislation and regulation in Australia reveals that the extent of self-management is powerfully constrained by accountability requirements, confirming a view expressed earlier in the chapter that decentralization is as much a matter of dispersion of authority and responsibility as it is about delegation. Expressed another way, it is a form of administrative decentralization rather than political decentralization (Caldwell, 1993), with authorities and responsibilities constrained by the Minister, who exercises a capacity to withdraw these at any time.

The case of Victoria is cited here for it has the most extensive system of self-management in the nation. It was noted earlier that the concept of 'charter' is a much weaker concept than that envisaged in some proposals (see Gannicott, 1997) and already in place in the United States (see Bierlein and Bateman, 1996). For Victoria, the Education Act asserts that 'A school charter (a) does not create any contractual relationship between any persons; (b) does not give rise to any rights or entitlements, or impose any duties, that are capable of being enforced in a legal proceeding' (Victoria, Education Act, 1958, Section 15L).

Bierlein and Bateman (1996, pp. 161–3) proposed the following as 'essential elements' for charter schools in the United States:

- A charter school must be allowed to seek sponsorship from a public entity other than a local school board and / or be allowed to appeal a school board decision.

- Any individual or group should be allowed to develop and submit a charter school proposal.

- Charter schools must have fiscal and legal autonomy.

- There should be no limits on the number of charter schools which can be established in a given state.

- Charter schools must be permitted to employ non-certified teachers.

Regulations in Victoria under the Education Act 1958 are comprehensive and constraining if exercised as stated (Victoria, Education Act 1958, Section 82). These refer to the capacity of the Governor in Council to make regulations on such matters as the standard of instruction and the subjects and courses of study in which instruction is to be offered; the system on which the standard of education in state schools shall be determined; scales of fees to be paid by parents of or by pupils attending state schools and the conditions under which exemptions from payment of fees may be granted; and the inspection of and reports upon the work of state schools.

With a significant portion of a state's education funds deriving from the Commonwealth Government, the constraints of accountability to the Commonwealth should also be noted. The States Grants (Primary and Secondary Education Assistance) Bill 1996 (Commonwealth of Australia, 1996) specifies that the State must certify that funds were used only for the purpose for which the assistance was granted, that amounts may be returned, and that, among other things, the State will take part in the preparation of a national report on the outcomes of schooling and take part in evaluation of outcomes of programs of financial assistance.

While constraints in respect to Commonwealth grants have been reduced in recent years through the elimination of some grants and incorporation of specific grants into broader bands of assistance, it is clear that accountability requirements are as strong as ever. To the extent that these constrain the states in the use of funds for schools under their jurisdiction, this may be viewed as a constraint on school autonomy. On the other hand, such constraints are understandable, for the Commonwealth has as much interest as the states in monitoring the efficiency and effectiveness of policies and programs. At the very least, the Commonwealth must require recipients of grants to account for their use in relation to the terms and conditions of those grants.

The issue was at centre stage in 1997 during discussions and debates on standards of literacy and the manner in which the Commonwealth may withhold or withdraw funds from states which do not take part in evaluation of outcomes of programs that are supported by financial assistance in this area. In this and other areas, the Commonwealth's view was that the reporting of outcomes was an important aspect of building public confidence in education.

The Commonwealth may give grants of assistance to individual non-government schools or to organizations representing non-government schools. An interesting matter for contemplation is the impact on school autonomy were the Commonwealth to express an interest in making assistance available directly to individual public schools, circumventing the state.

## 2  Inertia and tendencies for re-centralization

Progress toward the creation of self-managing schools has been slow in most states of Australia and in many other nations. Setting aside for the moment the problematic nature of the phenomenon and the powerful arguments that have been mounted for and against, it is clear that structural arrangements in respect to constitution and governance, along with the difficulty of effecting change in large and complex systems of public education, have proved to be a constraint on the introduction of self-managing schools. These are described in this section as 'inertia'.

### Inertia

Australia and the United States have encountered inertia in efforts to decentralize. Each has federal and state parliaments or legislatures, many of which have two houses. Constitutional powers to make laws in relation to school education lie with the states yet a significant portion of the funding from schools comes from the federal level. Having different parties in government at federal and state levels is a phenomenon common to both nations.

In addition to these complexities, each nation has an array of legislation in other fields that impinges on efforts to make change in school education along the lines under consideration, including industrial relations, health, welfare, law enforcement and transport. In the United States, in particular, but increasingly in Australia, there is a mountain of legislation and regulations affecting the operation of schools, and to make comprehensive and coherent change consistent with intentions in self-managing schools, especially where links are made to practice in classrooms, as suggested in Chapter 3, is very difficult indeed.

These experiences contrast to those in Britain where there is a unitary system of government and the parliament in Westminster may make sweeping changes that will affect what occurs in each of more than a hundred local education authorities. This was the case with the 1988 Education Reform Act and will surely be the case again with the legislative agenda of New Labour.

Resistance by bureaucrats is also a phenomenon that ought to be frankly acknowledged. A shift to self-management invariably calls for a reduction of the size of central offices and their regional agents. There is a diminution of authority and responsibility in key areas and a reluctance to give up power. Instances are documented in recent books by Kenneth Baker (see Baker, 1993), former Secretary of State for Education in Britain before and after the 1988 Education Reform Act and, in Australia, by Don Hayward who served as Minister for Education in the first term of the Kennett Government from 1992 to 1996 (see Caldwell and Hayward, 1998). Baker referred to the intransigence of officials much earlier, when former Labour Prime Minister James Callaghan called for major change in his famous Ruskin Speech in 1976, and he documented the potential for similar difficulties in relation to events surrounding the 1988 reform. Hayward reported the same and referred to the need for strong and direct involvement of the Minister in driving the reform agenda. Caldwell and Hayward called for strong leadership, alignment of interests and the will to follow through on intentions for a reform of the kind under consideration. They referred to a policy model proposed by Guthrie and Koppich (1993) to account for the success of large-scale reform, and the conditions proposed in the model were manifest in the window of opportunity that was presented to the Kennett Government in 1992. The political context in other states makes it difficult to achieve the same outcome.

Caldwell and Hayward (1998, pp. 167–8) cited an instance of inertia in the United States with LEARN (Los Angeles Educational Alliance for Restructuring Now). An initiative of the corporate sector, LEARN is a partnership of business, teacher unions and the Los Angeles Unified School District (LAUSD) to decentralize the operations of LAUSD. The reform is proceeding much slower than intended, with 'chronic delays in transferring power and money to schools' (citing Pyle, 1997, p. 6).

Experience in the charter school movement in the United States is also instructive as far as inertia is concerned, especially in the light of recent proposals for such schools in Australia (see Gannicott, 1997; Caldwell and Hayward, 1998). Bierlein and Bateman (1996, pp. 164–7) reviewed the development of charter schools in the United States and proposed optimal conditions for their success, in the manner cited earlier in this chapter. They also identified opposing forces and include the following:

- The overall number of states with strong charter laws is too small to make a significant difference.

- There is a lack of organized, well-financed support for the charter school movement.

- Those groups opposed to the charter school concept are becoming more sophisticated in their opposition.

- Charter schools are being forced to operate within state school financing structures which were designed to fund districts, not schools.

- Only a small fraction of the current education profession has the interest and motivation to undertake the implementation of a charter school.

- There is a question of whether unbiased research of charter schools can and will be conducted by those traditionally involved in K–12 education research.

Bierlein and Bateman conceded that they painted a 'bleak picture for the long-term future of charter schools':

> Reforms must fit within the current power structure of education: local school boards, state boards of education, state departments, legislators, the federal government, and the unions. The current power structure seeks to mould legislation to meet its needs, not necessarily the needs of students, and it is difficult to break down this ingrained system of power. (Bierlein and Bateman, 1996, p. 167)

While conceding that the limited movement of 250 (now approaching 1,000) out of about 85,000 schools nationwide has had a ripple effect, their final conclusion is pessimistic:

> . . . the odds are currently stacked against the ultimate success of charter schools. Unless well-coordinated efforts are undertaken to battle the many opposing forces, we predict that the charter school concept will simply not be strong enough medicine to become a broad-based reform initiative. (Bierlein and Bateman, 1996, pp. 166–7)

The 'ripple effects' of which Bierlein and Bateman wrote came in the form of school districts becoming more responsive to schools, with even the largest union, the National Education Association, launching a support project for teachers involved in charter schools. In this respect, the ripple effect is not unlike that in Britain where most local education authorities, which were dramatically down-sized and disempowered following the 1988 Education Reform Act, developed a much improved capacity to support schools than was evident in the past.

The opposing forces identified for the United States by Bierlein and Bateman may be envisaged for Australia should a charter initiative or counterpart be mounted.

*Re-centralization*

In addition to inertia, there is the phenomenon of re-centralization or pressures for re-centralization following an initiative toward more autonomous schools. In some cases this follows a change of government, as evidenced in New South Wales following the election of the Carr Labor Government, when plans for the local selection of teachers were finally abandoned in the wake of union resistance during the Greiner and Fahey years.

In Britain, the Blair Labour Government has similar plans to rein in grant maintained schools. Associated with the latter is concern about school places, identified earlier in a report of the Audit Council. Traditionally, in Britain, local education authorities had the task of ensuring a distribution of student places among schools in their jurisdiction. Under the local management of schools, accentuated with the publication of test results in 'league tables', schools perceived to be good attracted more students to the point of creating pressure for expanded facilities, while schools perceived to be poor lost students, leading to many empty places. The phenomenon was especially evident with the growth, albeit constrained, in the grant maintained sector. Considerations of efficiency and effectiveness led the Audit Council to recommend a return to a more rational allocation of places and this has been taken up by the Labour Government. A stronger role for the local education authority, along with the curtailment of autonomy on the part of grant maintained schools, clearly constitutes a retreat from the levels of self-management and self-government achieved in the last years of the Conservative Government. Critics of more autonomous schools will also point to the measure as necessary to limit the 'residualization' of some schools that have been denuded of top students in recent years, to the alleged detriment of achievement levels for students who remain.

Another possibility for re-centralization in Britain stems from government intentions for local education authorities to set and monitor targets for improvement at the school level. Along with the need to support grant maintained schools that are returning to the fold, there is likely to be an increase in the number of appointments of staff at the authority level. At the same time, the government is expecting authorities to devolve more cash to schools. Head of Education for the Local Government Association, David Whitbread admitted 'We are torn between wanting to argue for adequate funding to do our jobs properly and not stopping money going into schools — because at the end of the day there is no point having a Rolls Royce machine if schools are running as Austin 7s' (cited in Barnard, 1998, p. 4). The same issue is likely to arise in Australia, especially in Victoria following extensive down-sizing, as governments are faced with the problem of what to do with 'failing' or 'cruising' schools, when evidence emerges from the processes of school review.

If the views of principals are counted, there is evidence of re-centralization in Victoria, or at the very least, a reluctance to 'let go'. Annual surveys of principals in the Cooperative Research Project have consistently revealed that principals in Victoria are not happy with what they term 'bureaucratic interference'. An expectation for Schools of the Future was that it would lead to less bureaucratic interference. The 1997 survey revealed that, on a scale of 1 ('low') to 5 ('high'), 55 per cent of principals provided a rating of 1 or 2 for the extent to which the expected benefit had been realized in their schools (Cooperative Research Project, 1998).

Leaders of principals organizations in Victoria (in research reported in Caldwell, 1998) referred explicitly to a reluctance of the centre to 'let go', citing instances of constant change in the way policy was implemented; a lack of willingness on the part of many bureaucrats to listen to the views of principals, who were subsequently proved right in their judgment of an issue; excessively close monitoring of routine matters at the school level, when the concept of self-management implied a relatively high level of discretion; and the breaking up of collegiate groups of principals that successfully brokered resource arrangements among schools. Some distinguished between the level of openness and trust in the first term of the Kennett Government and that experienced in the second.

### 3   Selection of staff to meet the needs of a system

Many of the concerns described by principals in Victoria were derived from the limitations placed on schools in the matter of Full Staffing Flexibility, a feature of Schools of the Future in which it was planned that schools would have the capacity to select staff on the basis of advertisement when vacancies occurred. A small group of schools achieved Full Staffing Flexibility in 1995 for full implementation for 1996, and all have been accorded the benefit in 1997 for implementation for 1998.

The difficulty arises from reducing the pool of teachers deemed to be in excess of requirements across the system, a phenomenon that dates back to the early years of the Kennett Government when up to 8000 teachers were considered to be 'in excess'. A range of redundancy and early retirement arrangements have been effected and the pool is now very small. However, on a school-by-school basis, there is a need to give priority to placing such teachers as vacancies occur, when such teachers have been placed in that school as part of overall system management. In addition, excess staff situations emerge for reasons that attach to the particular school situation:

> An excess staff situation arises where a school has a greater number of employees than is necessary for the efficient and economic operation of the school as identified in the school's preferred staffing profile. An excess staff situation may also arise due to technological change, changes to educational programs or other changes in work methods, or changes in the nature, extent or organization of the functions of the school. (Department of Education, Victoria, 1997, p. 21)

*The views of principals*

Leaders of principals organizations in Victoria (as reported in Caldwell, 1998) were unanimous in their view that they were constrained in their appointment of staff to the detriment of efforts to improve learning and satisfy the needs of their communities. They cited an incapacity to select teachers who matched priorities among learning needs; instances where relatively less competent teachers had to be accepted when they could have selected more able staff if they were not constrained; differences in philosophy of teachers who had to be accepted from the pool of excess staff from that which prevailed or was preferred at the school; and an unwillingness of staff selected under these circumstances to carry out additional duties in the extra-curricular area where this is a community expectation.

One indicated that the complexity of the operation was a significant factor in maintaining a regional office style of operation, suggesting that a less constrained approach would limit the need for this level of administration, especially in urban areas. This was contrasted with practice in large Catholic systems that did not require a significant regional presence.

It was acknowledged that overall levels of resources for public education accentuated the effect of constraints on the selection of staff. An associated concern was the level of conflict generated among some principals in their competition for scarce resources, including staff. Reference was made to the workload of some principals in managing the staff resource, with one instance cited of a school enjoying full staffing flexibility having to fill several dozen vacancies. The task of advertising, receiving and sorting applications, short-listing and filling was very heavy indeed.

*A system perspective*

Traditionally schools have had limited control over the management of their workforce. Staffing formulae and promotion profiles were rigid, allowing little flexibility to meet local needs. Many personnel decisions, such as the granting of leave or selection of teaching staff, were made outside the school.

The Schools of the Future program has seen an unprecedented transfer of responsibility, authority and accountability to government schools in Victoria. Key personnel decision making is now located at the school level and resources are provided through the school global budget. The role of the principal has been significantly enhanced in all areas of personnel management.

The key objective of Full Staffing Flexibility is to provide principals the freedom to select the best available staff (teaching and non-teaching) to best meet the educational needs of students. Full Staffing Flexibility enables the maximum possible degree of operational autonomy over human and financial resources at the school level within school global budget allocations.

While principals exercise a significant degree of discretion in staffing decisions they continue to be subject to the requirements of relevant federal and state legislation, federal awards and Government policy. Importantly, this includes the obligations imposed by the Victorian Teachers Redundancy Award 1994 for consultation, identification and redeployment of excess teachers.

Prior to the introduction of Full Staffing Flexibility, the system was responsible for the management and placement of the annual cycle of teacher excess caused by demographic movements and curriculum changes. This involved the placement of between 1200 and 1500 excess teachers in vacancies through a central process. The staffing arrangements which have been established through Full Staffing Flexibility now enable the management of teacher excess without the need for central intervention:

- schools prepare three-year workforce plans and staff are recruited for either fixed term or ongoing employment on the basis of projected staffing needs. The increasing proportion of fixed term teachers will, over time, likely reduce the number of excess staff.

- comprehensive redeployment arrangements have been made for the management and resolution of excess staff situations in schools to ensure compliance with the Victorian Teachers Redundancy Award 1994. Principals work within guidelines, however, the identification of employees who may be the subject of retrenchment is managed centrally.

It has taken some time for these policies to become effective in all schools due to the large number of leave returnees and excess staff. However, by the end of 1997, considerable progress had been made and principals are now able to advertise vacancies as they occur and, in most cases, appoint the preferred applicant.

### 4    Curriculum and standards frameworks

The emergence in recent years of curriculum and standards frameworks is, by definition, a constraint on self-management, regardless of the setting: state or nation, government or non-government school. All schools in receipt of public funds are required to work within such frameworks. In Australia, there are no truly independent schools, such as in Britain where private schools are not required to work within the National Curriculum.

Despite the constraint, the fact that these constitute a 'framework' rather than a 'syllabus' allows a fair measure of school discretion in the particular content that will be addressed and approaches to learning and teaching that will be utilized. However, even these become constrained when there is a tight connection with system-wide tests, and this is the trend in Australia and comparable countries. Growing interest in and utilization of international benchmarks may further constrain the approach in schools.

Benchmarking against international best practice may help enhance student achievement. This may be illustrated with the work of James Stigler and his colleagues at the University of California Los Angeles (UCLA) involving videotapes and computer analysis of scores of lessons in Grade 8 mathematics in Germany, Japan and the United States. The outcomes have been a revelation, especially in respect to findings from Japan that reveal that some goals for learning in mathematics in the United States, and arguably Australia and Britain, are more likely to be achieved in classrooms in Japan. This finding places the spotlight on practices in classrooms, and a school ability to develop the capacities of teachers that underpin the connections between self-management and learning outcomes as set out in Chapter 3. The capacities of teachers to take up best practice is a constraint as well as a driving force, and further attention is given to it later in the chapter.

The matter of curriculum and standards frameworks, learning outcomes and self-management comes into sharp focus when recent findings in early literacy are considered. Findings in Victoria in the Early Literacy Research Project (see, for example, Crevola and Hill, 1997) demonstrate that substantial gains in student achievement in early literacy can be obtained, but a minimum of 90 minutes per day must be devoted to structured learning and teaching, an expectation which may clash with requirements of the curriculum and standards framework that calls for attention to each of eight Key Learning Areas. A similar finding has emerged in Britain. The issue here is the manner in which a school, taking up the authorities and responsibilities of self-management, especially in respect to focusing on a learning area where a high level of student need has been demonstrated, takes measures on time and utilization of staff that mean some compromise must be made on the extent to which the curriculum and standards framework is addressed. If improvement in learning outcomes is to lie at the centre of efforts at the school level, it is likely that revisions ought to be made to the framework, or the interpretation of it.

The Labour Government in Britain effectively 'suspended' the National Curriculum at the primary level in early 1998 to enable schools to adopt the National Literacy Strategy that recommended 90 minutes per day for reading.

Paradoxically, a system-wide attempt to legislate on findings in studies of school and classroom effectiveness may further constrain the capacity of schools for self-management. The findings relate to class size, because there is support for the view that smaller class size is desirable in the early years of primary school when literacy skills must be developed. Even the strongest critic of the class size issue concedes that this is maybe one circumstance where a case can be made (see Hanushek, 1996, p. 38; 1997).

The Blair Government acted on the matter of class sizes in the early years of primary school, taking into account research in early literacy. The intention is to limit primary classes to 30 in the early years. This has brought a strong reaction from those who see this as constraining the capacity of schools for local management. Dean reported in this manner under the headline 'Class size pledge risks parent anger':

> The Government's commitment to cut primary classes to 30 or under for every five, six and seven-year old is non-negotiable, civil servants have told local authorities. Ministers are prepared to sacrifice parental choice, the appeals system and the

right of schools to spend their budgets how they wish in order to meet the manifesto pledge — even where parents prefer bigger classes. A class of 29 children with one teacher is considered a 'good thing', a class of 31 with extra support would be unacceptable, officials currently visiting local authorities have revealed. (Dean, 1997, p. 3)

The budget implications of this pledge are serious indeed for small schools, especially in the many cases where a single class exists at a particular level and that class increases from, say, 29 to 31 and a new teacher must be employed.

The class size issue in the early years will likely remain on the agenda in Australia, especially when developments in Britain gain a higher profile, along with similar developments in California where millions of dollars have had to be spent in hiring additional teachers and building new classrooms. It is interesting that class size is not a matter specified in the current award for teachers in Victoria.

### 5   Registration requirements and the employment of teachers

The National Office of Overseas Skills Recognition (NOOSR) provided the following information about registration requirements for teaching in Australia (NOOSR, 1997). In Queensland and South Australia, all teachers must be registered before they can be employed in either a government or non-government school. Registration does not, however, guarantee employment. In Victoria, teachers in non-government schools must be registered by the Registered Schools Board. Eligibility to be employed in government schools is determined by the Department of Education. In New South Wales, Tasmania, Western Australia, the Australian Capital Territory and the Northern Territory, eligibility to teach is determined by the employing authority, that is, the State or Territory Department of Education, non-government school system or individual non-government schools.

Registration requirements and matters related to the employment of teachers and others who work in schools serve as constraints on school autonomy. Most with a stake in the quality of school education will contend that this is a necessary constraint, if teachers and others are considered to be professionals. After all, one expects no less than formal registration for those who work in health care and the legal field.

There is, however, a counter argument to formal registration when it constitutes credentialism, and where there is an absence of evidence that higher qualifications are associated with improved practice, or where certain kinds of expertise can be deployed with success in the absence of formal teacher training. The former is argued by Hanushek in the light of outcomes in recent decades in the United States:

Schools currently have record-low pupil–teacher ratios, record-high numbers for completion of master's degrees, and more experienced teachers than at any time at least since 1960. These factors are the result of many specific programs that have contributed to the rapid growth in per-pupil spending but have not led to improvements in student performance. (Hanushek, 1996, p. 39)

The second position is put by Bierlein and Bateman in their list of 'essential components' for charter schools in the United States. In arguing that 'charter schools should be permitted to employ non-certified teachers' they describe current arrangements and the case for an alternative in terms which are cited here in full:

> This component is critical because it challenges one of the education system's most strongly held beliefs and brings additional expertise to the classroom. The completion of a set number of College of Education-based courses and a student teaching practicum has long been the standard required to be considered 'fit' to teach ... Teachers must also acquire a set number of graduate-level courses to maintain their certification. Universities benefit from a steady stream of students (especially at the graduate level), while the teaching profession benefits by remaining a 'closed shop'.
>
> The allowance of a certain number of non-certificated individuals within a charter school does not mean anyone off the street should be placed into the classroom. Instead, it tests whether a focus on results, rather than inputs ... is achievable in public education. When a school is placed on a contract, will it still choose to include only certified teachers or might it include some part-time specialists such as retired engineers or college professors? Stronger charter school laws allow this and other questions to be tested. (Bierlein and Bateman, 1996, p. 163)

A scheme for the entry of specialists along the lines envisaged by Bierlein and Bateman is now in operation in Chicago, with a consortium of business, teacher unions, schools of education and the school system working together to ensure rapid entry. It appears to be a model for the kind of flexibility that is consistent with the concept of the self-managing school, yet at the same time reflects expectations for a profession. It warrants closer attention in respect to its applicability in other settings.

Efforts to implement national schemes will likely run counter to the capacity that Bierlein and Bateman propose for autonomous charter schools. The General Teaching Council in Scotland is generally held to be a model, and was an option considered prior to the creation of the unsuccessful Australian Teaching Council. It is also under consideration in Britain to fulfil an election pledge of the Blair Government, but early indications are that it will be very difficult to achieve a consensus among stakeholders. The Australian Council of Deans of Education has pressed for a consistent scheme across the nation. Such a scheme was proposed in the Report into the Status of the Teaching Profession (Senate Employment, Education and Training References Committee, 1998).

The case for formal recognition is strong in a field of professional practice such as school education, regardless of whether a national scheme or a collection of state schemes remain. The exercise of school authority and responsibility through self-management may, however, be most appropriately focused in incentive and reward schemes, including those that may secure additional high level recognition. A useful lead is provided by Richard Murnane from Harvard University:

A variety of studies confirm that incentives matter. Incentives influence who goes into teaching, where teachers teach, how long teachers stay in teaching, and whether teachers return to the classroom after a career interruption. To conclude that incentives matter is not the same as knowing what set of incentives will best contribute to staffing the nation's schools with skilled teachers. In fact, many policy initiatives designed to improve the quality of teachers in our nation's schools have had negative results. Examples include merit pay for individual teachers and extra pay for earning a master's degree. (Murnane, 1996, p. 255)

Murnane proposes a range of measures, including flexible salaries for teachers in fields with shortages of teachers, large pay increases for passing performance-based licensing examinations one or two years after an initial appointment, and incentives for licensed teachers to improve their teaching skills (Murnane, 1996, pp. 254–5). These proposals take on some of the features that are the norm in other professions. It will require a powerful capacity within the profession to design and implement the last two of these, with highly skilled professionals who themselves are licensed at an advanced level having responsibility. In the United States, such a role has been assumed by the National Board for Professional Teaching Standards (NBPTS) that charges a fee for those who seek the advanced level of licensing, but several states and school districts have agreed to pay the fee for those who go through the process and to pay a substantial salary bonus for those who succeed. Such proposals will challenge faculties of education in universities whose roles have become less certain in recent times, given a loss of faith in their capacities in some settings, as was the case in Britain under the former Conservative Government; or where demand for teachers declines, as has been the case in many places; or where the demands of teaching and doubts about the pay-off have led many teachers to withdraw from formal study at the postgraduate level. Similarly for professional associations of teachers, including those in the subject disciplines. None of these approaches is inconsistent with the concept of the self-managing school.

### 6 Stance of teacher unions

The stance of teacher unions in Australia and some other nations is a constraint on efforts to create systems of self-managing schools to the extent that they limit the alignment of interests in pursuit of lasting school reform. They were part of a successful alignment in the early years of the Cain Labour Government in Victoria when initiatives in a series of Ministerial Papers were enshrined in legislation, or derived from existing legislation, that gave school councils the capacity to set policy within guidelines provided by the Minister and to approve the school budget. However, later in the life of this government, along with parent organizations and key parts of the bureaucracy, unions baulked at efforts to extend self-management to include most of the resources, including staff, in the proposal supported by Minister Ian Cathie in 1986 entitled *Taking Schools into the 1990s*.

The opposition of the New South Wales Teachers Federation was instrumental in ensuring that a key element of plans to create self-managing schools in New

South Wales in the early 1990s was thwarted. This related to the local selection of teachers. This was also the case in New Zealand in attempts to introduce the bulk funding of schools.

*The experience of government*

In an account of his years in government, former Premier of Victoria John Cain made clear that the unions were a stumbling block in efforts to effect change in education:

> In education, so many good things were done with disadvantaged and disabled children, but we should have been firmer in our stand against the unions. We found ourselves locked into a number of industrial agreements that prescribed in great detail a vast array of teacher conditions and salaries that bore little relation to education. We got little cooperation from the teacher unions unless staff numbers or classroom sizes were affected. (Cain, 1995, pp. 277–8)

In health and community services, Cain noted the difficulty of effecting any changes because of the industrial implications, citing the integration of disabled pupils into regular schools. He described government efforts to work with the unions as 'trench warfare' and suggested that 'the prevailing culture was one of settling disputes, perhaps largely because the industrial officers appointed to it [Industrial Relations Taskforce] were former union officials' (Cain, 1995, p. 278).

Such a culture was described in equally graphic terms in relation to the experience of Don Hayward, Minister for Education responsible for the design and implementation of Schools of the Future in the first Kennett Liberal National Coalition:

> The power of teacher union officials derives from their ability to create a collective industrial dispute, usually concerning pay rates and working conditions, and then to use 'industrial action', such as a strike or the imposition of work bans, or threat thereof, to attempt to force the employer to grant their demands. (Caldwell and Hayward, 1998, p. 168)

Hayward was able to take a firmer stand against the unions than Cain, in retrospect, would wish to have taken.

*The union position on self-managing schools*

The position of the Australian Education Union on decentralization and privatization is set out in two publications (Martin, McCullow, McFarlane, McMurdo, Graham and Hull, 1994; Devereaux, Edsall and Martin, 1996).

In general, the Australian Education Union sees recent efforts in decentralization and the creation of self-managing schools as essentially a market-driven reform of the New Right, focused on increasing central control and diminishing resources to public education, in contrast to earlier efforts that were seen as socially democratic and empowering in their intentions. As a consequence, the union opposed virtually every recent initiative in self-management, although it is engaged in implementation to the extent that matters associated with awards (teaching conditions) are raised.

Developments in two nations are of interest in relation to the stance of the Australian Education Union. The first is in Britain, where all political parties gave their support to the concept and practice of local management in the election of 1 May 1997, and the Blair Government has made clear to unions that this is one practice among several mainstays of the Conservative Government's reforms that is non-negotiable. New Labour proposes a shift from 'structures to standards' and 'balancing pressure and support' in the pursuit of school improvement. In each instance, teacher unions are challenged to change their previous view about the nature and intent of reform to date and in the foreseeable future.

Such a shift in strategic intention is already under way for unions in the United States where leaders of both major teacher unions have an understanding of change in society and its implications for schools. Respected long-serving President of the American Federation of Teachers, the late Albert Shanker, repositioned his organization as early as 1987, appreciating that the system had become bogged down in a mass of regulation due in part to the complexity of agreements secured through collective bargaining. He was a powerful supporter of national goals for schooling, school-based management, new approaches to incentives and rewards, and changes to the workplace. He immediately became a key player in all decisions of note in the ongoing reform effort. Shanker's counterparts in the larger National Education Association (NEA) came to the same view.

## The experience of principals

Leaders of principals organizations in Victoria report that their members were usually able to work with local officials of the teachers union when it came to implementation of the terms and conditions of awards and where a degree of local flexibility was required (Caldwell, 1998).

The capacity of principals to negotiate with unions at the local level was likely developed during the years of the Cain and Kirner Labor Governments when principals were required to consult a Local Administrative Committee (LAC) on virtually every matter related to the operation of schools. The LAC included or was controlled by local union officials. Many principals also belong to the Australian Education Union.

Victorian experience can be set against the broader background of developments in the professional and industrial representation of principals around Australia. There is a trend to strengthening these organizations, with an increasing number of full- and part-time support officers. Some principals in several states are ceasing their membership of teacher unions, preferring instead their own organizations for representation. The Victorian Principals Federation is an example of a strong body whose recent disputes with government have the hallmarks of traditional government–union tensions.

## 7  Industrial relations frameworks

Industrial relations frameworks in Australia constrain the exercise of school auto-nomy to the extent that they prescribe salaries and working conditions for teachers and other staff through related state and federal awards. These prescriptions extend to hours of work, size of classes, processes for consultation, balance of continuing and contract staff, and procedures for dealing with virtually every aspect of human resource management, including performance appraisal and procedures for chang-ing the pattern of staffing in the school (such as when some teachers are considered in excess of requirements). For the most part, these same constraints are a feature of awards for non-government schools, so this is a broad impediment to the exercise of responsibility and authority at the school level.

Particular attention is given to constraints in Victoria, where the Schools of the Future program has delivered what is ostensibly a high level of self-management to schools. As noted earlier in the review in connection with inertia and re-centralization, principals continue to be concerned on matters related to the exercise of Full Staffing Flexibility, especially in respect to the management of staff considered excess to requirements and the filling of vacancies. A close inspection of the procedures on redundancy (Department of Education, Victoria, 1997; Luebbers, 1997), for example, reveals a complex procedure for consultation with staff and the union that are likely to be found in every setting, in government and non-government schools, in edu-cation and elsewhere in different workplaces. For the most part, these constraints should be seen as a necessary aspect of self-management in school education.

On the other hand, there is evidence that current frameworks for industrial relations are being utilized for seeking a centralized determination in relation to relatively routine management of staffing issues at the school level. For example, a stop-work action at a secondary college in Victoria to protest the allocation of a small number of 'extras' was placed in the context of a larger campaign to secure Certified Agreements in the workplace through the Industrial Relations Commis-sion. Henderson (1997, p. 1) asserted that 'it is clear that the AEU will have to demonstrate to the Minister the sort of industrial commitment that the Australian Nurses Federation demonstrated recently, to achieve their Certified Agreement' (nurses were associated with the shut-down of most services in many hospitals as part of their campaign to achieve this outcome).

Still to be tested are the implications of the Workplace Relations Act 1996 that involves fundamental change to and a renaming of the Industrial Relations Act 1988. A feature of the new legislation is that it allows employers and employees to make individual or workplace agreements with or without union involvement. This development clearly removes some of the constraints on school autonomy where individuals seek a more flexible arrangement. In the case of Victoria, the historic referral of the state's industrial relations powers to the Commonwealth is of inter-est, but only marginally so since teachers are currently on a federal award and will retain its protection, regardless of the nature of workplace agreements (see Senate Economics References Committee, 1996, for accounts of issues arising from the Workplace Relations Act).

The context for workplace relations is potentially turbulent, but marked with paradox. Surveys reveal employee concerns about escalating hours of work and proportion of jobs that are part-time and contract, but also declining union membership (see Hannan, 1997; Morehead, Steele, Alexander, Stephen and Duffin, 1997). These same conditions and paradoxes are evident in school education. The context is generally freeing rather than constraining of self-management for schools.

### 8   Commonwealth–State arrangements

As in the United States, constitutional arrangements and relations between national and state governments are generally a constraint on autonomy for schools to the extent that they add levels of complexity and accountability. The difficulty in obtaining a nationwide initiative in school autonomy in these two nations contrasts to what has been accomplished in Britain and New Zealand that have unitary systems of government.

Arrangements will be simplified if an equivalent in the education sector can be achieved along the lines of what occurred when Victoria referred its industrial relations powers to the Commonwealth, with the constitutional framework most likely to lead to referral to the state level in the case of school education. This can be done by the simple mechanism of the Commonwealth waiving accountability requirements (untying Special Purpose Payments to the states). There appears little prospect of this occurring if the climate surrounding the debate on literacy standards in 1997 is an indicator.

Matters of fiscal equalization must be addressed in any arrangement between state and Commonwealth, with the Commonwealth Grants Commission (CGC) recommending on the distribution of Commonwealth funds to address issues derived from vertical imbalance (the Commonwealth raises more taxes than it spends while the states spend more money than they raise) and horizontal imbalance (arising from variations at the state level in taxing capacity and costs of services). The first principle of fiscal equalization is that:

> each State should be given the capacity to provide the same standard of State-type public services as the other States, if it makes the same effort to raise revenues from its own sources and conducts its affairs with an average level of operational efficiency. (Commonwealth Grants Commission, 1993, p. 6 cited in Martin, 1996, p. 7)

It was CGC concerns about operational efficiency that led to reductions in Federal Assistance Grants to Victoria in the late 1980s and early 1990s.

### 9   Funding mechanisms for public and private schools

Funding mechanisms for public and private schools may be a constraint in Australia but they may change to driving forces, especially if the provisions of National

Competition Policy are tested and barriers between public and private schools are weakened.

Until recently, at the Commonwealth level, the New Schools Policy made it difficult to establish new private or non-government schools. With the abandonment of this policy and with the Education Resource Index for the Commonwealth support of such schools under review, the establishment of new schools in the private sector may be facilitated and resource arrangements may become more equitable. On the other hand, there has been no change to state registration requirements for private schools. The net effect may be a further shift of students from the public sector to the private sector but, while there has been an increase in the number of low-fee private schools, it will be some time before any conclusion of cause-and-effect relationship between Commonwealth initiatives and increased enrolment in the private sector can be drawn.

Proposals by the Association of Independent Schools of Victoria (AISV, 1997) called for a basic funding entitlement for all children, as did Caldwell and Hayward (1998). Caldwell and Hayward proposed that all schools that receive funds from the public purse should be classified as public schools and that all should receive the same entitlement of funds to meet recurrent costs, determined as a grant that attaches to the student, with different levels according to stages of schooling, special education needs and location of school. A higher level of cooperation among Commonwealth and states is preferred in the disbursement of grants.

Implementation of proposals along these lines may serve to drive the movement to greater autonomy for schools in the public sector because differences between approaches to funding the two sectors will narrow. Expressed simply, the narrowing of differences between the two sectors is likely to create a more supportive culture for school autonomy.

## 10   International obligations

Levels of resources are, by definition, a constraint on school autonomy and are not considered here except in one respect, namely, the capacity of public schools to raise revenue by setting fees. While different states allow schools to set a 'levy', these do not apply to meeting the cost of tuition, thus preserving the spirit of Australia's systems of free, compulsory and secular government schooling. The issue is highly contentious because the amount of money raised from parents in this fashion is increasing. Constraints on the setting of fees may be considered a constraint on the autonomy of public schools. This constraint is likely to be tested (see proposals in Caldwell and Hayward, 1998).

Australia has signed a range of United Nations Conventions affecting education and a case can be made that the introduction of fees is an infringement at two levels: that primary education must be free and compulsory; and that secondary and higher education must be available to all and must be made progressively free. The enforcement of these Conventions is through bodies such as the United Nations Human Rights Committee which hears complaints, often by citizens of nations that are claimed to have infringed. While the matter has not been tested in respect to developments in Australia, the existence of such international conventions should be considered a constraint on autonomy (see Salvaris, 1995, for a discussion of the possibilities).

### 11   Knowledge and skills of staff

The knowledge and skills of staff were identified earlier in the chapter as a driving force. It should also be considered a constraining force. This derives from findings reported in Chapter 3 that direct and indirect links between a capacity for self-management and learning outcomes are critically dependent on the capacity of teachers to utilize knowledge about what works and how in improving the quality of learning.

A case study was cited in Chapter 3 of how a primary school in Victoria created a team of teachers committed to raising literacy levels in the school. Intensive professional development as part of the Early Literacy Research Project was identified as an important factor in the achievement of success. High levels of energy and enthusiasm were reported. Powers that came to the school in the self-managing reforms of Schools of the Future were also cited.

Perceptions of self-management are likely to be reinforced by stories of this kind. In contrast, schools that are not able to take up their powers, or cannot make the link to learning, are likely to be indifferent to self-management or downright hostile, if the experience is seen as an imposition of busy work.

The implication is that the absence of adequate preparation and professional development programs, and an incapacity or unwillingness of schools to invest resources in helping teachers and other professionals gain knowledge and skill in learning and teaching are likely, in the broader picture, to constrain the further adoption of self-management. There is a daunting agenda here, for the areas of knowledge and skill that require attention are many, including early literacy, mathematics and information technology.

### 12   Values in public policy and the matter of trust

The final constraint on the movement to self-managing schools is the lack of alignment among key interests. The clearest example is the manner in which teacher unions have consistently opposed the various initiatives around the country, especially over the last decade, with these judged almost without exception to be market-driven reforms of the New Right. Even if a wider perspective is adopted, there is clearly a lack of trust among the various parties about the nature and purpose of reforms that involve the creation of more autonomous schools, especially when implemented at the same time that measures have been taken to deal with state debt or budget crisis, a condition that has affected most Australian states and comparable nations on at least one occasion over recent decades.

The issue of trust is implied in Green's analysis of the key difference between nations of the East and West as far as educational achievement is concerned. For the East, notably Japan and Singapore:

> ... as nations they place great emphasis on educational achievement, engendering high educational aspirations amongst individual learners. They tend to have a 'learning culture' in which parents and teachers have high expectations of their children's educational achievements, where the education systems are designed to provide opportunities and motivation for learners of all abilities, and where the labour market and society in general, reward those who do well in education. (Green, 1997, pp. 117–18)

Such a high level of consensus and commitment, or social capital, cannot be achieved with fragmentation or lack of alignment among key interests.

Achieving trust in public policy is now moving to centre stage in the literature and in public discussion. It is evident in the program of New Labour in Britain, modelled in the call for new partnerships in the implementation of the tough agenda for further reform in school education in that country. Fukuyama's (1995) distinction between 'high trust' and 'low trust' countries is often invoked, with the former depending on a healthy and dynamic 'civil society' for their vitality. Similar arguments are canvassed by Handy (1997) in reference to the limits of markets in capitalist societies. For Fukuyama:

> 'Civil society' — a complex welter of intermediate institutions, including businesses, voluntary associations, educational institutions, clubs, unions, media, charities, and churches — builds, in turn, on the family, the primary instrument by which people are socialized into their culture and given the skills that allow them to live in the broader society and through which the values and knowledge of that society are transmitted across the generations. (Fukuyama, 1995, pp. 4–5)

Fukuyama contends that Germany, Japan and the United States were examples of 'high trust' nations but that the United States has fallen behind with the fragmentation of its intermediate institutions. The same analysis has been applied to Britain in respect to education (see Barber, 1996) and it appears that this is the case in Australia. Rebuilding that trust and securing the alignment necessary to achieve lasting school reform will require strong leadership in all organizations and institutions. The concepts of 'trust' and a 'civil society' are considered in more detail in Chapter 7 (see also Rifkin, 1996).

## The Balance of Driving and Constraining Forces

In weighing the balance of driving and constraining forces, it seems that there are few impediments to achieving a higher level of autonomy for schools if governments have the will and parliamentary mandate to take action. Expressed another way, there are few impediments in existing legislation to the achievement of a higher level of autonomy. This is graphically illustrated in the actions of the first

Kennett Liberal–National Coalition through its Minister for Education, Don Hayward, who was able to drive the far-reaching Schools of the Future reform by utilizing powers in the existing Education Act. The reform was achieved largely by regulation and the government had the numbers in the Legislative Assembly and the Legislative Council to prevent any attempt to thwart the action. The broader political circumstances at the time allowed the government to override the opposition of the teacher unions, who were largely side-lined throughout the change, even though they had secured a shift from State to Federal Award early in the piece.

Recent initiatives in Queensland and Tasmania suggest that these governments were able to achieve the same because they had the will to make the change although parliamentary mandates were not as strong as in Victoria, indeed, in the case of Queensland, the government was dependent on the support of an independent member to remain in office, as is the case with the new government elected in June 1998. Western Australia could if it wished take the same initiatives under existing legislation. The proposed new Education Act explicitly provides for an increase in authority, responsibility and accountability for schools and their principals.

The opposition of teacher unions is, of course, a significant constraint but governments have proved that they can proceed, even within an industrial relations framework that is at first sight a further impediment. Efforts to achieve local selection of teachers have been thwarted by union opposition, as in the case of New South Wales, but not in Victoria, where the complexity of achieving 'full staffing flexibility' has been demonstrated for other reasons.

In general, it is the inertia of government that constrains school autonomy, especially when traditional ways of working with peak bodies of teachers and parents have been conducive to maintaining the status quo. Angus (1998) documented in comprehensive fashion the nature of this culture in his account of inertia in putting into effect the lessons from the National Schools Project that found that there can be important gains in student outcomes if flexibility in work practices can be achieved at the school level.

The willingness of governments to proceed may be dependent on establishing the link between school autonomy and student outcomes, and this remains problematic, despite the evidence that is emerging in some places. This evidence is opinion-based in most instances, with limited support in studies based on measures of student achievement. The paucity of evidence is frequently used by sceptics or opponents of school autonomy as grounds for opposition. Many have then resisted the very action that could settle the issue, namely, the use of a wide range of achievement measures and other indicators of student performance, and then using these as a basis for research. It seems that the debate on measures can be sustained for years unless governments are willing to take decisive action on this matter alone. An increasing number are willing to do this.

The existing levels of knowledge and skill among teachers are both a driving force and a constraining force. Given its prominence in case study accounts of how schools have used their autonomy to target professional development in areas of high learning needs, it is clear that governments that seek to enhance autonomy can energize the process through their support of school-based professional development.

**Shifting the Balance**

Unless a significant initiative appears on the scene to either add to the driving forces or mitigate the constraining forces, there is unlikely to be a change to current patterns of authority, responsibility and accountability in Australia. The Schools of the Future program in Victoria, with an option of self-governing status for some schools, is likely to be the high water mark in school autonomy for the foreseeable future.

It will take a 'significant initiative' to change the balance of driving and constraining forces. Possibilities include:

- the appearance on the scene of a new reforming government at the state level, with initiatives that extend autonomy, possibly on the lines of charter schools in the United States;

- a change in leadership and world view among teacher unions, as is starting to occur in other places, notably the United States, where support for charter schools is now bi-partisan, extending to unions;

- removing distinctions between government and non-government schools, especially in relation to the funding mechanism, and in other ways fostering a culture that minimizes differences and reinforces autonomy;

- application or extension of the Workplace Relations Act to provide for Workplace Agreements at the school level;

- allocating Commonwealth grants directly to schools rather than to the state, as is currently the case in allocations for independent, non-systemic, non-government schools;

- a dramatic expansion of business and other corporate support for schools that similarly targets funds to schools rather than systems, especially schools where there are high priorities for improvement; and

- building a culture that values local decision-making based on student needs by targeting professional development funds directly to schools and profiling the outcomes.

Most of these are incremental in nature. The achievement of a dramatic breakthrough seems remote. The probability of such a breakthrough will increase if actions of New Labour in a unitary system of government in Britain are seen to bear fruit. In Britain, the self-managing element of the Thatcher era is non-negotiable, and unions must 'come on board' if they are to be partners in a comprehensive program that, in rhetoric and action thus far, places 'education, education, education' at the top of the nation's priorities. Success will energize parallel efforts and align interests in other nations. Failure will place the future of public education at even greater risk, in other nations as well as in Britain.

The risk to public education seems to have triggered the creation of a new alignment of interests in the United States where 'the leaders of 12 education organizations are putting aside their past differences and forming a new coalition to focus on raising student achievement and boosting support for public schools' (Jacobson, 1997, p. 21). Rather than lobby for more funds, the Learning First Alliance will focus on action at the local level. The first major project of the group was a meeting in January 1998 to discuss research about improving student achievement and to design specific projects. Significantly, the alliance brings together every major teacher union and principals organization as well as associations representing the interests of states, school districts and parents. The only line drawn by its members derives from a common antipathy to vouchers. The initiative demonstrates, however, that new alignments can be created if the focus is on student achievement and there is openness to a range of possibilities. Given that a higher level of school autonomy is in virtually every option or program of action at this time, it is likely to be central to the reform agenda that is likely to flow from this initiative, and this is the agenda for Track 2: an unrelenting focus on learning outcomes. How that agenda is being shaped is the first matter to be addressed in Chapter 5.

### Strategic Intentions for Schools
### Completing the Journey on Track 1

1   Schools seeking more autonomy will utilize every capacity that is made available under existing schemes of self-management, including where possible and feasible the outsourcing of services where there is a benefit to the school.

2   Schools will take the initiative in building strategic alliances with individuals and organizations possessing or supporting a higher level of self-management, including providers in the public and private sectors of education and training, and will provide support to students who are engaged in home schooling.

3   Schools will place a high priority on staff selection and professional development to ensure that knowledge and skills are consistent with professional capacities that will sustain as much autonomy as possible.

4   Schools will place a high priority on building their capacities in communications and information technology, including advanced cost accounting and management information systems, reducing as far as possible their dependence on the system in these matters.

5   Flexibilities in workplace arrangements will be utilized to the full, subject to the legal and industrial frameworks that apply, in order to secure an optimal mix and match to needs and priorities in programs for learning and the support of learning.

6   Schools will reduce their dependence on system support for learning and teaching, seeking other sources in the public and private sectors, consistent with school priorities, but without sacrificing what is needed to deliver programs of the highest quality.

7   Schools will resist through every means available to them any attempt on the part of the system to re-centralize, especially in respect to matters that link to learning outcomes, including a capacity to select staff and deliver professional development programs that reflect school priorities.

8   Curriculum and standards schemes will be regarded as frameworks rather than prescriptions, and every attempt will be made to balance time and effort in key learning areas to reflect school needs and priorities, especially for, but not limited to, programs in literacy and numeracy.

9   Principals and other school leaders will be skilful in their dealings with teacher unions and other organizations representing the interests of their staff, creating alliances whose first priority is learning, and building high levels of trust.

10  Without sacrificing any source, schools will seek to reduce their dependence on funding from the public purse by seeking other substantial support, avoiding approaches that yield minimal resources from effort that diverts time and energy from the support of learning.

*Track 2*

# *Unrelenting Focus on Learning Outcomes*

# Chapter 5

# The New Agenda in School Reform

Chapter 4 concluded on a challenging note, pointing to initiatives in Britain under New Labour, where the priorities are 'education, education, education', and slogans like 'standards not structures' and 'balancing pressure and support' are in vogue. Attention was drawn to developments in the United States, where most of the powerful players have formed the Learning First Alliance, perhaps sensing that public education is at risk, and that the starting point to make it safe is an assessment of student achievement, and working backwards to determine what ought to be done, rather than commencing with an assumption that more resources will solve the problem. These are signs that reform on Track 2 is gathering momentum.

The purpose of Chapter 5 is to critically examine what governments in these and other countries are actually doing, or intending to do, in order to discern the agenda for the journey on this dimension of school reform. In most instances, there is ample evidence that the descriptor of 'unrelenting focus on learning outcomes' is an accurate one. The starting point is the agenda of Labour in Britain, especially that connected to 'standards not structures'. Reference is made to the setting of targets in literacy and numeracy, the creation of education action zones where conditions are difficult and much improvement is needed, concern about the education of boys, the drive to make use of a wider range of communications and information technology, and the use of symbols to communicate the new agenda. Attention is then given to the need for a broader agenda, reflecting anxiety that there has been an unduly narrow focus in recent times, in society at large as well as in school education. Charles Handy's (1997) notion of 'the hungry spirit' sets the stage; MacGilchrist, Myers and Reed (1997) provide the pieces in their view of 'the intelligent school'. The response of the school to an expanding and changing agenda cannot be random, haphazard, or unplanned. High levels of strategic and operational planning will not suffice. There must be a framework of values, programs and approaches that will shape the work of a school for a period of time and will be a source of stability, but within which there is ample room for change and development. The concept of 'school design' captures intentions in this regard.

## Standards Not Structures

Except in respect to grant maintained schools, there has been no reversal of direction on Track 1 as far as the structural aspects of reform in Britain are concerned. The major features of the 1988 Education Reform Act remain, notably, the National

Curriculum, to be reviewed on schedule, although it was 'suspended' at the primary level to accommodate the National Literacy Strategy; the local management of schools; and the testing of students at various points in their schooling, with publication of school results in 'league tables'. The market rhetoric was abandoned. Except for abolition, restructuring or restaffing of some agencies of government, the key structures remain.

There is no doubt that further change will occur on Track 1 to improve efficiency, effectiveness and equity in implementation, but the focus is now clearly on the achievement of high standards for all students, hence the slogan of 'standards not structures'. What many perceived as a mindless denigration of the efforts of schools and their teachers in the past has given rise to another new slogan of 'balancing pressure and support'. These two themes were sounded in the White Paper that appeared in July 1997, within three months of Labour coming to power (Secretary of State for Education and Employment, 1997).

There were, however, mixed messages with the release within a month of gaining office of a list of failing schools, and the critics were recalling the alleged 'name and shame' strategies of the former government. There was consternation in some of these schools because measures had already been taken following an earlier naming, and insufficient time had elapsed to see the effects.

By early 1998, however, the legislative agenda had taken shape and priorities for action had emerged.

### Standards and Effectiveness Unit

The Standards and Effectiveness Unit was established within days of assuming power, headed by Professor Michael Barber, former Dean of Innovations at the Institute of Education, University of London. Many of the directions for reform, and the major themes of the White Paper had appeared in Barber's book *The Learning Game* (Barber, 1996). This unit has responsibility for the implementation of government policy in respect to standards. The Office for Standards in Education (OFSTED) remains, with responsibility for inspections as in the past.

### Targets for Literacy

Targets for improvement in literacy were announced in January 1998. The baseline for 11-year-olds was the result achieved in each local education authority in 1996, when, across the nation, just 57 per cent reached the standard required for their age in reading and writing. The target for 2002 is 80 per cent. The low-achieving authority in 1996 was Tower Hamlets in London, with 38 per cent, and it must improve to 70 per cent in 2002. The high achieving Richmond-upon-Thames, 77 per cent in 1996, must reach 88 per cent in 2002.

The Minister for Education responsible for the scheme, Stephen Byers, made clear that the market rhetoric had been abandoned and that adoption on a school-by-school basis of strategies that were known to work must be adopted.

This marks a radical change, setting targets for local authorities and making them public.

It's a different approach to public service. The previous government thought market forces would deliver. We are saying we can't leave it to the vagaries of the market. We have set the target, but will offer a system of support. We aren't just setting them and walking away.

We don't want excuses for failure. Many local authorities are in deprived areas [Tower Hamlets is an instance], but poverty is no excuse for underachievement — it is a reason for targeted support.

There is clear evidence that some schools in depressed areas are already reaching above the national average — if they can improve, all schools can improve. (cited by Rafferty, 1998a, p. 4)

The government announced a National Literacy Strategy in September 1997 and commitments were given that are consistent with an intention to balance pressure and support. The pressure is for 80 per cent of 11-year-olds to reach standard by 2002. The support comes in the form of training for all with leadership responsibilities in literacy and three days of training for every primary teacher. Two hundred literacy consultants are available to support schools around the nation.

These announcements assumed, with good reason, that there is a body of knowledge and skill in literacy that can be acquired and made effective. The task for schools is to see that the capacities of their staff are developed accordingly. Implications for teacher professionalism are explored in Chapter 6.

*Targets for Numeracy*

Targets for numeracy were not far behind in the new agenda for reform on Track 2. Labour established a Numeracy Task Force headed by Professor David Reynolds of the University of Newcastle-upon-Tyne, eminent in the school effectiveness movement (he is a founder of the International Congress for School Effectiveness and Improvement). Reynolds' international comparative studies for OFSTED during the last years of the Conservative era focused attention on classroom practice in different nations, especially in the East where there were high levels of achievement and more use of whole class teaching and learning than in the West. The report of the task force was released in January 1998 and national strategies similar to those for literacy are intended for implementation in 1999.

Achievement in mathematics moved to centre stage in 1996 and 1997 with the release of the findings of the Third International Mathematics and Science Study (TIMSS) that involved 41 nations, which makes it the largest international comparative study ever undertaken in a single area of the curriculum. Britain finished toward the top of the tables, with the top ranked nations coming from the East and Eastern Europe. There was a call in Britain, as in comparable nations, including Australia and the United States, for schools to lift their game in the teaching of mathematics. As with the earlier studies by Reynolds, comparisons were made in respect to classroom practice in different nations.

There is no consensus on what ought to be done and what ought to constitute good practice in schools. There is no doubt, however, that raising the standards of achievement in numeracy is now and will continue to be an important item on the agenda for change on Track 2.

### Education Action Zones

A key strategy in supporting schools is the creation of 'education action zones'. These are areas in the most disadvantaged parts of the country. They will be supported by funds of about £15 million per year, with each zone receiving £250,000 from the Department for Education and Employment to be matched by business and the locally managed budgets of two or three secondary schools and their feeder primary schools. Each zone will be managed by a forum which the government intends to be led in some instances by business.

Head of the Standards and Effectiveness Unit, Professor Michael Barber, observed that 'the zones will be test-beds for innovation in a post-modern world' (Rafferty, 1998b, p. 5). In a presentation to the North of England Education Conference in January 1998, Barber announced that much of the management could be carried out by the private sector. Implementation along these lines raised the possibility that the zones may be freed from many of the constraints on local authorities, extending even to pay scales, curriculum, and conditions for work. This was subsequently confirmed by the school standards minister Stephen Byers (Barnard and Rafferty, 1998, p. 1). Graham Lane, Education Chair of the Local Government Association, was reported to have 'raged that it was tantamount to privatization of schools and the end of local democracy' and that 'it was a conspiracy hatched by civil servants and shadowy ideologues to do away with local education authorities' (as reported by Rafferty, 1998b, p. 5).

### Public Private Partnerships

Plans for education action zones indicated that Labour is continuing a strategy adopted by the Conservatives in seeking alliances of government and business in school reform. The first instance of the latter was the attempt to create City Technology Colleges, but this stalled with fewer than 20 such institutions created around the nation. More successful were special technology schools where grants from government had to be matched by grants from other sources, raised by the schools themselves.

The new partnership in special education zones is similar to schemes that have been in place for several years in the United States, where the major grants from individuals, corporations, foundations and trusts have usually been targeted at schools in disadvantaged communities, with management by teams representing the corporate sector, the school district and the teacher unions. An example is the Annenberg

Foundation that allocated $750 million for reform in a number of urban school districts around the nation.

In Britain, the private consulting firm Arthur Andersen worked with the Department for Education and Employment in determining ways to expand the number of Private Finance Initiative Schemes in education, the first of which involved the rebuilding of Colefox School in Bridport, Dorset. All buildings will be maintained for a period of 30 years by a private company. A similar scheme is the Public Private Partnership Program (see account in Sears, 1997, p. 6) in which school repairs are tackled in partnership with private enterprise.

### The Education of Boys

Britain is one of many nations where there are concerns about the achievement of boys and strategies for addressing the problem are unfolding, including research at Cambridge University, sponsored by OFSTED, to examine how school, authorities and government can reverse a trend that sees boys lagging behind girls, examining factors such as teaching methods, and numbers of male and female teachers in primary and secondary schools. Minister for Education, Stephen Byers, reported at the 1998 International Congress for School Effectiveness and Improvement that boys made up 83 per cent of students excluded from schools and that poor performance was evident across all areas of the curriculum. He asserted that raising achievement should not be at the expense of gains by girls in recent years. He suggested that cultural factors were at play:

> We must challenge the laddish anti-learning culture which has been allowed to develop over recent years and should not simply accept with a shrug of our shoulders that boys will be boys. (cited by Lepkowska, 1998a, p. 8)

Changes in culture require broad across-the-nation strategies, and many of these depend on fundamental social change before school effort is likely to have effect. Australian psychologist, Steve Biddulph, who has written extensively on the topic (see Biddulph, 1997) has claimed that Britain is raising 'the most under-fathered generation that has ever lived on this earth' (reported by Lepkowska, 1998b, p. 9).

There are, nonetheless, examples of school success and the relevance of a capacity for self-management. St Thomas Roman Catholic School was able to achieve a 33 per cent gain by boys in GCSE results by monitoring achievement, setting targets for improvement, selecting five boys in each class in Years 10 and 11 for special attention, which included close monitoring of work and additional praise (Lepkowska, 1998c, p. 9).

### Information and Communications Technology

An expanded role for information and communications technology (ICT) is as evident in Britain as it is in most other nations. ICT is seen as part of the curriculum and part of a broad-based strategy to support learning and teaching. It is considered in more detail in Chapters 8 and 9, but it is included here as part of the new agenda for change on Track 2. No school can ignore it.

Governments are wrestling with the issue of how to resource schools with ICT, bearing in mind the need for access and equity. Boundaries are being broken and new partnerships are being forged, as evidenced by the earlier Conservative initiative in creating special technology schools and requiring schools to obtain matching grants from the private sector. Government is working in partnership with industry to ensure that cables are brought to the schoolhouse door. Industry is a willing partner in most instances, given the size of the market in school education.

*Adding Value*

Labour has continued the testing program and the league tables that were intro-duced following the 1988 Education Reform Act. This appears astonishing at first sight, given that they were initially opposed by virtually every interest in the pro-fession and the manner in which they were frustrated by teacher boycotts. There is now broad community acceptance and they appear irreversible. Schools and teachers must come to terms with the practice.

One of the arguments against the tests and tables was that the results were misleading if they were intended to communicate the relative merits of programs offered by different schools. Schools have different intakes, reflecting different entry levels in student achievement and attitudes for learning. One way to address this concern is to provide a 'value added' adjustment to scores so the real contribu-tion of schools in 'adding value' to learning can be assessed. Outstanding work has been done in this regard by Carol Taylor Fitz-Gibbon, Peter Tymms and their colleagues at the University of Durham (see Fitz-Gibbon, 1995, 1996).

Value added measures in the Durham program do not involve school-by-school comparisons, although these can be made if desired. Schools receive data for their own students on a subject-by-subject, even classroom-by-classroom basis.

Given initial concerns about testing and tables, it might be expected that adoption of value added measures would be an item in the agenda for Track 2, but no national initiative has yet been taken. Apart from the technical issue of 'scaling up' the approach to all schools across the country in each of the key learning areas, there is the matter of understandability as far as the wider community is concerned. MacGilchrist, Myers and Reed (1997) highlight the complexities, and urge that a 'health warning' should also be applied to their use. Where school-by-school comparisons are made on the basis of value added measures, they draw attention to the manner in which high turnover can be masked and refer to the limitations of making comparisons on the basis of samples. On balance, however, they support the practice:

Using value-added data is most useful for helping individual schools to pinpoint areas of good practice and aspects of school life that need to be improved . . . The technique enables a school to take account of 'givens' that may have an impact on pupil outcomes such as prior attainment, socio-economic status, gender and ethnicity. Value-added data can also be used as a screening device to identify individual pupils whose 'predicted' and 'expected' are very different from those observed . . . Pupils who depart markedly from their expected levels of achievement can be identified and, if necessary, can become the focus for additional support. (MacGilchrist, Myers and Reed, 1997, p. 2)

Given these benefits, it seems important for the technical and transparency issues to be addressed so that schools can make use of such a powerful tool as part of their strategies to achieve an 'unrelenting focus on learning outcomes'.

### Symbols

Symbols are words, actions or artefacts that communicate meaning. Without entering a debate about whether the substance has changed, the symbols in Britain under New Labour certainly have. Five sets of symbols are selected for illustration, and each is intended to communicate a change in substance and a change in the agenda.

The first is the change in language. The slogans 'education, education, education', 'from structures to standards' and 'balancing pressure and support' are intended to signal a shift in substance and style, in contrast to the previous government, that was perceived or alleged to have different intentions and a language that had the effect of alienating teachers and educationists. There is a shift away from the rhetoric of the market, as illustrated in Minister Byers statement, cited above, that 'The previous government thought market forces would deliver. We are saying we can't leave it to the vagaries of the market' (reported by Rafferty, 1998a, p. 4).

A second symbol is the choice made by significant people on what events they will attend and which people they shall meet. Given that there are literally hundreds of options available each day in these matters, the choice is powerful in terms of communicating meaning. One of the first public acts of Prime Minister Tony Blair after election to office was to visit a school. It seemed that not a week passed without him visiting a school and being seen and photographed with children.

A third symbol is in honours and awards. The New Years Honours list in 1998 was flagged as having a larger than usual number of awards for those who worked in schools, ranging from heads to support staff. These are intended to communicate meaning about what is valued and ought to be celebrated and rewarded. One recipient was Pat Collarbone, former head of Haggerston School in Hackney, now Director of the London Leadership Centre, and a member of the committee to recommend on the future of the Hackney Education Authority. Dame Pat led the transformation of Haggerston, demonstrating that significant school improvement can be achieved under seemingly intractable conditions (see Collarbone, 1997, for an account of her work at Haggerston). She modelled professional development for principals by completing a Master of Business Administration in Education at Leeds Metropolitan University and undertaking a Doctor of Education in the School of Management at the University of Lincolnshire and Humberside. She now leads the professional development of heads and aspiring heads through her work with the London Leadership Centre.

A fourth symbol is in the substance and style of appointment to key roles and committees. These are, of course, substantive in their own right because they bring expertise to bear on an issue. Two instances concern Her Majesty's Chief Inspector, Chris Woodhead. One was the decision of Labour to keep him in this post following his service to a Conservative Government. It sent a signal to the profession that there was to be no let-up in attention to standards. Another was the decision of government to appoint Woodhead and Professor Tim Brighouse, Chief Education Officer in Birmingham, as joint chairs of a standards task force. Brighouse was a critic of aspects of reform by the previous government and won a large civil action against a former Secretary of State for Education and Employment. Brighouse is highly respected by practitioners. Apart from its substance, the joint appointment communicated meaning about the importance of building an alliance of interests if there is to be significant progress in raising standards in schools.

The fifth symbol was the manner in which the Secretary of State for Education and Employment chose to release the White Paper in 1997. It was decided to place a summary in supermarkets across the country and to invite the community at large to make comment on proposals for change. A relatively small number chose to respond and the largest group among these were teachers who had access to the document through their workplaces. Symbolically, however, the strategy was intended to communicate the government's wish to consult and listen.

Taken together, these are powerful symbols that help define the agenda, certainly in terms of style and to some extent, its substance. Governments in other nations and leaders in schools and school systems should give careful consideration to the symbols to be adopted in helping to energize change along Track 2.

### Broadening the Agenda

An important item on the agenda for change on Track 2 arises from the question 'What outcomes are counted to be worthy if there is to be an unrelenting focus on learning outcomes?' Given the priority attached to literacy and numeracy, and the limited range of learning areas that are addressed in tests, the results of which are published in 'league tables', it would seem that the range of outcomes is rather narrow. This is, of course, the subject of much of the criticism of school education in general and the reform agenda in particular. There is evidence, however, that a broader perspective on these matters is now being taken or is being restored, and this covers not only what counts as worthy in learning but also how the school should cope, indeed flourish with the weight of expectations.

*The Hungry Spirit*

This broader perspective is a reflection of concerns being raised about the nature of change in society at large and the need for the restoration of values that have been lost or subsumed in the events of recent times. One influential writer who has drawn attention to this issue is Charles Handy who, with writers such as Peter Drucker, has been so helpful for those who seek to understand the nature of change and what the future holds (see, for example, his two books *The Empty Raincoat*, 1994; and *Beyond Certainty*, (1996)). In *The Hungry Spirit* (Handy, 1997) he is concerned about the nature and effect of many of these changes and calls for a new agenda:

> What good can it possibly do to pile up riches which you cannot conceivably use, and what is the point of the efficiency needed to create those riches if one third of the world's workers are now unemployed or under-employed . . . ?

> Organizations, as well as individuals, have therefore got to decide what they are about before they decide what they have to do. (Handy, 1997, pp. 2–3, 8)

Schools have an important role to play in the matter, and Handy makes a powerful contribution to the new agenda by proposing an extension of Howard Gardner's (Gardner, 1983) list of seven 'intelligences' that ought to be addressed in schools: linguistic, logical mathematical, spatial, bodily-kinaesthetic, musical, interpersonal, intrapersonal. Handy concedes that three intelligences — factual intelligence, analytic intelligence and numerate intelligence — 'will get you through most tests and examinations and entitle you to be called clever' (Handy, 1997, p. 211) but he suggests eight more: linguistic intelligence, spatial intelligence, athletic intelligence, intuitive intelligence, emotional intelligence, practical intelligence, interpersonal intelligence and musical intelligence (Handy, 1997, pp. 212–13).

It is the first set of three intelligences that are crowding the agenda and it is the last eight that ought now be capturing attention if schools are to make a contribution to the well-being of society in the manner envisaged by Handy. While he concedes that few individuals can be competent in more than a small number of these, his list is helpful in broadening the agenda as far as learning outcomes are concerned. A school should be unrelenting in its efforts on all or most fronts, with different emphases according to the needs, interests and aspirations of students and their communities. Expressed another way, using the language in the passage cited above, without sacrificing effort on matters such as literacy and numeracy, schools ought to decide 'what they are about' before they decide 'what they have to do'.

*Learning Organizations and Intelligent Schools*

There is a school counterpart to learning outcomes for students. With school considered to be all in its community, but especially staff, students and parents, the following questions are critical: 'What should the school "learn"? How should the school "learn"?'

The concept of 'the learning organization' helps shape the answers to these questions and the work of Peter Senge has assisted in this regard (Senge, 1990). Carol Johnston (1997) adapted Senge's five disciplines — systems thinking, personal mastery, team learning, shared vision and mental models — to frame a doctoral study exploring the extent to which three self-managing secondary schools in Victoria's Schools of the Future had taken on the characteristics of learning organizations. She found evidence of the disciplines in each school and they were highly developed in one. She proposed a further adaptation of the Senge model to suit schools, highlighting collaborative structures, effective communication channels, integrated and inclusive professional development programs, and learning focused leadership. Her findings on collaborative structures confirmed earlier doctoral research in Victoria, before the Schools of the Future initiative, conducted by Helen Telford in schools in inner Melbourne (this doctoral research was published in Telford, 1996).

MacGilchrist, Myers and Reed (1997) adapted Gardner's notion of multiple intelligences to describe the kinds of intelligences a school should nurture if it is to thrive under conditions that prevail on Track 2. Their book brings together key findings from research on school and classroom effectiveness and improvement. They present a portrait of an 'intelligent school' which 'conveys the wholeness of the enterprise in which schools are engaged' (p. 103). While acknowledging that 'the intelligent school is greater than the sum of its parts' (p. xvii), they propose the following as key components:

- Contextual intelligence, which includes the capacity to see the school in relation to the wider world.

- Strategic intelligence, that includes a capacity to utilize the findings from research on school and classroom effectiveness and improvement.

- Academic intelligence, that places a high value on scholarship.

- Reflective intelligence, referring to a capacity for collecting, analyzing, interpreting and acting on a wide range of data from many sources: the intelligent school 'is comfortable in its ability to interpret and use information and put it to the service of its pupils and the organization as a whole'. (p. 107)

- Pedagogical intelligence, that characterizes a school that seeks to become a learning organization, committed to learning about its core business, which is learning.

- Collegial intelligence, describes the capacity of staff and others in the school community to work together to improve practice.

- Emotional intelligence, reflecting the work of Goleman (1996) and Salovey and Mayer (1990), with the latter highlighting self-awareness, managing emotions, motivating oneself, recognizing emotions in others, and handling relationships. (p. 108)

- Spiritual intelligence, characterized by 'a fundamental valuing of the lives and development of all members of a school community: that they all matter and have something to contribute'. (p. 109)

- Ethical intelligence, which concerns 'the way a school conveys its moral purpose and principles'. (p. 109)

Noteworthy are the last three in the list, given the concerns expressed by Handy about the toll on personal well-being from recent changes in society. There are major implications for school leaders, some of which are taken up in Chapter 10.

A masterful illustration of emotional intelligence is given by David Loader, principal of Australia's largest school, Wesley College in Melbourne in his book *The Inner Principal* (Loader, 1997). While many observers see Loader as a model of contextual intelligence in the list provided by MacGilchrist, Myers and Reed, especially through his pioneering leadership in the adoption of technology in his previous position as principal of Methodist Ladies College in Melbourne, it was of his emotional life that he chose to write.

Pioneering research on compassion in leadership was undertaken by Russell Swann at the University of Melbourne (Swann, 1998). Drawing on the work of Matthew Fox, he identified eleven elements of compassion — celebrative, passionately active, justice-making, benevolently loving, creative, non-elitist, networking, transpersonal, pain relieving, transcendent and fun-filled — and constructed a framework for surveys and case studies that allocated each element to four leadership frames based on the classification of Bolman and Deal — structural, human resource, political and symbolic. He found strong confirmation of a model for compassion based on this framework in his study of compassionate leadership in Melbourne schools.

### School Design

The response of the school to an expanding and changing agenda cannot be random, haphazard, or unplanned. High levels of strategic and operational planning will not suffice. There must be a framework of values, programs and approaches that will shape the work of a school for a period of time and that will be a source of stability, but within which there is ample room to change and develop. The concept of 'school design' captures intentions in this regard.

*Illustrations of School Design*

*United States*

International attention has been focused on school design as a result of a major initiative in the United States by the New American Schools Development Corporation, founded in 1991. The program is known as New American Schools (NAS). NAS was established by business and foundation leaders who were prepared to invest in efforts to transform schools, free of public funding in the design phase of five years, after which schools and school systems were to take charge as efforts were made to achieve scale-up on the basis of lessons learned. Partnerships were established with school systems toward the end of the initial phase. Nine designs were approved on the basis of a Request for Proposal, each taken further in NAS through the work of a Design Team.

Detailed accounts of NAS are contained in Stringfield, Ross and Smith (1996) but the following give an indication of the design features of seven projects selected for wider scale-up.

- Atlas Communities based in Boston combines the work of James Comer, Howard Gardner and Theodore Sizer. The goal is to create school communities of learners in K–12 feeder patterns. Teams of teachers from across the pathway work together to define standards and formulate curriculum.

- Audrey Cohen College in New York organizes programs around a complex statement of purpose, with student-centred learning to mastery involving the wider community.

- Co-NECT Schools in Cambridge, Massachusetts, has a design based on the Outward Bound program, keeping teachers and students together for more than a year in specially-designed learning expeditions that develop intellectual and physical knowledge, skills and attitudes.

- Modern Red Schoolhouse in Indianapolis focuses on the fundamentals of education in core academic areas, with highly individualized instruction using sophisticated learning technologies.

- The National Alliance for Restructuring Education based in Washington has a design for system restructuring to support the transformation of schools. Work is organized around five key tasks: standards, learning environments, community services and supports, public engagement and high performance management.

- Roots and Wings is based on Robert Slavin's pioneering work at Johns Hopkins University in Baltimore, with 'roots' referring to the outstanding Success for All program in literacy in elementary (primary) schools, and 'wings' referring to secondary counterparts in mathematics and science.

### United Kingdom

Case studies of successful school improvement in different nations suggests that each school has adopted its own design in respect to values, programs and approaches. Examples may be found in the Report of the National Commission on Education that provides accounts of effective schools in disadvantaged areas in the four countries that make up the United Kingdom. Entitled *Success Against the Odds* (National Commission on Education, 1996), special design features can be found in each of the eleven schools. For example:

- Fair Furlong Primary School addressed behaviour policy, display policy and management systems;

- Crowcroft Park Primary School focused on leadership styles, staff working in teams, clearly defined processes for curriculum development, shared purpose, excellent communications and engaged students;

- Blaengwrach Primary School developed a design based on shared vision, common philosophy, high expectations, a community 'open door' policy, and a commitment to excellence;

- Columbia Primary School highlighted leadership and an ethos that takes a strong stand on ethical issues and community self-confidence, the capacity of staff to work in teams, and a behaviour and discipline policy developed by the school in partnership with its community ; and

- Burntwood Secondary Girls School stressed values (clarity of aims and ethos, focus on quality, collegiality), mechanisms (leadership that was stable, secure, committed, with attention to detail and high expectations, as well as efficient management, good communications, systematic monitoring, participatory decision-making and parental and community involvement) and other contributory factors (including grant-maintained status and outstanding site).

These schools and the others in the project (Hayward High School, Hazelwood Integrated College, St Michael's Roman Catholic Comprehensive School, Sutton Centre, Selly Park Girls' School) demonstrated to a high level each of the 10 characteristics of highly effective schools that were postulated by the National Commission on Education as required for success in raising student achievement.

1 Strong, positive leadership by the head and senior staff.
2 A good atmosphere or spirit, generated both by shared aims and values and by a physical environment that is as attractive and stimulating as possible.
3 High and consistent expectations for all pupils.
4 A clear and consistent focus on teaching and learning.
5 Well-developed procedures for assessing how pupils are progressing.
6 Responsibility for learning shared by pupils themselves.
7 Participation by pupils in the life of the school.
8 Rewards and incentives to encourage pupils to succeed.
9 Parental involvement in children's education and in supporting the aims of the school.
10 Extra-curricular activities that broaden pupils' interests and experiences, expand their opportunities to succeed, and help to build good relationships within the school.

(National Commission on Education, 1996, p. 366)

In a sense, this list of 10 provides a blueprint for schools to prepare their own designs for the particular ways they will focus on learning outcomes, taking account of their circumstances. The schools featured in *Success Against the Odds* appear to have had no such blueprint but developed their own approach. As was noted in the synthesis of the 11 case studies:

> But the major lesson of this study is plain for all to see. It is that every school has the opportunity to succeed against the odds. None of the schools studied holds itself out as exceptional or puts success down to any particularly gifted individual. Nor does the opportunity for success arise as a once-for-all, 'gift-wrapped' opportunity. On the contrary, it arises every day in a hundred different ways, large and small, and what matters is that the school should form a consistent habit of creating or taking advantage of these fleeting opportunities. It is the steady accumulation day on day, and week on week, of positive progress which emerges so clearly. (Maden and Hillman, 1996, p. 362)

These case studies seem a step removed from the concept of design that is evident in New American Schools to the extent that the latter are working to a blueprint. On the other hand, the schools and school systems that furnished the blueprint had for the most part to work through the 'hard slog' that is described in the synthesis by Maden and Hillman. The challenge for schools is to develop and acquire a blueprint, or for systems or even whole nations, it is to achieve scale-up from design to wider implementation, a matter that is taken up in the final part of this section.

Before leaving the accounts in *Success Against the Odds*, it is worth noting that the structural features of reform on Track 1 do not feature to any great extent. They seem to have been taken on board without a fuss, and Maden and Hillman describe local adaptations as instances of 'colonization' by schools and conclude that:

> Perhaps the most important lesson to be learned is that the energy released in these schools is generated primarily by what the school believes it can and must do . . . government policy and statutory requirements are part of the larger context within which the school operates and moves forward. (Maden and Hillman, 1996, p. 354)

## *Australia*

The concept of design is also evident in Australia. System-wide reforms such as Schools of the Future in Victoria, Leading Schools in Queensland, and Directions in Education in Tasmania are examples of blueprints for restructuring schools. For the journey along Track 2, they require the addition of a core element that focuses on learning. An example of such an element is the design for literacy that is part of the Early Literacy Research Project described in Chapter 3.

In Australia and other nations, there is a priority on developing a design for the middle school, generally considered to be a stage of learning that spans Years

5–8. The intention here is to redress some of the dysfunctions of the traditional year of transition from Year 6 to Year 7, from a primary (elementary) school to a secondary school. The National Middle Schooling Project (NMSP) is a project of national significance, funded by the national Department of Employment, Education, Training and Youth Affairs (DEETYA), managed by the Australian Curriculum Studies Association (ACSA). A number of middle school design features have emerged in particular schools, including Holy Eucharist Primary School in Victoria, Kurri Kurri High School in New South Wales, Lanyon High School in the Australian Capital Territory, and Oatlands District High School in Tasmania (see accounts in Education Review, 1997).

George and Alexander (1993) list the requirements for this stage of schooling and these might shape design on a school-by-school basis: classroom-based guidance efforts, often in the form of 'advisory programs'; interdisciplinary team organization of teachers; common planning time for teams of teachers; flexible scheduling, often in a block format; a curriculum emphasizing balanced exploration and solid academics; arrangements that permit the development of longer term relationships between teachers and the students they teach; heterogeneous grouping whenever appropriate; instructional strategies that consider the characteristics of the learner; a wide range of special interest experiences keyed to the development of middle school youth; and collaboration between and among teachers and administrators as they work to improve middle school programs.

An example of a middle school design that crosses international boundaries may be found at two schools in Australia — Eumemmerring Secondary College and the Grange Secondary College. Both schools have adopted the Team / Small Group Model (TSM) pioneered in the Saarland in Germany by Klaus Winkel. Teachers work in teams at a particular year level and teach as few students as possible for as many subjects as possible. Where practicable, students work in small groups of four as they complete their tasks in the various subjects, working as a team to share their knowledge and skill (see Taylor and McKenzie, 1997, for an account of practice at Eumemmerring).

School designs based on or stimulated by technology are increasing in Australia. The first comprehensive design was developed at Methodist Ladies College in Melbourne under the leadership of David Loader. All girls from Grade 4 to 12 have their own laptop computers. While this was the core design, what followed indicates the impact of technology, for virtually every aspect of school operations then changed, including building design, furniture, the role of teachers, the timetable and relationships between different learning areas in the curriculum. Further information about this design is contained in Chapter 8 in the context of the journey along Track 3, namely, creating schools for the knowledge society.

*Scaling up Success in School Design*

This review of school design contained illustrations of designs that were based on a blueprint, present from the outset, and others that evolved, based on key values and clear goals, forged by a combination of experience and knowledge gleaned from research. In each instance, once established, they may be viewed as blueprints for others, with adaptations to suit particular settings and the needs, interests and aspirations of schools and their communities. The challenge here is to achieve scale-up from one or a few schools to many schools, if not an entire system. Consistent with the notion of the self-managing school, it is a task for each school to create, select or adapt a design to suit its circumstances, and this will be a requirement for success on Track 2.

Achieving large-scale take-up of effective school design has been an important issue in the New American Schools (NAS) initiative in the United States. A Memorandum of Understanding with NAS forms the basis for action by states and districts as scale-up proceeds. The contents of these documents are illuminating because they highlight the common features of NAS designs:

- The willingness to give schools wide authority and autonomy to make decisions regarding all aspects of schooling, including staffing, budgeting, curriculum and scheduling.

- Common publicly supported standards for achievement for virtually all students, accompanied by institutional mechanisms through which schools or systems of schools can petition for the acceptance of self-developed standards as equivalent to or exceeding the established standards.

- Rich and reliable systems of assessment that help schools demonstrate that they are meeting the standards and help teachers make improvements in their programs.

- Sources of assistance in choosing and developing curriculum and instructional strategies that are consistent with the standards and responsive to individual students' needs . . .

- A system for professional development and certification that is responsive to the needs of schools and school professionals, and assures that their instructional staff can help students meet high standards.

- Technology that supports teachers and students in the instructional process, assists in the management of schools, and generally supports the restructuring of schools to provide students with the individual attention and opportunities they need.

- A services and support system that strengthens community and family engagement in the school, reduces health and other nonacademic barriers to learning and promotes family stability.

- A multifaceted plan to engage the public in the transformation in serious and meaningful ways and to develop a broad and deep public understanding of and support for the transformation.

- A capacity and willingness to allocate and reallocate the resources necessary to transform individual schools, at both the system and school level.

- A management and governance system that ensures that schools have the broad guidance, individual autonomy, and support necessary to achieve their mission.

(Kearns and Anderson 1996, pp. 18–19)

The self-managing school is a central concept in this strategy. The different elements illustrate the kinds of linkages that are required if self-management and the design under consideration are to be effective. While most are concerned with the system–school relationship, all point to capacities that must be developed at the school level, including 'rich and reliable systems of assessment', 'assistance in choosing and developing curriculum and instructional strategies', professional development that 'assures that instructional staff can help students meet high standards', and technology that 'supports the restructuring of schools to provide students with individual attention and opportunities they need'.

There is early evidence of impact on learning with the adoption of whole-school designs. Researchers from the University of Memphis, University of Tennessee at Knoxville, and Johns Hopkins University in Baltimore found that 25 elementary schools in Memphis that began implementing whole school designs in 1995–1996 showed significantly greater gains on state tests (that by 1997–1998 incorporated a 'value-added' approach) by 1997–1998 than did a control group of schools (Olson, 1998, p. 9).

*Toward a world-class education system*

Michael Barber, head of the Standards and Effectiveness Unit in Britain, offered a concise synthesis of the new agenda for change in Track 2, with an affirmation of the broad thrust of change on Track 1. Addressing the North of England Education Conference in January, 1998, Barber suggested that a world-class education system should have the following characteristics:

1 They will provide extensive autonomy at school level.
2 They will maintain a constant focus on teaching, learning and best practice.
3 They will be flexible and have a highly-developed capacity to manage change at all levels.
4 They will consciously prepare for the future through controlled and targeted experimentation.
5 They will actively pursue equal opportunities.
6 They will promote a culture — right across society — of high expectations, and a belief that education can make a difference.
7 They will provide steady and substantial funding targeted to meet need.

(Barber, 1998, p. 6)

Barber acknowledged the start on Track 1 that was made by the previous Conservative government. As far as autonomy in school management was concerned 'the present British government inherited a system at the global cutting edge', with implementation that 'was sometimes painfully slow but is now widely recognized to have been a success'. The chief problem, however, was 'its blatant unfairness in the distribution of funding and in admissions policy'. There is more work to be done to 'simultaneously ensure fairness and extend autonomy' (Barber, 1998, pp. 6–7). However, the main effort is certainly on Track 2, providing an unrelenting focus on learning outcomes.

### Strategic Intentions for Schools
### Setting the Agenda for Track 2

1    Primary (elementary) schools will select and develop teams of teachers that have state-of-the-art knowledge about strategies for success in literacy, and will ensure that these are effective and that all students learn to read well.

2    Teachers at all levels will critically examine approaches to learning and teaching in mathematics and science, guided by research, challenging assumptions and stereotypes where appropriate, and informed by the findings of international comparative investigations such as the Third International Mathematics and Science Study.

3    Schools whose communities place students at a disadvantage and where achievement is lower than it ought to be, will work with other schools, and will secure resources from many sources, public and private, in efforts to achieve higher standards of achievement.

4    Learning outcomes for boys will be monitored and appropriate strategies will be developed to address low levels of achievement where these are evident, without sacrificing their effort in respect to learning by girls.

5    In addition to its place in the curriculum, information and communications technology will be harnessed to support learning and teaching across all learning areas.

6    Schools will seek and take up opportunities to obtain value-added data on student achievement, on a classroom-by-classroom and subject-by-subject basis, and will use the information so obtained in the design of learning for students whose achievement falls short of 'predicted' or 'expected'.

7    A range of symbols will be devised by schools to communicate and reinforce their intentions to focus on learning outcomes in unrelenting fashion, including the language of communication, public behaviour and ceremony, selection and appointment, and style of involvement of the community.

8   Schools will ensure a much broader agenda than is evident in much of public discourse, including literacy and numeracy, and without sacrificing attention to these, will build their capacity to address a range of 'intelligences'.

9   The notions of 'the learning organization' and 'the intelligent school' will be embraced, and strategies will be designed and implemented to ensure success.

10  A high priority will be placed on determining a school design that suits the setting and the needs, interests and aspirations of the school and its community, with participation in system-wide efforts to achieve scale-up of particular designs where these have proved effective.

*Chapter 6*

# The New Professionalism

The roles of teachers and those who support their efforts have changed profoundly in recent years. In many respects, these changes have not been welcomed, especially in regard to the apparent politicization of the field, including efforts to establish a national or state curriculum, and the attendant uncertainty and changeability as different players have entered the arena. The curriculum has been crowded out, not only with requirements in key learning areas, but also in the way schools have been expected to address all manner of social issue, including driver training, drug education, water safety and a range of matters that may impinge on sexual behaviour and preference.

Resource provision has rarely been adequate and teachers have been expected to be fundraisers as well as teachers, counsellors, de facto parents, welfare providers and police officers.

It seems that traditional values such as respect for wisdom and authority are no longer upheld: within the school, from students or, outside the school, from the local community and society at large.

Incessant attention to measurement and comparison with other schools — locally, nationally and internationally — add to the pressure of being a teacher. Structures have changed and traditional sources of support and supervision have been down-sized, out-sourced or have disappeared altogether. Changes in technology that at once seemed so exciting became daunting in the face of mind-numbing change.

The profession is ageing and the exuberance of new teachers, eager to succeed and be different, is rarely found in the staffroom. The prospect of a stable, lifelong career in school teaching has all but vanished. The thought of a lifetime under the conditions just described is daunting. Nostalgia abounds. Will the days of the teacher as a true professional return?

### Purpose

What can be expected for teachers in the journey on Track 2, given the agenda for further change that is starting to emerge? Will it be more of the same, depressing even further any hope of gaining or regaining the elixir of 'being professional'?

These questions are addressed in Chapter 5. A sense of the 'new professionalism' is constructed by the process of 'backward mapping', illustrated earlier in Chapter 3 with the links between self-management and learning outcomes. The starting point is the core work of schools, namely learning. With due account of the conditions that attend this activity, a view is constructed of what a professional ought to be under these conditions.

The word 'new' is becoming a cliché, as in 'New Labour' in Britain and 'New American Schools' in the United States, both featured in Chapter 5 under the title of the 'New Agenda'. Its suitability is, however, worth testing, because the context and expectations for teaching are so different now. In the account of the knowledge society in Chapter 6, attention is drawn to Peter Drucker's (1993) view that the world is going through one of the great social transformations that come along every few hundred years. He suggests that schools will be affected more than any other social institution and will face the greatest challenge. A consequence is surely a profound change in the role of the teacher. Except in ways that will be readily accepted, this does not mean abandoning the traditional tenets of the concept; indeed, they are extended and enriched. The new view of the professional calls for the shedding of many aspects of the role that have recently become so tiresome or distasteful or, at least, more appropriate for others to perform.

This purpose is not completed in Chapter 5. The concern in this chapter is to deal only with those aspects of the role that respond to the needs of Track 2: an unrelenting focus on learning outcomes. The task is completed in Chapter 9, when the full impact of technology on Track 3 is explored, where the task is to create schools for the knowledge society.

## Backward Mapping

The starting point for constructing a view of the professional, who contributes with success and satisfaction to schools that provide an unrelenting focus on learning outcomes, is to look at success in learning under these conditions. Considered here are the requirements for success in early literacy and mathematics; the adoption of information and communications technology; a broader view of outcomes to attach a fuller and richer meaning to the concept of 'value added'; and practice in 'the integrated school'. This list of practice is not complete, but it is a sufficient sample to construct a new image of the professional in schools.

### Literacy

In Chapter 3 a case study was provided of success in early literacy at Mackellar Primary School in Victoria. The purpose was to show how capacities that accrue with self-management may be linked, directly and indirectly, with improvements in literacy in the early years of primary (elementary) education. For the purposes of the current chapter, the task is to work backwards from this account to describe the characteristics of the teacher as a professional.

The outcome in this instance was an improvement in reading after the school had identified in the course of writing its charter that there was general dissatisfaction with levels of literacy. The school became part of an important research and development effort known as the Early Literacy Research Project led by Professor Peter Hill, with the key developmental role played by literacy expert, Carmel Crevola, both at the University of Melbourne. The new principal had expertise and a commitment to literacy. The capacity for local selection of staff was used to employ a teacher to lead a team that would build its capacities in this key learning area. New staff were employed, intensive training was conducted, and practices changed. Teachers needed to become skilful in using a battery of assessment instruments and protocols as a basis of determining the particular approaches to be used at each level of need. Progress and outcomes were continually monitored, serving as the starting point in conversations about what worked and why, and what could be done better. Others were involved, notably parents, consistent with what has been found in other successful projects in literacy in different nations. Dozens of national and ethnic classifications appear in the school profile, so teachers needed to be effective in cross-cultural communication. Resource requirements were substantial, but still limited, so teachers needed to set and reset priorities to ensure optimal deployment.

What are the important dimensions of professional practice that emerge from this account? Teachers acquired new knowledge and skill in a learning area for which they were already qualified to teach. They needed to be skilful in using an array of diagnostic and assessment instruments to identify precisely what entry levels and needs existed among their students, and these were different in each classroom. Each child had to be treated as an individual, in reality as well as in rhetoric. Teachers needed to have a capacity to work in a team and devote much time out of class to preparation and in briefing and debriefing meetings, to assess the effectiveness of approaches and to plan new ones. Cross-cultural communication and the effective involvement of parents as partners in the enterprise were also required. Also evident was a commitment to the program, appreciating that existing approaches were not good enough, though good enough to get by on in the past, and a high shared expectation that all children could succeed.

These are the hallmarks of the new professional in teaching. The experience offers a blueprint for what should occur and what is needed in every learning area. It is emphasized that none of these capacities call for abandonment of the traditional tenets of professionalism. They are reinforced, extended and enriched. The effective professional in the past will likely be well-suited to the new circumstance, albeit with an updating of knowledge and skill. But there should be no doubting that the new professional in this field has a more sophisticated body of knowledge and skill than in the past, and a new and very demanding set of expectations to live up to.

One contrast with past practices in the profession is in order, as is a comparison with professional practice in other fields. In respect to the former, it is clear that the isolation of the past has gone. This is not a teacher working alone, who is expected or expects to teach her or his class behind closed doors. This is a professional who is at ease working in a team and at ease in sharing complex sets of data about student entry points, progress and outcomes. This calls for a willingness to share and also a willingness to be vulnerable.

The comparisons with other professions, particularly the caring professions, are immediately apparent. One expects doctors, general practitioners and specialists, to make use of an increasingly sophisticated battery of tests and select a treatment. There is distress at the prospect that doctors might not keep up to date with the latest developments in their fields, through their private reading and successful participation at regularly organized programs of professional development that are provided as a matter of course by their professional associations. At a place where there is a concentration of doctors, such as a clinic or a hospital, there is an expectation of regular conferences where there is a sharing of information about what does or does not work. We expect full accountability.

This comparison with the health care field is not new. Papert (1993) used it in respect to the adoption of information technology, as is done in Chapter 8 in this book. David Hargreaves, Professor of Education at Cambridge University, has employed it to good effect (see, for example, Hargreaves, D., 1994, 1997). It is not an entirely appropriate comparison, for education involves concern about students who are learning whereas, in medicine, doctors deal with patients who have an ailment. It is, however, entirely appropriate to show that the new professionalism for teachers can be as fully professional as for doctors, whose status in this regard is held in society to be unquestionable.

### Mathematics

Concern about achievement in literacy is on the agenda for the further reform of school education, as illustrated in Chapter 5. Also making an appearance is achievement in mathematics, as reflected in the high level of international cooperation that was required to conduct the Third International Mathematics and Science Study (TIMSS), and the wide public dissemination and discussion of the findings and their implications. This was the largest international comparative study in education ever undertaken, with 41 nations participating in part or all.

Nations whose practices are illustrated in this book did relatively well, usually falling around the 10th rank. Those who did best were those in the East — Singapore, Hong Kong, South Korea and Japan — and some in the West. Reactions have been mixed, ranging from 'the nation has done relatively well, so any notion that there is a crisis in this area of learning is inappropriate', to 'schools had better lift their game to match it with the high flyers'. What there is agreement on, however, is that some students do not do well, and that there is a range of achievement within schools and across schools that ought to be addressed, given a commitment to redress disadvantage and inequity in these matters.

The implications for teachers as professionals include those identified above for literacy. Others can be gleaned from the findings of research in an important international investigation that was part of the Third International Mathematics and Science Study (see Lawton, 1997a, pp. 20–3). James W. Stigler, Professor of Psychology at UCLA, was commissioned by the United States Department of Education's National Centre for Educational Statistics and the National Science Foundation to conduct a $2 million international comparative study of mathematics teaching in Grade 8 in Germany, Japan and the United States. The methodology is as interesting as the findings. A total of 231 classrooms were selected, 81 in the United States, 100 in Germany and 50 in Japan. Researchers videotaped one day of lessons in each classroom. No fewer than 50 research assistants then transferred the videotapes to CD-ROM and then analyzed the content and style of each lesson from multiple perspectives so that searches could be conducted in seconds, and international comparisons made, according to a range of key words. Transcripts of each lesson were prepared.

The results were surprising. Those of particular interest were that Japanese lessons tended to focus on single concepts, whereas those in the United States and Germany tended to focus on multiple concepts. In the United States, there were far more interruptions to lessons on extraneous matters on the public address system than in the other nations. Noteworthy was the fact that, contrary to international stereotyping, there was much discovery learning in Japanese classrooms, with less teacher direction than is widely held to be the case. For example, in introducing a concept, a Japanese teacher would set a problem and invite students to work individually and in groups to come up with a solution that was then shared with the class as a whole. The concept and the manner in which it should be applied were then developed by the teacher. In classrooms in the other nations, teachers would typically explain the concept, demonstrate its use, and then have students drill its application. The Japanese approach is known as *jiriki kaiketsu*: to solve under one's own power. In this respect, Japanese teachers were addressing the goals in the standards of the National Council of Mathematics Teaching (NCMT) in the United States to a greater extent than were teachers in the US!

Other points of difference were the time taken up with preparing for and discussing homework in classrooms in Germany and the United States. It was not that homework was not set or expected in Japan, it was just that it was left to after-school schools and home for drill. Consistent with stereotype, Japanese classrooms were more teacher-directed, despite the focus on discovery learning, and use of hand-held computers was rare.

In a presentation to Australian educationalists at a conference on the TIMSS study, Stigler highlighted an important feature of professional practice for teachers in Japan. While there is a national curriculum in mathematics, and standards and expected outcomes are clear and consistent, teachers spend a considerable amount of time sharing and planning how they will go about the task, and what they learn from the experience, as part of an expectation that teaching and learning will be honed and shaped so that all students will reach the standards. Regular meetings are organized within and among schools for this purpose.

The implications for teacher as professional are noteworthy. One is the value of keeping in touch with the international comparative literature in one's field of interest, for the findings may challenge assumptions about practice in one's own country. This was the case for teachers in the United States who were surprised to find that Japanese teachers were teaching to NCMT standards more consistently and effectively than many teachers in the United States. Another is the high level of school-based discretion and professional activity that is possible, indeed necessary, when working within a curriculum and standards framework. The need for schools to make time for such professional activity is evident. Other implications are particular to the subject, such as the need to reduce the number of concepts that are attempted in some lessons.

The research methodology also has implications for professional practice in education. Stigler's study was an expensive one using sophisticated technology. A spin-off has been the development of a desktop version of the software that was used in the analysis, to sell at about $200. Mary Lindquist, Professor of Mathematics Education at Columbus State University, suggests that the digital database 'gives us real power to look at classroom instruction in many different ways with many different eyes over a long period of time' (cited by Lawton, 1997a, p. 22). Wide application in the classrooms of self-managing schools may be some distance off, but it illustrates the way in which the new professional will be empowered in the search for more effective ways to design learning experiences that can ensure the highest possible standards of achievement for every student.

There are some resource implications that pertain to professional practice. An early reaction to a national call to raise standards in mathematics in Australia was that class sizes should be reduced. More realistically, a higher priority should be an investment in preparation and professional development of teachers so that knowledge and skills for teaching along the lines indicated can be nurtured. There should be provision of planning time, supported by data on achievement, as illustrated with literacy, so that wise professional judgments can be formed about what has been effective and why, and how things can be done better. Further down the track, or even now for some, there will be the use of advanced technology in the manner anticipated by Lindquist. Marginal reductions in class size will have nowhere near the effect of these actions, judging from research on class size and the relative costs of alternatives in this domain. While there are cultural explanations for how Japanese schools can achieve high standards with larger classes, it is noteworthy that a high level of discovery learning occurs in these settings.

*Information and Communications Technology*

The same process of backward mapping can be used in respect to the professional capacities of teachers that arise from developments in information and communications technology. While the impact of such technology is problematic in some aspects of its application to learning and teaching, there are other aspects where benefits are beyond doubt. These lie in the manner that large amounts of important information can be accessed quickly, enabling students to focus their time and attention on higher levels of learning. For example, a study project on life in another country or on relationships between climate and economy can draw information from a CD-ROM in just a fraction of time that it would take to access the same information from print sources in a library.

The benefits in terms of higher order learning were confirmed in a 10-year study of the placement in schools in 1985 of computers, videodisc players, video cameras, scanners and CD-ROM drives. Researchers concluded that:

> . . . students in the technology-rich classrooms performed no better than students in traditional classrooms on standardized achievement tests, but that the classes were reaping other kinds of benefits. Students were writing more and finishing units of study more quickly. They were becoming independent learners and self-starters, working cooperatively, expressing positive attitudes toward the future, sharing their expertise more spontaneously, and representing information in a variety of forms. (Viadero, 1997a, p. 17)

There seems to be no debate about the merits of educational technology for disabled or disadvantaged students. Viadero (1997b, p. 14) reported that 'Technology has literally helped open schoolhouse doors for disabled students and given impetus to the "full inclusion" movement, which calls for teaching disabled students in regular classrooms whenever possible'. Pyke (1997, p. 1) described a project 'equipping seven-year olds with executive style "pocket book" computers [that] is reversing the inner-city reading blight in two of the London boroughs officially savaged for low standards of literacy' and noted that Professor David Reynolds, then a member of Labour's task force on reading, had described the results as 'phenomenal'. Hayward provided a detailed account of how information and communications technology had transformed learning in a Koorie Open Door Education (KODE) school in Gippsland, Victoria (Caldwell and Hayward, 1998, pp. 64–5). These aboriginal children had used the internet to learn with their counterparts in a Zuni Reservation school in New Mexico.

There is, of course, much that is of little or no value, and other material that is downright harmful as far as the use of technology is concerned.

What can be discerned from these brief accounts about the role of the teacher? The most obvious is the need for new knowledge and skills in the use of the technology that can have benefits for learning. Another obvious implication is the capacity to discriminate between what is beneficial and what is not beneficial, and under what conditions these benefits can be secured. More fundamental, however, is the change in role. While teaching in its traditional sense, even lecturing, will remain in the repertoire, the teacher adopts a wider range of behaviours including coach, mentor and conductor.

The level of penetration of technology in schools suggests that these capacities need to be developed on a large scale and relatively quickly. In the United States, for example, *Education Week* reported the following for 1997: 21 students per multimedia computer; 55 per cent of schools with videodisc players; 74 per cent of schools with cable TV; 28 per cent of schools with satellite access; 65 per cent of schools with a Local Area Network (LAN); 30 per cent of schools with a Wide-Area Network (WAN); 21 students per CD-ROM and 70 per cent of schools with internet access (Education Week, 1997, p. 20). A National Assessment of Educational Progress survey in the United States in 1994 found that 43 per cent of Grade

4 students used a computer in the learning of reading compared to 38 per cent in history and social studies, and 42 per cent in geography. Findings for Grade 8 students were 17, 32 and 34 per cent, respectively (cited by Education Week, 1997, p. 16).

These findings suggest a high level of take-up of technology in schools in the United States and comparable levels are likely in Australia and the United Kingdom. Governments in each of these three countries have set even higher targets. Even though some schools have much higher levels than these, especially fee-paying schools in the private sector, there are grounds for satisfaction, and a convincing argument that teacher professionalism is changing to accommodate the new role.

A more negative picture emerges if comparisons are made with the use of technology in health care. These levels of penetration would be unacceptable in a public hospital. In this respect, the criticisms of education in the early 1990s are still pertinent, including that of Gerstner, Semerad, Doyle and Johnston (1994, p. 12) that 'schools transmit information as they have since Gutenberg', and of Dixon (1994, p. 362) that 'Worldwide, school is a pufferbelly locomotive chugging incongruously through a high-tech landscape'.

The comparisons with the medical field were presented most graphically in the opening lines of Seymour Papert's *The Children's Machine* (1993). He asked the reader to imagine time travellers from the 1890s, including a group of surgeons and a group of teachers, eager to see what changes have occurred in their fields when they visited in the 1990s. For the visitors to the hospital, 'they would in almost all cases be unable to figure out what the surgeon was trying to accomplish or what was the purpose of the many strange devices . . . the surgical staff were employing'. For the visitors to the school, 'they would fully see the point of most of what was being attempted and could quite easily take over the class' (Papert, 1993, pp. 1–2).

These are harsh words, and they cannot be applied to schools that have taken up the new technologies and are staffed by teachers and other professionals who are adept in their use. For these schools, the concept of the 'new professional' in school education is more like that which applies to a doctor or other health professional than to a teacher in the traditional sense. The implication is that such professionals should be trained and rewarded in like manner, and should be represented by organizations that in style and substance are like those in the field of health. This matter is taken up later in the chapter.

*Adding Value in Learning Outcomes*

The image of the 'new professionalism' in school education that derives from a comparative analysis of the work of teachers and doctors, and that favours the latter, is strengthened when one carries out the same backward mapping exercise on the manner in which teachers and other professionals make use of data. This calls for what MacGilchrist, Myers and Reed (1997) described as 'reflective intelligence' in their view of 'the intelligent school' (see Chapter 5, this volume). Whether it be in Britain, utilizing information in inspection reports or making sense of the league tables, or in Schools of the Future in Victoria, with data drawn from a complex array of indicators that are employed in compiling a school's annual report or completing a triennial review, the level of knowledge and skill required is far higher than ever before. Compare these high expectations with what applied to most teachers until recently, when all that was required was a capacity to devise and administer classroom-based tests and report the results to parents each term.

The role is even more demanding if value-added measures are used, where data may be provided on a classroom-by-classroom, subject-by-subject basis, with account taken of learning outcomes controlled for prior attainment, socio-economic status, gender and ethnicity.

This kind of professional knowledge and skill is expected of specialists in the medical field. Making sense of the data can only be accomplished if teachers and other professionals in schools are up to date with the literature. Is not this the same expectation and a requirement for professional survival in medicine? Indeed, for the latter, regular access to selected and authoritative web-sites is required to keep pace with knowledge. The same capacities are surely required in school education.

## The Integrated Services School

Change on Track 2 is manifested in a special way with the emergence of the integrated services school or the full services school (see Dryfoos, 1994, for an account of the full services school). The need for such schools became evident when it was found that the needs of some students, particularly the disabled or disadvantaged, were not being met in many settings. Data were either not collected or were not acted on, or the required professional services were either not available or were not deployed.

The response has been to bring together at or near a school site all of the professional and para-professional support services that are required to ensure the best possible conditions for learning. This has been a complex process, for these services have invariably been delivered separately and often in uncoordinated fashion in the past, by different providers in the public or private sectors. Different levels of government have been involved. These services include education, health, welfare, law enforcement and social service. For a particular child in an integrated service school, there may be many professionals from all of these fields who will work as a team to provide the necessary support. The concept of case management comes into play, for a detailed database must be compiled and monitored by a skilled manager who can then deploy the required professional support.

This is a demanding development, politically and economically, for organizational boundaries must be crossed and expensive expertise must be acquired. For these reasons, the movement is still in its infancy, but it is an imperative if the journey on Track 2 is to be completed for all students. In a sense, this is one manifestation of the concept of school design that was featured in Chapter 5.

The integration of education and health, as well as other fields of professional practice, make this development a particularly apt one to demonstrate the new levels of professionalism required in schools. A large team of professionals and para-professionals attend to patient needs in hospitals. In pre-care, in the operating theatre, and in post-care, there may be dozens. Along with developments in technology highlighted above, this is a far cry from basic services in the hospital of a century ago. The same progress has not been made in school education except where the concept of the integrated services school has been implemented.

While this appears at first sight to make the role of the teacher more complex, the opposite is in fact the case. It recognizes that the teacher cannot provide all or even most of the care that many students need and that a large team of other professionals will be required. Some teachers will play key roles in leading and managing the integrated services school. Most will be able to focus their energies on the core work of teaching, in the fullest and richest sense of that word.

### Issues to be Addressed in the New Professionalism

There are a range of issues to be addressed in bringing this concept of the 'new professionalism' to realization. While the case is strong that the medical image for doctors in particular is more appropriate than the traditional image of the teacher, there are dangers in pushing the matter too far. After all, doctors are treating medical conditions, dealing with illness in most cases, and often death. Teachers are concerned with learning. That part of the image adopted here is that in professional matters, there are some valuable guides from the medical field on what ought to be accomplished in the educational field.

#### *Curriculum and Standards Frameworks*

The first issue relates to the nature of curriculum and standards frameworks. Are these so prescriptive as to remove the level of professional judgment that matches what might be expected in medicine? This issue extends to the manner in which such frameworks are developed as well as to how they are implemented. Ivor Goodson provided a scathing account of the absence of expert input in the development of the National Curriculum in Britain, at least on the first attempt:

> It was not a case of competing expertises when the National Curriculum was launched, but of ignoring existing research and theoretical expertise and pushing ahead in denial and defiance of it. To ignore expertise, whether you stigmatize it as trendy theory or not, is not a very smart move; this is being clearly indicated by the fate of the National Curriculum exercise. (Goodson, 1997, p. 37)

The National Curriculum had to be re-worked under the leadership of Sir Ron Dearing and a better job was done in using the expertise of the profession. The efforts of Dearing were acknowledged with the award of a life peerage in the 1998 New Year Honours List. A better job was done for Schools of the Future in Victoria, where as many as 10,000 teachers were involved in one way or another (see account in Caldwell and Hayward, 1998, pp. 56–7).

There is a counterpart in medical practice, for doctors must work within strict protocols and clearly defined standards, often with relatively detailed prescription of what treatments can and cannot be utilized. To develop these protocols and standards without professional input would be a nonsense.

Once established, practitioners in both domains then exercise their professional judgments, and teachers and other professionals in education are no more constrained than their counterparts in medicine.

### Role of the Union and Other Professional Associations

The difference between education and medicine are stark when it comes to representation by unions and professional associations, yet on the basis of analysis presented thus far in the chapter, they ought to be similar, and more similar to that found in medicine than in education.

Taking Australia as an example, doctors typically belong to the Australian Medical Association that attends to professional matters and to workplace arrangements, with the latter including levels of fees for service within the framework of a nationally funded medicare system. Doctors also belong to a professional association that relates to general practice (Royal Australian College of General Practitioners) or one or more specializations (for example, Royal Australian College of Obstetricians and Gynaecologists). These professional associations determine entry requirements, determine standards of professional practice, and prescribe what has to be done to maintain membership, with the latter including regular professional development.

The counterparts in education vary from country to country. In Australia, practice does not reflect the medical image that has been constructed thus far. Membership in teacher unions is not compulsory and is declining, and these bodies are primarily concerned with industrial matters. While they have been partners in promising projects that opened up the possibility of far-reaching change, for the most part they have opposed virtually every initiative in reform along Tracks 1 and 2 in the manner described in Chapter 4. They advocated a higher level of professionalism and the professionalization of teaching, but little progress was made. From a union perspective, this was the fault of government, which side-lined them in planning the reform agenda in many instances, notably in Schools of the Future in Victoria, and which were unable or unwilling to provide the resources to sustain a vibrant system of public education and high levels of professionalization. The central issue here is trust, and the long term solution is building high levels of trust, consistent with the analysis of Fukuyama set out in Chapter 4.

Many teachers belong to professional associations like the Australian Curriculum Studies Association or the Australian Mathematics Teachers Association, or their state counterparts, but membership is voluntary and, while professional development is organized and encouraged, these bodies play no role in the setting of standards for professional practice.

There is urgency in the task of moving these organizations closer to the roles played by their counterparts in medicine, especially in relation to determining standards of professional practice, including requirements for professional development to maintain membership and right to practise.

### 'New Unionism'

Is there a 'new unionism' that matches a 'new professionalism'? What is the outcome of backward mapping if one starts with the description of teacher as professional that was built up earlier in the chapter and then asks: 'What structures and processes are required to collectively support teachers in such an endeavour?'

Questions like these have been addressed in the United States in each of the two largest teacher unions. The late Albert Shanker took the lead from the mid-1980s as President of the American Federation of Teachers. Bob Chase, President of the National Education Association (NEA) articulated the shift from an industrial paradigm to an approach that suits further reform on Track 2, with self-management a central concept:

> What are the sounds of a paradigm shifting? Listen closely. Linda Bacon is president of the local NEA affiliate in Florida that has made school quality a top issue at the bargaining table. At a recent union gathering, one member rose to challenge her priorities: 'Your job isn't to look out for the children; your job is to look out for *me*!' Bacon respectfully disagreed: 'Our bedrock purpose as an association must be to improve student learning'.
>
> These are the clashing voices of teachers working at the fault line of a remarkable paradigm shift. New schools are being created in our midst. And teachers like Linda Bacon are striving courageously to reorient — more accurately, to reinvent — their local union for a new era.
>
> True, most educators are still stymied by the old industrial paradigm. Factory-style schools with as many as 4,000 students are managed badly — by a top-heavy, top-down bureaucracy. Teachers are relegated to the role of production workers, with little say in decision-making.
>
> But today, this old world is ending — not with a bang, but through countless acts of 'subversion'. For example, public charter schools, many of them founded and run by teachers, are proliferating rapidly. So are schools where principals and teachers collaborate in 'site-based' management.
>
> In all of these new-style public schools, teachers and other employees are co-managing — and sometimes self-managing — the education enterprise. Talking with these professionals, you quickly realise that they are preoccupied with issues of school quality and renewal. (Chase, 1997, p. 7)

Chase promoted the notion of a 'new unionism' by asserting that 'We can't just continue to do things the same way and think it'll work . . . It won't' (cited by

Archer, 1997, p. 27). Along with leaders of many other unions, he drew inspiration from the Saturn project of General Motors. General Motors and the United Auto Workers faced the threat from Japanese imports in the early 1980s by acknowledging that dramatic change was required. An outcome was a slimmed down collective agreement that allowed a high level of flexibility in work practice. Saturn requires all employees to complete 92 hours of job training each year, a level exceeded by more than 30 per cent in recent years. There is a focus on teams. Employees have the opportunity to receive bonuses of $12,500 per year if performance targets are reached, an outcome achieved in all but two quarters from 1992 to 1997.

Archer drew the parallels for education of the challenge that was successfully met in the automobile industry:

> Instead of Japan, they face a growing myriad of alternatives to one-size-fits-all public schools, including charter schools, privately managed schools and the rapid increase in the number of parents who home school their children. The push for vouchers continues. And perhaps more significant is the perception of customer dissatisfaction underlying these operations. As with the car industry, teachers' unions are seen as hampering rather than driving needed school improvement. [In 1997], an NEA-commissioned study entitled 'An Institution at Risk' reported that 'the NEA is now painted as the number-one obstacle to better public schools'.... New unionism is both an answer to such critics and an attempt to revitalize the massive union. (Archer, 1997, p. 28)

The significant features of the NEA response lie in its recognition of the need for sweeping change, embracing the concept of a 'new unionism'; a focus on quality of learning in defining the primary purpose of activity, consistent with reform on Track 2; supporting the concept of self-management, providing momentum to continue on Track 1; and an approach to a 'new professionalism' that is consistent with the image conveyed in this chapter, including high levels of professional development. The employer–employee trust evident in the Saturn model requires a counterpart in education if the vision of a 'new unionism' is to be brought to realization.

*Incentives, Recognition and Rewards*

A driving force for change is the effort to create systems of incentives, recognition and rewards for teachers and other professionals in education. A coherent scheme for accomplishing this is set out in the book by Allan Odden and Carolyn Kelley entitled *Paying Teachers for What They Know and Do* (Odden and Kelley, 1997). They described the changing context of teaching in the same terms as employed in this chapter in building the case for a 'new professionalism' that should be the hallmark of the journey on Track 2. They described new schemes for compensation across all workplaces and suggested that these ought now apply to teachers:

These evolving new notions about how to pay knowledge workers, including teachers, are compatible with and even reinforce the broader reform context surrounding teaching and education. First, serious efforts are being made to transform teaching into a much stronger profession. These efforts include a new understanding of what constitutes good teaching, actions by teachers to describe and assess what beginning and advanced teachers know and can do, and creation of incentives for teachers to learn these new teaching practices. Second, the standards-based education reform movement, in which teachers play leading roles, is identifying curriculum content standards and student performance standards that require a higher level of professional competence to implement. The standards-based reform movement includes notions of school restructuring and site-based management, both of which require that teachers play new and key roles in organizing and managing their work environments; these roles also require additional teacher competencies, as well as incentives for teachers to develop them. (Odden and Kelley, 1997, p. 14)

In the new compensation arrangements for knowledge workers, job-based pay, experienced-based pay, and individual merit and incentive pay are replaced by skill-based pay, competency-based pay, pay for knowledge, pay for professional expertise, collective rewards for adding value to performance, gainsharing, and team-based performance awards. 'In short, compensation has been changed to align organizational incentives and rewards with the strategic needs of the workplace' (Odden and Kelley, 1997, p. 13).

Odden and Kelley show how old arrangements have proved ineffective and how new arrangements can work in schools. In a counterpart to the concept of school design set out in Chapter 5 (in this volume), they provide a design framework for teacher compensation based around five key principles, each of which has multiple elements as summarized below:

- Process principles (10 elements): involvement of all key parties, broad agreement on the most valued education results, comprehensive evaluation systems, adequate funding, investments in ongoing professional development, no quotas, general conditions of work, management maturity, labor maturity and persistence.

- General technical design principles (3 elements): fairness, comprehensibility and incentive-behaviour compatibility.

- Competency-based pay principles (2 elements): clear, specific and measurable skill blocks; and an objective, sound and credible assessment system to determine skill attainment.

- Contingency-based pay principles (2 elements): identification of tasks critical to a system's top education goals and its reform efforts, and selection of one or two tasks that both teachers and the district can readily implement.

- Performance award principles (7 elements): provide awards only on a group (probably a whole school), not an individual basis; be very clear about what performance is most valued; base the performance standards for each school on improvements over some historic base; provide an integrated and protected funding pool; provide awards that are valued by teachers; if the award is a salary award, provide it as a bonus, not as an addition to base pay; and provide teachers professional control over the work environment.

(Odden and Kelley, 1997, pp. 157–62)

Developing a system of incentives, recognition and rewards based on this design clearly calls for the re-engineering of current compensation schemes. It is beyond the scope of this chapter to describe how this will be done and what will be the outcome. The design of Odden and Kelley is recommended as a starting point for this important task. Two issues are taken up, however, and these concern the setting of standards for professional practice, and the place of universities and other providers of preparation and professional development programs.

### Setting Standards for Professional Practice

The concept of 'new professionalism' is dependent in so many ways on the setting of standards for professional practice. The key issue is who shall have responsibility for this task. In medicine, it is relatively clear cut, with the professional associations playing the central role, as they do in law and engineering. This ought to be the case in education.

Considerable attention has been given to the potential for a body styled as a General Teaching Council, based on the highly respected model in Scotland. New Labour has committed itself to such an approach for England and Wales and a discussion paper on the matter was released in 1997. Andy Hargreaves has included such an organization in the broad directions he proposed for a 'New Deal' for teachers. These directions are similar to those suggested in this chapter. For Hargreaves, a General Teaching Council should be:

... controlled by an elected majority of teachers, which will be independent of unions and employers, and will control teacher licensing and registration, define and apply codes of professional ethics, discipline its members where appropriate, establish and apply standards of professional practice, create a national framework for professional learning, work with Government to ensure policy initiatives support teachers' professional learning, and work with higher education to accredit programs of initial teacher education, and accredit providers of in-service teacher education. (Hargreaves, A., 1997, pp. 123–4)

Governments in some countries are wary of bodies such as a General Teaching Council, and it is likely that Labour will be cautious in its approach in Britain. The Australian Teaching Council was intended to meet needs along the lines in Andy Hargreaves' formulation but it was not successful, even under the former national Labor Government that supported and partly funded it. While its members were elected, it was generally viewed as a creature of the unions, and the successor

Liberal National Coalition Government would not work with it. The Australian situation is made difficult by each state having its own teacher registration requirements, as summarized in Chapter 4, and attempting to reach agreement on a national framework is proving more difficult than establishing a national railway gauge after a century of state specifications.

David Hargreaves believes such a body may be coming too late, and takes up the medical analogy in proposing an alternative:

> A General Teaching Council modelled on a General Medical Council may be established — I fervently hope it will — but it will survive and prosper only if it becomes a highly elite institution, somewhat like the royal colleges of medicine in which membership is reserved for a small body of well-qualified and demonstrably competent . . . educational experts, at the top of a complex pyramid of para-educators . . . The stark alternative is progressive de-professionalization: a learning society where everybody teaches and learns and nobody is an expert. (Hargreaves, D., 1997, p. 19)

A range of approaches is in place or being developed in the United States (see Odden and Kelley, 1997, pp. 17–18 for an account of these). The National Board for Professional Teaching Standards (NBPTS) was established following the report of the Carnegie Forum on Education and the Economy in 1986 with the purpose of developing an assessment system to certify experienced teachers who met or exceeded high standards of professional practice. The first certificates were awarded in 1995 and certification in about 30 areas is planned by the end of the decade. Each set of standards is contained in a document of 30–40 pages. Similar schemes have been set up by the Interstate New Teacher Assessment and Support Consortium (INTASC) at the Council of Chief State School Officers in Washington, DC, and the PRAXIS project of the Educational Testing Service. There is also the Professional Teacher Initiative of the National Council for the Accreditation of Teacher Education (NCATE) that sets standards for the accreditation of university-based teacher training. NCATE 2000 was announced in late 1997, with greater emphasis on the performance of teacher candidates in the evaluation of schools of education, an approach intended 'to bring teacher education in line with the broader movement to set higher academic standards for students and teachers' (NCATE President Arthur C. Wise, cited by Bradley, 1997, p. 1). NCATE 2000 is designed to mesh with the programs of NBPTS and INTASC.

Odden and Kelley (1997, p. 18) noted that 'for the first time, efforts were being made to describe in detail, on paper, what good teaching entails'. The task is clearly complex and demanding and will take several years to complete. It is made more difficult in countries like Australia and the United States where there are national and state governments. The teacher unions in the United States are playing a key role in these developments, partly because they embraced much of the reform agenda, short of vouchers, and are partners in the design and implementation of most projects. Despite this, Odden and Kelley urged an indirect role for unions in the establishment of bodies to set standards for professional practice. They suggested that the two national teacher unions — the American Federation of Teachers and the National Education Association — should take the lead because such a scheme is consistent with their strategic interests, which lie mainly in the area of teacher compensation. However:

> To ensure that the set of teaching standards and accompanying system were truly professional in nature, the unions would be wise to create an independent board of teachers, much along the lines of the NBPTS, to create both the standards and the assessment system. It would also be prudent for the unions to formally link the standards and assessments to INTASC, PRAXIS and the national board . . . (Odden and Kelley, 1997, pp. 92–3)

This call for an indirect and prudent role seems applicable in Australia and Britain, indeed, more so, given the apparent lack of trust that presently exists in these countries. This trust will need to be earned, and a series of smaller steps may need to be taken to establish it before a national body along the lines of a General Teaching Council can be established and prove effective.

## The Role of the University

Universities through their faculties, schools or colleges of education, have a vital role to play in the future of public education. With the demise of teachers' colleges, they have been the chief provider of pre-service and postgraduate education; professional development; research to guide and critique policy and practice; and consultancy support to schools, school systems and governments. Like schools, the advent of the knowledge society presents a challenge to the university as the sole provider, suggesting the importance of a high degree of alignment with the reform effort.

Recent experience in Britain suggests a weakening of faith by government in the role of the university in school education, with schools given the opportunity to provide an important component of the pre-service program for teachers, and for universities to enter into service agreements.

The new arrangements are a far cry from the situation where universities worked closely with central authorities for assured employment of graduates. Arrangements with individual schools were no more complex than practicum placements for student-teachers, reaching agreement on roles for cooperating teachers in schools, and scheduling occasional visits by university supervisors. Research was invariably negotiated with an official in central office. Now, in places like Australia and Britain, the university makes all arrangements with individual schools, resulting in operations far more complex and uncertain than ever before. When combined with a decline in demand for teachers, increasing dependency on funds other than from government, and pressures to internationalize and adopt new information technologies, the work of the university will change as dramatically as will the work of schools.

The challenge for the university comes in many ways, First, to ensure that all graduates have knowledge and skill in state-of-the art approaches to learning and teaching consistent with the 'new professionalism' described earlier in the chapter, which for many will require an upgrade for members of staff, most of whom did their own school teaching at least a decade ago. Many of the teaching practices of these times are now being challenged, for good reason, especially in the areas of literacy, numeracy and school and classroom organization. Second, to play a role in the ongoing professional development of teachers, through award and non-award programs, and this means highly flexible modes of delivery that render virtually obsolete the once per week late afternoon lecture. New information technologies will enable distance learning to occur, locally, nationally and internationally. Third, high priority should be given to research that addresses issues of significance for policy and practice. Fourth, high level consultancy service should be made available to schools and school systems, to practitioners and policy-makers, to ensure that the findings of research can be deployed constructively and critically. Increasingly, the reform effort will be research driven, as evidenced by the influential role now played by researchers in the field of school and classroom effectiveness and improvement. Fifth, to contribute to vigorous debate and critical scrutiny of developments in school education. Sixth, to contribute to the setting of standards of professional practice.

If universities can align themselves with the transformation of school education on all three tracks for change, without sacrificing their critical role and capacity to propose new and often different directions, then their future is secure.

### Strategic Intentions for Schools
### The New Professionalism in Action

1  There will be planned and purposeful efforts to reach higher levels of professionalism in data-driven, outcomes-oriented, team-based approaches to raising levels of achievement for all students.

2  Substantial blocks of time will be scheduled for teams of teachers and other professionals to reflect on data, devise and adapt approaches to learning and teaching, and set standards and targets that are relevant to their students.

3  Teachers and other professionals will read widely and continuously in local, national and international literature in their fields, consistent with expectations and norms for medical practitioners.

4  Teachers and other professionals will become skilful in the use of a range of information and communications technology, employing it to support learning and teaching, and to gain access to current information that will inform their professional practice.

5    Schools will join networks of schools and other providers of profes-
     sional services in the public and private sectors to ensure that the needs
     of all students will be diagnosed and met, especially among the disabled
     and disadvantaged, employing the techniques of case management to
     ensure success for every individual in need.

6    Professionals will work within curriculum and standards frameworks, as
     well as other protocols and standards of professional practice, with the
     same level of commitment and rigour as expected in medicine.

7    Schools will advocate, support and participate in programs of unions and
     professional associations that are consistent with the new professional-
     ism in education.

8    Working within frameworks established for the profession, incentives,
     recognition and reward schemes will be developed at the school level
     that are consistent with the strategic needs of the workplace, with com-
     ponents that are skill-based and contain provision for collective rewards,
     gainsharing and team-based performance awards where these are pos-
     sible and appropriate.

9    Staff will seek recognition of their work that meets or exceeds standards
     of professional practice, and will support and participate in the programs
     of professional bodies established for this purpose.

10   Schools will work with universities and other providers in a range of
     programs in teaching, research and development that support and reflect
     the new professionalism in education.

# *Creating Schools for the Knowledge Society*

# Chapter 7

# Education and the Knowledge Society

Peter Drucker coined the term 'knowledge society' in 1959 and it is now part of the language. In this respect, schools have been part of the knowledge society for some time, but it is only at the dawn of the third millennium that there is broad recognition that the kinds of schools that will best meet the needs of the knowledge society might be very different to those that have proved successful for much of the last century.

Some schools are being transformed in response to the challenge and many are planning a major effort in this direction. Others are not sure what to do, being wary of continuing, escalating change. The nature of society in 10 or 20 years' time might be difficult to discern in many respects, and so is the nature of schools that will serve it, but there is enough to guide a major project in school design. The purpose of the third part of this book is to share what has occurred thus far and explore possibilities for schools as they continue their journey on Track 3: creating schools for the knowledge society.

The nature of the knowledge society is explored in Chapter 7, guided by insights from the work of Peter Drucker, William Bridges, Dale Spender and Jeremy Rifkin. Implications for schools are drawn, setting the scene for Chapters 8 and 9 that provide some of the detail. It is acknowledged that parts of the vision or *gestalt* are not clear because they are not known. Schools that are leading the journey will help complete the picture. Chapter 10 addresses requirements for leadership and management in schools of the third millennium.

### The Knowledge Society and Its Impact on Schools

Peter Drucker was born in Vienna in 1909 and educated in Austria and England. From 1937, he worked in the United States, first as an economist and management consultant and then as a distinguished professor. He was appointed Clarke Professor of Social Science at Claremont Graduate School in California in 1971. His books span more than half a century, publishing a book every year or two in recent times. Few can match the length, breadth and depth of his understanding of leadership and management in the context of broad societal movements over the course of the 20th century.

In *Post-Capitalist Society*, Drucker (1993) described the scale of societal transformation and the challenges that face the school:

Every few hundred years in Western history there occurs a sharp transformation . . . Within a few short decades, society rearranges itself — its worldview; its basic values; its social and political structures; its arts, its key institutions. Fifty years later, there is a new world . . . We are currently living through such a transformation. (Drucker, 1993, p. 1)

According to Drucker, knowledge as a resource lies at the heart of such transformations over the last three centuries. Until the Industrial Revolution knowledge had been seen as applying to being. It then became a resource for doing. Following the Industrial Revolution until about World War II, knowledge was applied to improving the doing. These transformations characterized a capitalist society in which the factors of production were capital and labour. Since World War II, however, knowledge has been applied to knowledge itself so that 'knowledge is fast becoming the sole factor of production, sidelining both capital and labour' (Drucker, 1993, pp. 19–20). It is now a post-capitalist society. The implications for schools, writes Drucker, are profound:

As knowledge becomes the resource of post-capitalist society, the social position of the school as 'producer' and 'distributive channel' of knowledge, and its monopoly, are both bound to be challenged. And some of the competitors are bound to succeed . . . Indeed, no other institution faces challenges as radical as those that will transform the school. (Drucker, 1993, p. 209)

Drucker expanded his view of the scale of transformation, and the impact on schools, in *Managing in a Time of Great Change* (Drucker, 1995). The nature of work over more than a century is traced, from an era when agriculture and domestic service were the dominant fields, through the early twentieth century when the blue-collar or industrial worker gained ascendancy, to the late twentieth century and the rise of the knowledge worker, a term coined by Drucker to describe those whose work requires a great deal of formal education, a capacity to acquire and apply theoretical and analytical knowledge, a different approach and a different mindset and, above all, 'a habit of continuous learning'. By the 1990s, observed Drucker, for the first time since the industrial revolution, the largest single group of workers — the knowledge workers — own the chief factor of production, knowledge itself. When the expanse of this change is appreciated, it is more than a social change: 'It is a change in the human condition' (Drucker, 1995, p. 203).

Many of the seemingly intractable social problems are connected to the difficulties of transition and the condition of some groups in society. In the United States, for example, the plight of the urban Black has been accentuated, for most remain in blue-collar, unionized, mass production work, which provide the jobs that are rapidly disappearing.

Drucker spelt out the opportunities and threats to school education. It is, indeed, a knowledge society that is emerging, but:

Paradoxically, this may not necessarily mean that the school as we know it will become more important. For in the knowledge society clearly more and more knowledge, and especially advanced knowledge, will be acquired well past the age

of formal schooling, and increasingly, perhaps, in and through educational processes that do not centre on the traditional school — for example, systematic
continuing education offered at the place of employment. But at the same time,
there is very little doubt that the performance of schools and the basic values of the
schools will increasingly become of concern to society as a whole, rather than be
considered 'professional' matters that can safely be left to the 'educator'. (Drucker,
1995, pp. 204–5)

Drucker pointed to the need to redefine what it means to be an 'educated
person', who will likely be somebody 'who has learned how to learn and who
throughout his or her lifetime continues learning, and especially learning in and
through formal education' (Drucker, 1995, p. 205). He warns against sterile
credentialism, an over-valuing of immediately usable knowledge, and an under-
rating of fundamentals and wisdom itself (p. 205). Drucker reinforced the view that
knowledge workers work in teams and should have access to organizations, even if
they are not employees of organizations. These organizations will be more like
symphony orchestras than hierarchies of superiors and subordinates, and management will be an artistic endeavour:

> Management, in most business schools, is still taught as a bundle of techniques . . . to
> be sure, management, like any other work, has its own tools and its own techniques
> . . . [but the] . . . essence of management is to make knowledge productive. Man-
> agement, in other words, is a social function. And in its practice, management is
> truly a 'liberal art'. (Drucker, 1995, p. 219)

Drucker stressed the importance of the social sector in the light of the high mobility
of the knowledge society and the decline of the family and the church; people no
longer have 'roots'. He has little confidence in the welfare state, with its huge
welfare bureaucracy:

> . . . in every developed country, society is becoming sicker rather than healthier,
> and social problems are multiplying. Government has a big role to play in social
> tasks — the role of policy maker, of standard setter, and to a substantial extent, the
> role of paymaster. But as the agency to run social services, it has proven itself
> almost totally incompetent . . . (Drucker, 1995, p. 221)

The solution does not lie with the employing organization in the style of the
modern Japanese corporation because, increasingly, knowledge workers will not
have lifetime or even extended security with a single organization. It is 'neither
"the government" nor "the employing organisation"'. It is a separate and new social
sector' (p. 223), with the task of the social sector being 'to create human health'.
There are thus three sectors in the knowledge society: a public sector, a private
sector and a social sector. The nature of this third sector is developed by Rifkin and
addressed later in the chapter, because there are important implications for schools.

Drucker was unambivalent in his view that school and education lie at society's
centre, but the context presents a challenge to the traditional view of schooling.

Schools and education will increasingly involve partnership of the three sectors and, with new arrangements in this partnership, they are bound to remain political issues. It is no wonder, then, that three of Drucker's (1995) six priority tasks for society in the twenty-first century involve knowledge and education:

- We will have to think through education — its purpose, its value, its content. We will have to learn to define the quality of education and the productivity of education, to measure both and manage both. (p. 236)

- We need systematic work on the quality of knowledge and the productivity of knowledge — neither even defined so far. On those two, the performance capacity, and perhaps even the survival of any organization in the knowledge society will increasingly come to depend. (p. 236–7)

- We need to develop an economic theory appropriate to the primacy of the world economy in which knowledge has become the key economic resource and the dominant — and perhaps even the only — source of comparative advantage. (p. 237)

Matters related to the quality and productivity of knowledge have, of course, been part of the reform agenda and have been contentious in most settings, but Drucker's analysis is convincing, and the stakes are high. Further developments are certain. Many educators who have been sceptical, if not critical, of efforts to tie curriculum and the work of schools to the needs of an international economy will be encouraged by the third item in the list of tasks set out above. It may be that the failure to develop an economic theory that takes account of knowledge as the key economic resource has helped form the chasm between critics in education and policy-makers and decision-makers in other settings. Critics on the other side would counter that many educators, despite claims to the contrary, still see schools in the factory image as they hanker for solutions to current problems that reflect a bygone era. Drucker offered a means of bridging the chasm, but it will be a long-term endeavour.

### The Changing Nature of Work

More fundamental is the manner in which all work and the concept of a 'job' is changing. These changes were described by William Bridges in *Jobshift* (Bridges, 1995). He argued that 'the job is not going to be part of tomorrow's economic reality' (Bridges, 1995, p. x). He was referring here to the concept of a person working full-time and long-term for a particular organization. Arguing from a view that 'the job is a social artefact', he stated that:

> The job concept emerged in the eighteenth and nineteenth centuries to package the work that needed doing in the growing factories and bureaucracies of the industrializing nations. Before people had jobs, they worked just as hard but on shifting

clusters of tasks, in a variety of locations, on a schedule set by the sun, the weather and the needs of the day. The modern job was a startling new idea . . . Now the world of work is changing again. The very conditions (mass production and the large organization) that created jobs two hundred years ago are disappearing. (Bridges, 1995, pp. viii ix)

Bridges wrote almost exclusively about jobs in business, but the very forces he identified as shaping change in that field are impacting education, and chief among these is technology. Why should one expect that education will or should be buffered against such change, particularly when it may be the means by which a range of specialist professional and para-professional support can enhance the processes of learning and teaching in the manner proposed in Chapter 6?

Bridges noted that yesterday's organization located every person vertically in a hierarchy and horizontally in a functional unit, with a formal job description and a career path up the hierarchy with corresponding increases in power and reward (Bridges, 1995, pp. 50–1). He extended Charles Handy's view of tomorrow's organization as a three-leaf shamrock. For Handy, one leaf is the core of professional, technical and managerial staff; another is made up of external contractors who provide specialist support; the third consists of 'contingent' workers, who are temporary or part-time people who come and go as needed. Bridges suggested that the leaves are more permeable or transient than presented by Handy (Bridges, 1995, pp. 156–8).

These developments are, of course, already evident in education, but they have been generally regarded as dysfunctional and an aberration rather than extensive, fundamental and inevitable change in the sense described by Bridges. Nonetheless, many professionals in education are already accommodating this new (old) concept of 'job' and are finding themselves a rewarding and satisfying niche in a reshaped profession.

There are many implications of these developments for schools. One that is experienced in very harsh terms is that some schools are located in communities where industrial workers have been displaced and there are high levels of unemployment. Teachers in some schools have to work with children where no member of the family is working; indeed, the younger children may have no life experience of a member of their family who works. This makes the process of learning and teaching so difficult compared to a generation ago. Indeed, the process was relatively easy at that time when there was full employment, or close to it.

A second implication is that schools must prepare their students for a society where 'jobs' are disappearing. Dale Spender, who writes eloquently and persuasively about the new workplace, education, technology and gender in a manner illustrated further in Chapters 8 and 9, made this point very clear:

There is no point in educating people for jobs and work patterns that have passed . . . Not only is it ill informed and irresponsible, but to look for 'jobs' as a goal for schooling is to set schooling itself on the path to increasing irrelevance. (Spender, 1997, pp. 9, 11)

Spender placed herself in the new era, noting that 'I now have portfolio employment. I also employ five other people who have portfolio employment. Some have come from jobs that have disappeared; some have made a career choice for portfolio work. And education must take this into account' (Spender, 1997, p. 9).

A third implication for schools is that teachers and other professionals may themselves be portfolio workers. Without questioning the need for a core of permanent, full-time, continuing teachers, there will be increasing numbers who may serve several schools because of their particular expertise, for example, in support of information and communications technology, or because they serve a network of schools that provide integrated services, in the style described in Chapter 6. While there are other reasons for the phenomenon, it is noteworthy that schools with a capacity to select their own staff in systems of self-managing public schools are tending to make short-term contract appointments because a particular need can be addressed in a relatively short time.

David Hargreaves advocated such a system in his proposal for the staffing of schools in the twenty-first century. Such schools should:

- Have a core of full-time, highly trained professional teachers, on five-year renewable contracts, supported by a range of assistant teachers and part-time teachers who also work in other fields.

- Contract out substantial parts of their teaching functions, so that secondary pupils spend less of their time in schools.

- Be permeable to their community, to business and the world of working adults, so that the boundaries between the school and the outside world weaken.

(Hargreaves, D. 1994, pp. 53–4)

A fourth implication is in the form of a challenge, and it arises from the third implication. How does a school build up loyalty and commitment among its portfolio or short-term contract workers? This was a relatively simple task in the past when all or most staff were employed full-time on a continuing basis. Staff were loyal to their schools, where they served for many years, and to their school systems, over the course of a career in which promotion occurred at clearly defined points according to well-established criteria. The approach must now be individualized, and in many cases it will call for individual contracts where the nature of incentives, recognition and rewards will be determined according to the needs and values of both parties. The design of compensation schemes developed by Odden and Kelley (1997) described in Chapter 6 may be a useful starting point in this regard.

## The Downside of the Knowledge Society

The downside of the knowledge society has already been mentioned in connection with the high levels of unemployment in communities that contain factories and other industrial plants where workers have been displaced by machines. The social dislocation has been portrayed in movies like *Brassed Off* and *The Full Monty*.

Governments have been criticized for not providing support that will ensure a transition to the new workplace.

The same dislocation was evident in the decline of the agricultural workforce and the migration of workers to the cities to look for new opportunities. Novels like John Steinbeck's *Grapes of Wrath* told the story.

There is an assumption that displaced workers in the knowledge society will find work in similar fashion to the full employment that followed the decline of the agricultural sector. Governments around the world recognize the problem and new schemes have been created. Tony Blair introduced a welfare-to-work plan, imposed taxes on public utilities and reallocated funds from welfare to expanded programs in education and health. Some commentators, however, have suggested that things are different on this occasion and have questioned whether, in fact, new opportunities for work can be created. Michael Phelan (1998) suggested that this might not happen because workers are being replaced by machines and whole levels of management are being removed, never to be returned. Even radical schemes such as reducing wages to expand demand and make industries competitive with those in Asia will not work. '[T]his is just not feasible morally, politically or economically', observed Phelan, who cited research in the United States to show that:

> . . . it is automation rather than the cheap labour available to foreign competitors that is the principal threat to manufacturing jobs. In the global economy, where consumers want increasingly well-designed and better manufactured goods and services, automation is already threatening jobs in the low-waged as well as in the higher-waged countries. (Phelan, 1998, p. 40)

There is another downside to the knowledge society and that concerns the struggle to win a place among the elite of knowledge workers. Entrance examinations are conducted for young children entering private nursery and primary schools in Japan and thousands who aspire to enter are placed in cram schools where they are coached for what examiners expect. It is a large industry in Tokyo, where there are 150 nursery-level cram schools, with the largest enrolling about 8,000 children annually. Just four lessons cost about 50,000 yen. Aoyama Gakuin Kindergarten is part of a private system that culminates in the Aoyama Gakuin University, and 98 per cent of those who start the former reach the latter. There are 10 applications for each of its 40 places and entry tests assess the attitudes of parents, how children deal with instructions and how children manage among their peers (this account based on Watts, 1998). If this is a portent of what might occur in other nations, it is clear that major social tensions will exist within the ranks of those who aspire to be knowledge workers as well as between the successful elite and those who have been displaced with the advent of the knowledge society.

### Toward a Third-Sector Solution

Jeremy Rifkin, President of the Foundation on Economic Trends in Washington, DC, described the downside in the following terms in *The End of Work* (Rifkin, 1996):

Today, all three of the traditional sectors of the economy — agriculture, manu-facturing, and service — are experiencing technological displacement, forcing millions onto the unemployment rolls. The only sector emerging is the knowledge sector, made up of a small elite of entrepreneurs, scientists, technicians, computer programmers, professionals, educators and consultants. While this sector is grow-ing, it is not expected to absorb more than a fraction of the hundreds of millions who will be eliminated in the next several decades in the wake of the revolutionary advances in the information and communication sciences . . . The restructuring of production practices and the permanent replacement of machines for human labourers has begun to take a tragic toll on the lives of millions of workers. (Rifkin, 1996, p. xvii)

There is good news here for educators, but only for those equipped in the manner described in Chapters 5 and 6, in the short-term, and for the knowledge society, in the long-term, in the manner described in this and later chapters. Keeping the focus on the broader picture for the moment, Rifkin highlighted the dire consequences of the combined impact of communications and informa-tion technology and global market forces. He referred to two 'irreconcilable and potentially warring forces' — a cosmopolitan elite 'who control the technolog-ies and the forces of production' and the growing numbers of displaced workers 'who have little hope and even fewer prospects for meaningful employment in the new high-tech global economy' (Rifkin, 1996, p. xvii). The solution, he sug-gested, lies in making a transition from a 'market-oriented vision' to a 'third-sector perspective'.

The third sector includes privately owned, not for profit organizations, and volunteer services in either publicly-owned or privately- owned organizations that provide a multitude of services covering social support, health care, education, the arts, religion, and advocacy. Services include those provided to the aged, homeless, crisis centres, recycling, environmental protection, rape counselling, drug rehab-ilitation, firefighting, disaster relief, child abuse, theatre and music. In the United States, according to Rifkin, the total of funds that support these activities exceeds the gross national product of all but seven nations, cutting 'a wide swath through society' (Rifkin, 1996, pp. 240–1). Rifkin called this sector 'the civil society' and he described how it shrunk in recent times as more and more people expected the services to be fully provided by agencies owned and operated in the public sector, an approach that Drucker suggested, as cited earlier in the chapter, was not just ineffective: '. . . it has proven itself almost totally incompetent'.

Rifkin shared a vision in which those who have employment in the public and private sectors work fewer hours and contribute to the volunteer, third or civil sector, which employs an expanding number of people as a matter of course, drawing from those who would otherwise be permanently unemployed. He demon-strated how a value-added or consumption tax can raise funds to support the civil society, with this tax applied only to non-essential goods and services. Such a tax is not presently levied in the United States. Social wages for community services are also proposed.

Some observations can be made about this vision. First, the services provided by the civil society are not now, and never will be, an option. They are essential for the well-being of society. Second, the proposal is not a replacement of funds withdrawn from public sector services during recent times of cut-back. Public funds will be deployed, but mainly through non-public organizations. Third, there will be voluntary contribution on a large scale. Fourth, there are few options to the broad sweep of the proposal. The consequences of maintaining the present course are very grim indeed, especially when current policies and priorities are pursued, resulting in a decline in the civil society and an increase in the number of people in prison, exceeding 3,000,000 in the United States in 1998, with steady growth in budgets for police and private law-enforcement and security organizations.

In an analysis that could well be applied in several nations, Rifkin referred to the Reagan and Bush years when 'third-sector themes were continually manipulated in a cynical effort to mask a free-market agenda':

> 'Returning the government to the people' became a convenient euphemism to push for deregulation of industry, fewer corporate taxes and cutbacks in social services and entitlement programs for the working poor and those trapped by the poverty line. In the end the third sector was seriously compromised and undermined by the very political forces that professed to be its champions and advocates. (Rifkin, 1996, p. 251)

There is a long-term agenda for the knowledge society that will require strong leadership, an alignment of political interests and a powerful will to see it through. Of particular interest in this chapter are the implications for schools, which one might place in any one of the three sectors in Rifkin's classification. They can, however, make a contribution to the civil society in two ways. The first is to employ people on a contract or volunteer basis to contribute to programs that support teaching and learning. This is already done with parent and grandparent volunteers in literacy programs but the concept can be extended. The second is through teaching about the third sector and preparing young people for making a contribution.

An example of the possibilities is furnished by Montgomery Blair High School in Maryland. Students receive academic or community credit for setting up computer centres with donated equipment in low-income apartments where some students live (Zehr, 1997, p. 37). In the NetDay initiative, described in more detail in Chapter 9, 250,000 volunteers helped wire for the internet 50,000 classrooms across the United States.

The possibilities for schools are now being recognized in the literature. Dan Brown, whose book on decentralization and school-based management (Brown, 1990) made an important contribution to the literature on self-managing schools, has argued that voluntarism is an underestimated and undervalued field. He presents a vision for an expanded role (Brown, 1998).

### Strategic Intentions for Schools
### Securing a Place for Schools in the Knowledge Society

1   School leaders will help build an understanding among staff, students and others in the school community about the nature of the sweeping social changes over the last century, and of the particular ways that transformation has affected and will continue to affect education in general and their school in particular.

2   Schools will understand that many problems of motivation and negative attitudes to work are a consequence of the major social dislocation that has followed the decline of industrial work.

3   School staff will understand that the changing nature of work and the decline in jobs in society at large will affect the school as they affect all places of work, with a higher proportion of part-time and contract appointments than in the past.

4   Portfolio work for some teachers and other professionals will be part of the employment scene, with the possibility of multiple appointments in several schools and in other organizations in the public and private sectors.

5   School leaders will be challenged to design incentive, recognition and reward schemes that will help secure loyalty and commitment among portfolio workers.

6   Student expectations will be more realistic in respect to the prospect of a job, as traditionally understood, with prospects for portfolio appointments and third sector contributions explained and illustrated in a constructive manner.

7   Curriculum offerings and approaches to learning and teaching will reflect the expectation that most workers will be knowledge workers.

8   Studies of society in schools will address the changing nature of the workplace, including an account of factors that are polarizing opportunities for knowledge workers and those displaced by the decline of industry.

9   School leaders will be advocates for a civil society and will actively seek ways of making a contribution.

10   Schools will change their employment arrangements to accommodate contract appointments and volunteer contributions from those with a capacity to add value to the school program, reflecting a commitment to the development of the third sector in a civil society.

# Transformation of Learning:
# A *Gestalt* for Schools

Chapter 8 explores in more detail the possibilities for schools. In the previous chapter, the larger picture was painted with the aid of Peter Drucker who coined the term 'knowledge society' and others, including William Bridges, Dale Spender and Jeremy Rifkin. The place of this epic transformation among the great movements in society over centuries was established. The challenges and the opportunities for schools are as exciting as they are profound. The darker side of the picture was then exposed, for there is the prospect of polarization when it comes to employment and work. It is more a chasm, and it is getting wider and deeper, with elite knowledge workers, including the 'new professional' in education on one side, and the permanently unemployed on the other. Rifkin's vision of the 'civil society' must be included in the larger picture if the outcomes are not to be catastrophic in human terms. There are important opportunities and responsibilities for schools.

In Chapter 8, the focus is sharper, on how schools will change, but more specifically, how the processes of learning and teaching and the support of learning and teaching will change. As noted from the outset, the detail will become clearer as the years pass, with further advances in the new technologies and the seemingly unlimited capacities of humankind to be creative in their use. Particular attention is given in this chapter to how schools can be designed and redesigned to satisfy their roles in the knowledge society. The last part of the chapter is written by architects Andrew Bunting and John Wood of the Sainsbery Reed Group in Melbourne, who provide explanations and illustrations of school design based on their successful experience across all sectors of schooling, including the self-managing Schools of the Future in Victoria.

### A *Gestalt* for Schools in the Knowledge Society

The content of Chapters 8 and 9 is organized around a *gestalt* as illustrated in Figure 8.1. According to the Oxford Dictionary, a *gestalt* is 'a perceived organized whole that is more than the sum of its parts'. It is a simple model of a larger vision that could be better conveyed in a movie in which the elements are represented by events in the lives of learners in a variety of locations or, better still, in a visit to a school that is well down Track 3. Figure 8.1 is simply a starting point to guide the reader on a personal journey of exploration. Each element of the vision is described

Figure 8.1   *A vision for schooling in the knowledge society illustrated in a* gestalt

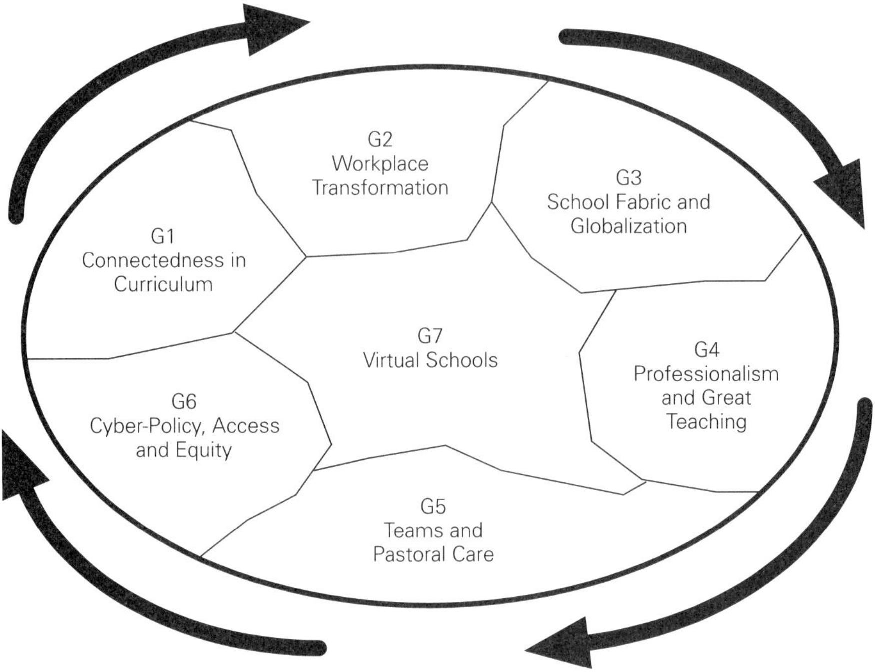

*Source:* Caldwell and Spinks, 1998

and illustrated with present events in schools that have already commenced the journey.


### 1   Connectedness in the Curriculum

*Dramatic change in approaches to learning and teaching is in store as electronic networking allows 'cutting across and so challenging the very idea of subject boundaries' and 'changing the emphasis from impersonal curriculum to excited live exploration', to use the words of Seymour Papert in* The Children's Machine *(Papert, 1993). At risk is the balkanized curriculum that has done much to alienate children from schooling, especially in the middle years of the transition from primary to secondary.*

The impact of information and communications technology on learning and teaching was described briefly in Chapters 5 and 6 in connection with change on Track 2, that involves an unrelenting focus on learning outcomes. While there have been mixed findings on the impact of technology on learning outcomes, there is no doubt that it is a means of accessing and managing a large amount of information and of individualizing the presentation of information in a powerful manner. These chapters were written as though the technology was still an option. This is not the case for the journey down Track 3, for everyone will have a computer.

The size and price of computers are declining to the point that they are likely to be given away before too long, much like mobile or cellular phones at the end of the 1990s. The cost is attached to the software and network charges. Imagine the situation where all have a palm size computer that can access far more information than the most powerful laptops and can process that information almost instantaneously. Imagine the software that can assist in advanced problem-solving and creative works across the spectrum of the arts. These are a reality for some at this time; they will be a reality for all in the first decade of the third millennium.

The realities correspond to those at the advent of the printed word (see Spender, 1995, for an extended account of attitudes to new technology since medieval times and the invention of the printing press). In medieval times, monasteries and a few universities were the sole places of book learning. With the printing press, a wider community, but usually only the privileged, had access to books, and there were no doubt many debates about the benefits and pitfalls of making them available to all. Books were by no means commonplace in systems of public education that made their appearance in the late nineteenth century. Every student had a slate, and classrooms had blackboards and a few maps and globes. Books were available but few students would have one or more that related to the subjects in which they were being taught. Schools had small libraries. Indeed, the public library was the place in the community where people went to borrow books for private reading. As in earlier times, there were no doubt many discussions and debates about the desirability and cost feasibility of requiring each student to own their own books. Issues of access and equity were as evident then as they were in the 1990s as far as the new learning technologies were concerned. These issues will be resolved as they have in most instances in the countries that provide the main point of reference for this book.

What will learning and teaching be like when all students have their own computers? This was the reality in some schools throughout the 1990s. Methodist Ladies College in Melbourne was one such school, with a strategic decision as early as 1989 to transform the school for learning through laptop computers. By the mid-1990s every girl above Grade 4 in this K–12 school of about 2200 students had her own laptop computer. A visit to a classroom revealed learning in the manner envisaged by Papert (1993), summarized in the description of g1: connectedness in the curriculum. For example, students in the upper years of primary school were accessing and utilizing resources on a CD-ROM and other locations and were constructing their own reports on the topic under consideration. Their activity cut across subject boundaries as pictures were selected, charts constructed, music composed, calculations made, and sophisticated analyses undertaken to determine impact on a range of variables. The possibilities for creativity were numerous. What was clear was that subject boundaries made little sense in this work.

Realities such as these raise important questions about the nature of the curriculum. Developments on Tracks 1 and 2 have involved the construction of curriculum and standards frameworks, often for the first time, and there is an assumption that they will continue. Teachers have worked hard to develop an understanding of these frameworks and have organized their work accordingly. What emerges in a scenario for learning with technology in the knowledge society is that curriculum boundaries will disappear and an approach to learning that gained momentum in the 1970s and 1980s will return. A key difference, however, is the unrelenting focus on learning outcomes that was rare in these earlier days. Under the new arrangements, there will likely still be the tests of student achievement, even in discrete learning areas, but also tests of capacity to work across subject boundaries, tapping high order skills in problem-solving and creativity.

Dale Spender challenged another aspect of learning within subject boundaries in a scathing comment about the preoccupation with literacy and numeracy, identified in Chapter 5 in the agenda for change on Track 2. She noted the high level of resources devoted to these areas, and suggested that this was a contributing factor in the widening gap between schools:

> And there are some people (often in high places) who want to get the school and the work place, back into synch, by putting the genie back into the bottle. By going back to what they knew — back to the print basics they were drilled in when they were at school. . . . And I would say — without qualification — that when it comes to education, this is the worst possible strategy for the future. . . . To start with, it is confined almost exclusively to state schools . . . While many private schools have moved towards computers and digital literacy — we can see certain state schools where students are being deprived of the new skills — as they are directed towards the old print proficiencies. (Spender, 1997, pp. 13–14)

In defence of people in high places, the relationship between capacity in literacy and numeracy and potential for obtaining worthwhile work is very powerful. The social consequences and cost of widespread failure in literacy and numeracy make it, understandably, a policy priority. Spender's argument is still relevant, however, for it raises questions about the kind of literacy and numeracy to be addressed, and what learning tools and learning environments are provided.

### 2    Workplace Transformation

*Schools as workplaces are transformed in every dimension, including the scheduling of time for learning and approaches to human resource management, rendering obsolete most approaches that derive from an industrial age, including the concept of 'industrial relations'.*

Adoption of the new learning technologies and learning that is constructivist in the sense illustrated above means major change on two dimensions, human and material. The first is considered as g2: workplace transformation in the *gestalt* presented in Figure 8.1 (p. 160).

Consider first the role of the teacher. With student projects that involve CD-ROM and other locations, including the internet, the teacher is no longer the primary source of information, organized into discrete learning areas. The teacher is at once a team builder, motivator, coach, skilled professional in the selection of source, critic, assessor of process and product, source of encouragement and feedback. Timetables that carve up the day into discrete time blocks for discrete subjects of study make no sense. Schedules that mean the ringing of bells and movement from place to place are foreign, even more so when it is appreciated that much of this learning by students can occur outside the classroom, at home and elsewhere, even for students in the primary school, certainly for students at secondary schools.

Concepts of standard class size under all conditions are rendered meaningless, when much highly productive learning through dissemination of information and explanation of abstract material can occur in very large groups, especially when the teacher is supported with advanced technology that allows large-screen projection and display on student hand-held or laptop computers. Similarly for students working in groups that are highly engaged, constructing their own learning, and teachers assume roles such as those listed in the last paragraph. There will be one-to-one individualized direct teaching or coaching support in many circumstances.

Under these conditions the concept of 'industrial relations' is obsolete, especially in respect to the way class size and 'contact time' might be specified. Conditions of work will, of course, continue to be important, but union-negotiated awards will likely address the broad parameters rather than the mind-numbing and constraining detail of the past (see 'new unionism' in Chapter 7). As in Chapter 6, resorting to a medical analogy might be in order, and the prospect of individual work contracts is likely to become a reality, sought by the teacher and preferred by employers. In similar fashion, whether or not schools are self-managing is an irrelevant issue, because there can be no other. How can a tightly centralized system of hundreds or thousands of public schools operate if approaches to learning and teaching are as indicated here.

Jane MacFarlane, a solicitor specializing in employment law, summarized developments and possibilities in Britain:

> ... stability is a thing of the past. Developments in employment legislation together with changes in education and in the wider employment culture mean that it is no longer possible to provide the flexibility to run a complex organization like a school by use of fixed-term and temporary contracts and the traditional supply teacher system ... Every week another shot is fired against the already crumbling wall of accepted norms. It is no longer unthinkable that some teachers will be paid more than others on the same scale, and school standards minister Stephen Byers has already hinted at moves to individually-negotiated contracts ... [but] There will always be a core of teachers on full-time permanent contracts. Schools need continuity and stability probably more than most other institutions. (MacFarlane, 1998, p. 27)

Attention thus far has been on the role of the teacher and the consequences for workplace relations and approaches to school management. As far as students are concerned, the changes are just as profound. In the illustration provided for the

Study of Society and the Environment, much of the work will be carried out individually but there will also be much activity in teams.

It is illuminating and exciting to watch students working with laptop computers in projects such as these. Rather than the image of lonely learning at stand-alone desk-top computers, one observes a buzz of excitement at key points as students huddle together to share information or solve a problem. They come together as a highly motivated high-performing team. They may be visited by a teacher from time to time, and one might leave the team and visit the teacher, carrying the laptop computer to demonstrate something or seek assistance. It is just as interesting with smaller children with such technology, when individual and team activity takes place in a variety of postures, even lying on the floor or in a pile of bean bags.

The assumption thus far has been that this learning occurs in a place called school — and most of it will be — especially for students of primary age. Much will also occur at home and in other places, and also in the workplace, for those whose learning is in an enterprise that might be privately owned, but in a strategic alliance with a school or a network of schools. These possibilities are considered further in Chapter 9 in the context of g7: virtual schooling.

### 3   School Fabric and Globalization

*The fabric of schooling is similarly rendered obsolete by electronic network-ing. Everything from building design to the size, shape, alignment, and fur-nishing of space for the 'knowledge worker' in the school is transformed. In one sense, of course, the school has no walls, for there are global learning networks. Much of the learning that previously called for the student to be located at school occurs in many places, at home, and in the upper years of secondary schooling and for lifelong learning, at the workplace.*

It is evident in the preceding accounts that the traditional size, shape and configura-tion of school buildings designed for the industrial era are rendered obsolete by the requirements of the knowledge society. Dale Spender made the point in graphic fashion, linking learning style to the structure of the workplace:

> The industrial revolution and mass education go together. And both are closely linked to the factory system. This is why the school day has been marked by bell ringing. Why the year has been divided into semesters. It is why students have been regimented into years, classes, grades and rows. . . . It is why teachers and lecturers have been the authorities, who not only keep students in line, but who have kept close control over information. It's why schools have been governed by content prescription. Examination orientation. And the hierarchical outcomes. (Spender, 1997, pp. 22–3)

Methodist Ladies College in Melbourne was faced with the issue when deci-sions were made that all girls from Grade 4 to Grade 12 should have their own laptop computers, and learning and teaching would occur in the style illustrated earlier in the chapter. Buildings constructed in the nineteenth and early twentieth century were not conducive to learning for the knowledge society. The fabric of the school needed to change in dramatic fashion, but the availability of resources required this be done stage by stage, at the same time that new buildings would be created to accommodate learning across a range of intelligences such as music, this being an 'intelligent school' in the image provided by Handy (1997) and MacGilchrist, Myers and Reed (1997).

An example at MLC is the transformation of the Cato Building for students in Grade 8, that was constructed in the old style, with classrooms of standard size laid end to end, one floor above another, with little flexibility for learning in the new order. The building was re-created, though it looked the same from the outside. Inside there is a variety of learning spaces, ranging from the traditional classroom, to larger space where several classes can come together, to informal working areas for small groups and finally, individual work space. Places for teachers to work in a style that suits the 'new professional' are also evident. New furniture was provided that is at once more attractive and flexible in the manner of its use.

This school is no longer bound by the site, either at its city location in suburban Kew, or its rural location at Mallacoota in Eastern Victoria, because learning is now global. Each student has her own e-mail address. Boundaries have also been broken in Schools of the Future in the public sector, including one described in Chapter 5 — the Woolum Bellum Campus of the Koorie Open Door Education school in Morwell. Learning for aboriginal students was transformed by an internet alliance with a Zuni Reservation school (A:Shiwi) in New Mexico (see Caldwell and Hayward, 1998, pp. 64–5, for a detailed account).

Experience at MLC, a relatively well-to-do private school, raises the issue of how the fabric of schools across the public sector will be transformed to meet the needs of schools in the third millennium. The costs will be staggering, given that there are about 85,000 schools in the United States, 25,000 in Britain and 8,000 in Australia, most of which will require refurbishing. In Britain, the Labour Government seeks a partnership of the public and private sector in accomplishing the task. In this chapter, however, the focus is on the 'what' rather than the 'how' and, in the remaining pages, we draw on the experience and expertise of those who have successfully redesigned schools for the knowledge society, and have plans for new facilities that will assist other schools in designs to meet their requirements.

### School Design for the Knowledge Society: The Sainsbery Reed Story

The Sainsbery Reed Group is a company of architects, planners and interior designers based in Abbotsford in Melbourne whose repertoire includes the design of schools for the knowledge society. They established a reputation for success in redesigning schools that were built in another age and that are now obsolete, given the needs of schools on Track 3. They have also designed new schools to meet these needs. Andrew Bunting and John Wood are two directors of the company who have specialized in this work. They are tuned to the needs of schools for this era and have a rare capacity to articulate what is required and a sensitivity to the needs and aspirations of teachers and others who seek to be 'the new professional'.

In the past, most work in education for people like Andrew Bunting and John Wood had been in the private school sector. The client was the school itself and there were no requirements for approval by others except to ensure conformity with Building Codes. For schools in the public sector, it was normal until recently for a public architect to determine a school design that would then be replicated hundreds of times, with little variation from setting to setting, and little consultation with professionals who had responsibility for learning and teaching.

Things have changed with the advent of the self-managing school, and the Sainsbery Reed Group now works in the public sector with the school as client. In the pages that follow, Andrew Bunting and John Wood tell this story, providing 'before' and 'after' designs to show what is possible in transforming industrial age schools for the knowledge society, and creating new ones from scratch. The setting is Schools of the Future in Victoria, but they have drawn many of their ideas from further afield, and the outcomes are widely applicable.

## School Building as Investment

In the late 1800s and early 1900s, many schools in Victoria and other parts of Australia were built of double brick construction, some with two levels. Reflecting a belief that education was an investment, these schools were viewed as investments, intended to last. Most are still in use today, having given stoic service with minimal expenditure to maintain their basic fabric. Until recent changes in approaches to learning and teaching and the introduction of information technology, few questions were asked as to their suitability.

Ironically, given recent change, it can now be argued that the strength of their construction was their greatest weakness, for in many respects, they are inflexible and cannot accommodate the new.

In contrast, from the 1950s to the 1970s, there was a large student population 'bubble' that moved through the school system, reflecting the post World War II baby boom and the welcomed influx of migrants. The Education Department in Victoria had to recruit thousands of teachers and build hundreds of schools very quickly. Double brick multi-level schools were not the answer as they would take too long to construct and would cost too much. The answer devised by the Office of Public Works was for a school of standard design with a long, low central corridor. The classrooms opening off each side of the corridors were mostly standard size (50m$^2$). The buildings were timber framed and clad in timber, cement tile or brick. They were known as LTCs (light timber construction). To staff, they were known as 'chicken coops'!

It was obvious in the economic climate of the time that 'quantity' was more important than 'quality'. These buildings were not meant to last. In fact, they were regarded as temporary at the time of construction, with a life span of about 25 years.

In construction terms, the LTCs were the opposite of what had gone before, but it would be incorrect to suggest that the government of the day regarded them as other than investments. The buildings may have been regarded as 'expendable' once the student bubble had passed through the system, but the education that took place within them was every bit an investment as the double brick constructions. The quantity and the standardization were a response to the times. In hindsight, it is hard to see that the government had any alternative.

What is interesting about the LTCs is that most of them were still operating many years after their 'use by' date. Less than buoyant economic times had meant that successor governments did not have the budget revenue to demolish and rebuild these schools. In general, the approach was to consolidate and upgrade. Fortunately, unlike their solid brick forebears, these schools are conducive to reconfiguration.

### *Reconfiguring Thornbury Darebin Secondary College*

An example of successful reconfiguration for the Sainsbery Reed Group was Thornbury Darebin Secondary College, a suburban secondary school in Melbourne that enrolled about 1100 students. The school is a consolidation of the Junior Grades 7–10 and the Senior Grades 11–12 on the site of the former, which was housed in a typical LTC building. Our task was to upgrade this building with a budget of $5 million to enable the use of the latest technology and teaching methods. The existing conditions were standard, as illustrated in Figure 8.2.

Our intention was to create an 'educational Shopping Mall' reflecting the following principles in school design:

- To create a central social spine;
- To have core elements, including specialist facilities, branch out from the mall;
- To provide information technology within the mall;
- To have the height of the mall increased to double storey which would increase the level of natural light in the centre of the school;
- To link arts and technology across the curriculum through a design centre;
- To provide alternative means for students to move to avoid overloading the mall with unnecessary traffic;
- To enhance curriculum links by breaking down isolated facilities through the development of commonalities.

The school design that resulted from the application of these principles is shown in Figure 8.3.

### *Reconfiguring the Boundaries: A New Design for the Middle Years*

For many years in Victoria, and in most other places, there has been a clear distinction between the first six years of school at the primary level, and the last six years,

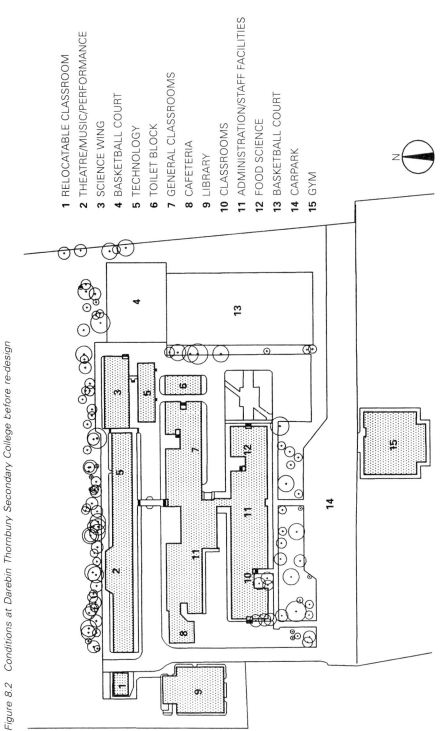

*Figure 8.2  Conditions at Darebin Thornbury Secondary College before re-design*

1 RELOCATABLE CLASSROOM
2 THEATRE/MUSIC/PERFORMANCE
3 SCIENCE WING
4 BASKETBALL COURT
5 TECHNOLOGY
6 TOILET BLOCK
7 GENERAL CLASSROOMS
8 CAFETERIA
9 LIBRARY
10 CLASSROOMS
11 ADMINISTRATION/STAFF FACILITIES
12 FOOD SCIENCE
13 BASKETBALL COURT
14 CARPARK
15 GYM

*Source:* Sainsbery Reed

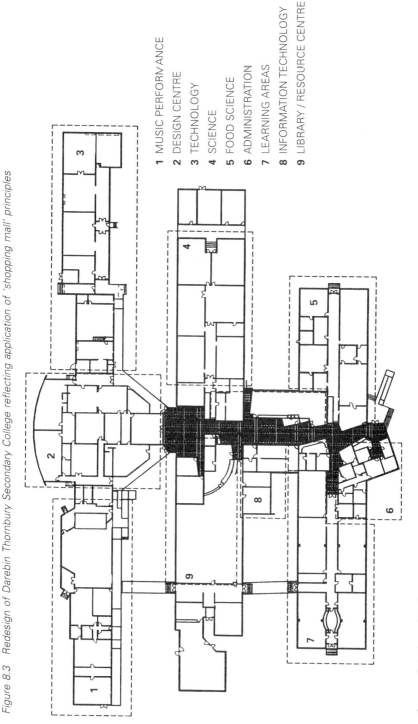

*Figure 8.3   Redesign of Darebin Thornbury Secondary College reflecting application of 'shopping mall' principles*

1 MUSIC PERFORMANCE
2 DESIGN CENTRE
3 TECHNOLOGY
4 SCIENCE
5 FOOD SCIENCE
6 ADMINISTRATION
7 LEARNING AREAS
8 INFORMATION TECHNOLOGY
9 LIBRARY / RESOURCE CENTRE

*Source:* Sainsbery Reed

at secondary, with tertiary education to follow. For a period of time, the boundaries between primary and secondary were blurred, so that some primary schools included eight years of schooling, and these were known as 'central schools'. Some schools in rural areas combined primary and secondary and these were known as 'consolidated schools'. The Sainsbery Reed Group has been involved in reconfiguring school design at the boundaries between primary and secondary and between secondary and tertiary.

Recent reports (see Australian Curriculum Studies Association, 1996, for example) have provided evidence that achievement and attitude to schooling have tended to 'flatten out' in the transition from the traditional primary to the traditional secondary. Many aspects of schooling change sharply at the point of transition, including building design, curriculum and approaches to learning and teaching (see Chapter 5 for a more detailed account of problems and possibilities in this transition).

We worked with consultant Darryn Kruse in the development of a 'middle school concept' that would break the mould of primary and secondary in the facilities domain, acknowledging that this would mean the redesign of existing buildings or the construction of new ones. We addressed two issues in our consultations: 'What is an appropriate generic design for a middle school that would address the key educational issues faced by students in this age range?' and 'How could existing buildings be reconfigured for this purpose?' We came up with two designs, illustrated in Figures 8.4 and 8.5.

The first generic design, illustrated in Figure 8.4, reflected the following characteristics:

- The intent was to create a series of sub-schools or home groups;
- Each classroom 'house' is located in landscaped surroundings and makes a strong connection to the environment;
- Specialist facilities are grouped together and inserted into the central space;
- The central space houses information technology;
- The buildings are colourful, including different textures, materials, heights and quality of lighting;
- The design is intended to create surprises and interest;
- A classroom cluster around a technology area, described as a 'technopod', or as described later for technology at the primary level, a 'technocubby'; and
- The buildings are able to be staged and developed according to enrolment pressures: additional classroom houses can be built if required.

The second generic design included the following characteristics, illustrated in Figure 8.5:

- To develop the classroom house concept;
- To develop flexibility in the classrooms to cater for further independent learning;

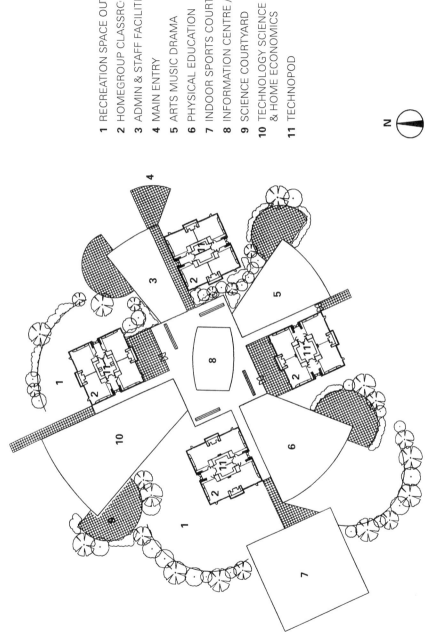

*Figure 8.4 Generic design 1 for the middle years of schooling*

1 RECREATION SPACE OUTDOORS
2 HOMEGROUP CLASSRCOMS
3 ADMIN & STAFF FACILITIES
4 MAIN ENTRY
5 ARTS MUSIC DRAMA
6 PHYSICAL EDUCATION
7 INDOOR SPORTS COURTS
8 INFORMATION CENTRE / LIBRARY
9 SCIENCE COURTYARD
10 TECHNOLOGY SCIENCE
& HOME ECONOMICS
11 TECHNOPOD

*Source:* Sainsbury Reed

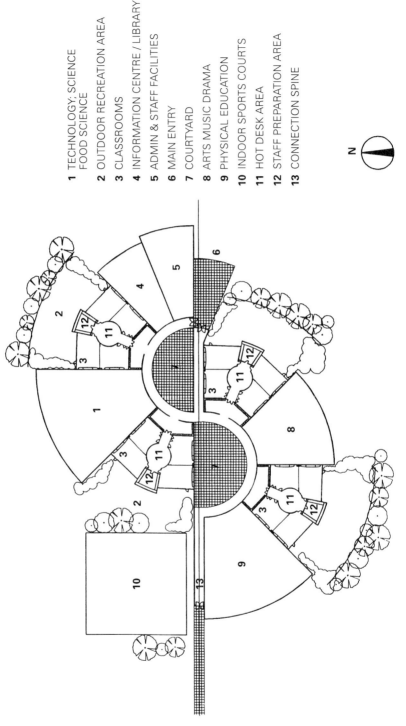

*Figure 8.5   Generic Design 2 for the Middle Years of Schooling*

1  TECHNOLOGY: SCIENCE
   FOOD SCIENCE
2  OUTDOOR RECREATION AREA
3  CLASSROOMS
4  INFORMATION CENTRE / LIBRARY
5  ADMIN & STAFF FACILITIES
6  MAIN ENTRY
7  COURTYARD
8  ARTS MUSIC DRAMA
9  PHYSICAL EDUCATION
10 INDOOR SPORTS COURTS
11 HOT DESK AREA
12 STAFF PREPARATION AREA
13 CONNECTION SPINE

*Source:* Sainsbery Reed

- To develop in each classroom house areas of open plan, computer resourced 'hot desks', each shared by several students;
- To develop a social spine which links the buildings together;
- To relate each component of the building to the environment;
- To provide for good quality natural light; and
- To have each component of the building relating to a central courtyard.

There are other issues to be addressed in school design. Young primary school children need security and intimacy, so they should not have to cope with threatening buildings and vast spaces. Older children at the secondary level appreciate space and facilities that foreshadow the workplace of further education.

### The Impact of Information Technology on School Design

The impact of information technology on learning is only now becoming clear. The speed of application is only constrained by the cost of hardware and software, although these are falling rapidly, and the capacity of teachers to appreciate and stay on top of developments and their application to learning and teaching.

There are significant implications for educational facilities. If learning can occur anywhere, in school or at home or in other places, and if teachers are becoming facilitators as well as instructors, what are the consequences for classroom design?

Students are more likely to work in groups than before and they will work across curriculum boundaries. In both instances, the conditions are approaching those found in the 'real world'. To accommodate this, some learning spaces should be configured as 'problem-solving spaces' with work stations for, say, five to six students in a semi-formal setting to facilitate layout of papers, discussion and computer use. Teachers and other professionals will 'hover' or be available in offices or at other work stations nearby, being available for guidance or consultation. In most respects, the pace and progress of learning is controlled by students.

### Reconfiguring the high school

We explored the reconfiguration of the high school and developed the design in Figure 8.6. It includes personal work stations with a range of spaces for group problem-solving and informal social interaction. It assumes that all students have personal, portable computers with access to appropriate software and on-line services, all seen as essential tools for learning in the information age.

### The 'technocubby' for the primary school: Big Hill Primary

One approach in the primary environment is to create shared areas for technology. We had the opportunity to create this from scratch, rather than reconfigure an existing building, when the Sainsbery Reed Group was invited to work with Big

1 GROUP WORK SPACE
2 GROUP DISCUSSION CENTRE
3 TEACHER PREPARATION ROOM
4 INSTRUCTIONAL AREA
5 ENTRY
6 RESOURCE STORAGE

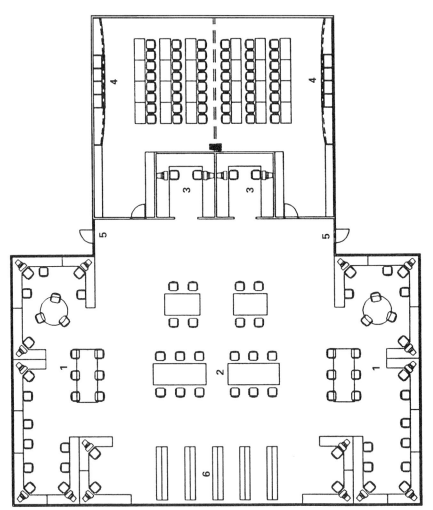

*Figure 8.6   Reconfiguring the high school for information technology*

*Source:* Sainsbery Reed

Hill Primary in rural Victoria, built for 300 students in 1996. We designed a 'technocubby' which is a technology-rich common area shared by four classrooms. The school consists of two pods of four classrooms, with a 'technocubby' in the middle of each pod. The design intentions were as follows, illustrated in Figure 8.7:

- To give teaching flexibility with room combinations so that teachers could work alone or in teams;
- To enable teachers to supervise an adjacent room or to visually connect to the next room;
- To provide internal or external access;
- To provide a central area that all classrooms can use;
- To have this central area visually connected to all teaching areas around it;
- To have the ability to divide the technocubby into two areas for smaller groups;
- To have the technocubby fitted out with power and data cabling;
- To provide fixed and mobile furniture which would allow flexibility in layouts to respond to varying teaching methods;
- To have a waterproof floor which would allow for hands-on activities within the classroom precinct rather than having the students travelling to another part of the school; and
- To provide natural light in the technocubby and ventilation for warmer climates.

*Flexibility and adaptability: Goulburn Ovens Institute of TAFE at Seymour*

Rural colleges typically provide many short courses in a variety of subjects. The major design component for one such college we designed was flexibility and adaptability in the use of technology. The Seymour Campus of the Goulburn Ovens Institute of Technical and Further Education (TAFE) was completed in 1996 with extensive use of operable walls, 'roll in–roll out' kitchen facilities and multi-use computer laboratories. These features gave the college enormous scope for teaching many programs at short notice.

As illustrated in Figure 8.8, the computer laboratories were designed to also operate as lecture theatres and general purpose classrooms, making three uses in total. Each room is 9 metres by 9 metres and accommodates 22 adult students with layout space beside each computer. When used as a general purpose classroom or lecture theatre, the space can accommodate 50 students.

Each computer room accommodates three rows of students, with each student having a computer. The three rows are at different levels, similar to a lecture theatre, and the students sit on swivel chairs between two benches. When the student faces the front, the room serves as a general purpose classroom or lecture theatre. The room is tiered, with a camera and monitor at the front of the room when video-conferencing is desired.

When the students face the back of the room and use the computers, the room functions as a computer laboratory. Large computer monitors are located on the

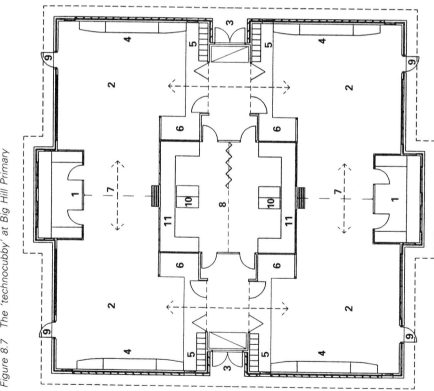

*Figure 8.7 The 'technocubby' at Big Hill Primary*

1 STAFF PREPARATION
2 LEARNING AREA
3 ENTRY
4 CLASSROOM STORAGE
5 STUDENT BAG / COAT STORAGE
6 BASIN / SINK
7 REMOVABLE WALL
8 TECHNO CUBBY LEARNING AREA
9 EXTERNAL ACCESS
10 MOVEABLE FURNITURE
11 FIXED FURNITURE
←→ INDICATES ACCESS & TEACHING
    CONTACT BETWEEN LEARNING AREAS

*Source:* Sainsbery Reed

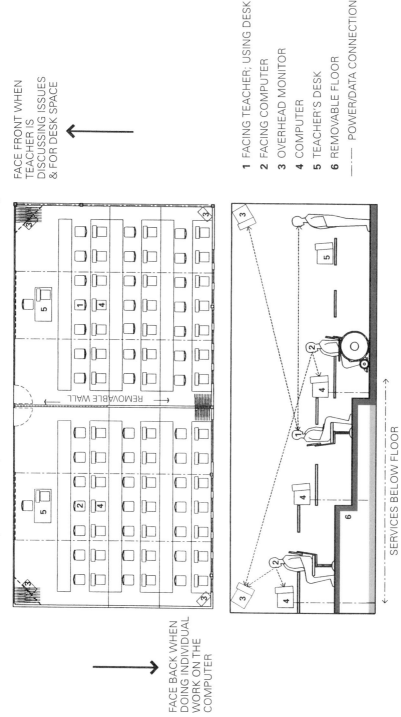

*Figure 8.8   Adaptability and flexibility in use of computers at the Goulburn Ovens Institute of TAFE at Seymour*

FACE FRONT WHEN
TEACHER IS
DISCUSSING ISSUES
& FOR DESK SPACE

FACE BACK WHEN
DOING INDIVIDUAL
WORK ON THE
COMPUTER

1 FACING TEACHER; USING DESK
2 FACING COMPUTER
3 OVERHEAD MONITOR
4 COMPUTER
5 TEACHER'S DESK
6 REMOVABLE FLOOR
---- POWER/DATA CONNECTION

REMOVABLE WALL

SERVICES BELOW FLOOR

*Source:* Sainsbery Reed

rear wall at a height visible to all students. The monitors show the lecturer's screen, which may be a stand alone computer or a laptop, which is operated from the front of the room. Because the students are sitting at tiered levels, the lecturer is able to see all computer screens and can determine student progress. Good sightlines were a prime consideration.

Flexibility is also increased by designing an operable wall which, when opened, increases the size of the room to accommodate twice the number for larger computer classes or lectures. Given the preponderance of computer applications in all subject areas and the multiple use of the two computer rooms, it is not surprising that this space is used almost 100 per cent of the time.

Even in the event of the college needing to change the function of these rooms in say, 5 to 10 years' time, the construction is adaptable. The tiered levels are made of timber panels and are easily demountable. Computer cabling from flush mounted outlets on the floor can be disconnected, allowing a now empty room to be reconfigured.

It is clear that buildings must be able to accommodate such flexibility, given the rapid change in information technology and curriculum. Existing campus buildings which are unable to adapt to constant modification are not only frustrating for teachers and students but they are decidedly uneconomic.

### Issues in Building Design

In this final section of the Sainsbery Reed story, we address four issues in general terms, without reference to particular designs in particular settings. These concern the use of technology in libraries; the challenge of change; ownership and use of school facilities; and the concept of 'form follows function'.

### Use of technology in school libraries

The impact of technology on school libraries is interesting. Libraries have traditionally been the repository of information in the form of books, with more space typically allocated to non-fiction than fiction. With the increasing rate of development in technology, non-fiction rapidly became out of date, especially with the advent of the internet. What are the implications for library design?

If non-fiction leaves the library, then the space required for a library of fiction only, either for reading or for borrowing, will be smaller. If librarians maintain a role of advising on access to non-fiction, then libraries need more computer work stations in place of non-fiction shelves.

There has been a trend in office design which implies 'high tech – high touch'. This means that the more technology there is, perhaps involving less human contact, the more important it is to balance this by high touch items such as indoor plants, art work and above average staff facilities and social programs. In other words, there is recognition that it is harmful to deprive people of significant human interaction when they are working with computers for much of the day. There is indeed a danger of losing interpersonal skills.

Such considerations are important in libraries and in other aspects of schools affected by the information age. Sporting, musical, drama and other artistic and cultural facilities will be more important than ever, and account must be taken of these in the overall design of the school.

### The challenge of change

The last quarter of the twentieth century presented some challenging times in school design, with expansion, contraction and change.

Expansion is more of the same; contraction is less of the same; change is doing things differently. Dealing with change in the public system is particularly challenging because it is large and, being a bureaucracy, the work is constrained by rules, regulations and schedules.

Another area where change presents particular challenge is at the upper end of secondary, where learning has again shifted from school site to industry and commerce. In one sense, these are the characteristics of apprenticeship, but there is now high technology involved.

The possibilities for lifelong learning are fascinating, with some developers looking at this concept as the focus of residential developments in the way post offices and town halls once played this role. It may be that the 'Educational Shopping Mall' will operate 24 hours per day, 365 days per year and will be the centre of the community.

### Ownership and use of school facilities

In many countries, including our own, public schools are owned by the State. In some places, notably Britain with grant maintained schools (foundation) or schools in the aided sector, the ownership of schools has passed to or is in the hands of a private body. A strong argument may be found for shifting ownership in this manner in order to locate the care, maintenance and management as close to the community as possible, so that the community itself can take pride and interest in its school.

Apart from churches, schools could well be the most under-utilized facilities in the community. Local ownership combined with the use of modern technology and the possibility of lifelong learning may lead to rapid change in this regard. The impact on school design is noteworthy, with the key concept being 'flexibility'. This will mean that rooms must be capable of reconfiguration on a daily basis. In the medium to long term, the key word is 'adaptability', for facilities must be capable of being refitted every five years or so without major structural inconvenience.

It is now desirable to have some rooms that are highly specialized, such as a science laboratory, and others that are highly generalized, such as an all-purpose classroom, with a range of spaces in between that can be rapidly configured for particular purposes. There are counterparts in a hospital, being an operating theatre, ward and recovery room, respectively.

These 'in-between' rooms are now technically feasible with the advent of 'roll in–roll out' equipment that can be plugged in and plugged out as needed. Services such as electricity, water, gas, telecommunications, and exhaust systems can all be deployed in this manner.

### The concept of 'form follows function'

The concept of 'form follows function' may be found in every field, including architecture. Its use has been illustrated throughout the Sainsbery Reed story. Dramatic change is occurring as 'schools' are being conceived as 'learning centres'.

There is, however, the converse: 'function follows form' as illustrated in the way the nature of a building shapes the attitudes and operations of those who work within it. Drab, boring and dysfunctional buildings may have the same effect on the people who work within them. Colourful, dynamic and functional buildings will be uplifting.

There is a third concept that 'form follows culture'. If each school has a unique culture, then its buildings ought to be unique too.

When we commence any form of school planning or school design, we make a point of spending a great deal of time at the school listening and talking to staff, students, parents and other interested parties. We like to ask these people 'What makes your school tick?' and 'Why is it different to others?' These questions become more critical than ever in the design of schools for the knowledge society.

### Reflections on the Sainsbery Reed Story

Andrew Bunting and John Wood have illustrated the manner in which schools may be designed and redesigned to carry out their role in the knowledge society. Indeed, the issues they raise and the developments they report touch on each of the elements in the *gestalt* in Figure 8.1 (p. 160), including efforts to integrate learning across the curriculum, the change in workplace arrangements that call for flexibility and adaptability, and the need for the fabric of the school to change in a new era for education. Their account assumes a high level of local decision-making and, in that respect, is an illustration of moving 'beyond the self-managing school'. Setting aside the need for building codes, central authorities in a system of self-managing schools often constrain school design by bureaucratic process. Their reference to the concept of 'form follows function' captures the need for new school designs. Their comment on the converse that 'function follows form' is a salutary reminder of the consequences of not making change. Their closing comments refer to the way they operate, being deeply sensitive to the needs and aspirations of staff, students and others in the school community, an approach captured in the notion that 'form follows culture'. It also raises the issues addressed in Chapter 9 that deals with the human dimensions of change in schools as they make the journey down Track 3.

## Strategic Intentions for Schools
## Transformation of Learning

1 Approaches to learning and teaching will change to accommodate the reality that every student in every setting will have a laptop or hand-held computer, making the new learning technologies as much a part of the learning scene as books have been since the advent of systems of public education.

2 Subject boundaries will be broken and learning will be integrated across the curriculum as the new learning technologies become universal, challenging rigidity in curriculum and standards frameworks, without removing the need for learning in discrete areas as well in learning that spans the whole.

3 Schools will critically examine their approaches to the teaching of literacy and numeracy to ensure that the new learning technologies are incorporated, and every effort will be made to resource the latter without sacrificing targets for success in the basics for every student.

4 Rigidity in roles, relationships and approaches to school and classroom organization will be broken down, with multiple but rewarding roles for teachers and other professionals, more flexibility in the use of time, and abandonment of narrow specifications of class size that are rendered meaningless in the new workplace arrangements.

5 School buildings designed for the industrial age will be redesigned to suit the needs of the knowledge society.

6 Staff in self-managing schools will have critical roles to play in school design, sharing needs, aspirations and visions with architects who are tuned to the requirements of schooling for the knowledge society.

7 Information technology will pervade school design for the knowledge society.

8 Schools that serve the middle years in the Grade 5 to Grade 8 range, or thereabouts, will require major change in school design, reflecting what is known about the causes of flattened levels of achievement and motivation across the years of transition from the traditional primary to the traditional secondary.

9 School design will feature high levels of flexibility and adaptability, with the former referring to multiple uses of the same facilities in the

short term, and the latter to a capacity for major redesign with minimal disruption in the medium to long term.

10   Schools will be adept at analyzing the relationship between function, form and culture in school design, helping to bring to realization a design that contributes to making schools exciting and uplifting places of work for staff and students.

# The Human Dimension: Completing the *Gestalt*

Chapter 9 is concerned with the human dimensions of creating schools for the knowledge society. There were, of course, important human considerations in each element of the *gestalt* explored in Chapter 8 (g1–g3) but the prime focus was the structural arrangements, including the curriculum, workplace arrangements and school design.

The remaining elements of the *gestalt* (g4–g7), as illustrated in Figure 9.1, are explored in Chapter 9. The notion of a 'new professionalism', considered first in Chapter 6, is extended in consideration of g4: Professionalism and great teaching. The new learning technologies can help lift teaching to great heights. It is already evident from earlier chapters that a capacity to work in teams is as relevant to schools as it is to workplaces in virtually every other setting, so particular attention is paid to this phenomenon in g5: Teams and pastoral care. Pastoral care refers to the need to nurture and care for students and staff, recognizing how sweeping are the changes on Track 3. They are proving traumatic for some staff. Concern about access and equity pervades the scene in the late 1990s as momentum for change on Track 3 gathers momentum. Many schools are being left behind, and the social chasm described by Jeremy Rifkin (1996), summarized in Chapter 7, may widen unless good 'cyber-policy' is developed at every level. The notion of cyber-policy was developed by Dale Spender (1995). The *gestalt* is completed with an exploration of the possibilities of virtual schools. In many respects, these possibilities have already been raised, but this is an opportunity to draw them together. The likelihood of lifelong learning represents a fundamental change in the human condition, so this section serves to integrate many matters related to the human dimensions of the journey on Track 3.

*g4 Professionalism and great teaching*

*A wide range of professionals and para-professionals support learning in an educational parallel to the diversity of support that may be found in modern health care. The role of teacher is elevated, for it demands wisdom, judgment, and a facility to manage learning in modes more complex and varied than ever. While the matter of intellectual capital must be resolved, the teacher is*

Figure 9.1 *A vision for schooling in the knowledge society illustrated in a* gestalt

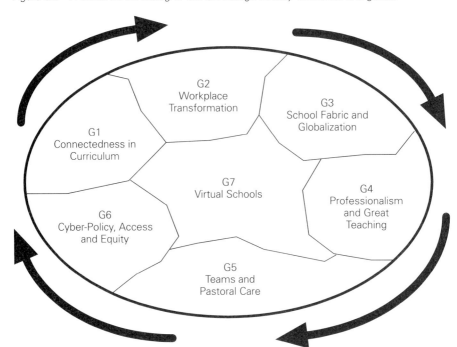

*freed from the impossible task of designing from their own resources learning experiences to challenge every student: the resources of the world's great teachers will be at hand.*

This element in the *gestalt* is a composite of many practices described throughout the book, but further possibilities are envisaged. The case was made in Chapter 6 for a 'new professionalism' and comparisons were made with the medical field, comparing teachers and others in the school setting with doctors and other health care workers. The range of professionals immediately available to support students and their learning is smaller than for care in the health field, as illustrated in the number and variety of staff who support a patient before, during and after an operation.

Current practice that best illustrates the possibilities are the integrated service schools described in Chapter 6. All services that might be needed to support every child are available at or near a school site, with every aspect of need and learning experience for every student monitored so that all support can be accessed and deployed. It is the school equivalent of case management in other fields. There will be few schools where all services will be available at a single site, but the image presented in this short description indicates the high level of planning and professionalism that will be needed if the rhetoric of an unrelenting focus on learning outcomes is to be brought to realization for every student.

The good news is that there are some fine examples of integrated services schools. A notable example is the Port Phillip Specialist School in Port Melbourne, Victoria. Formerly a small school serving students with moderate to severe physical impairment, the vision and drive of the principal, Bella Irlicht, and her community resulted in a much larger site being secured, with integrated services made available to a much larger population. An outstanding feature of the school is the partnership in resourcing the facility, with major enterprises in the private sector making donations of furniture, equipment, time and money. This is the stuff of the third sector that Jeremy Rifkin (1996) advocates.

The 'new professionalism' advocated in Chapter 6 provided parallels for teachers and doctors in the manner in which each should use sophisticated diagnostic data and determine a program for those in their care, working to strict protocols and standards of professional practice. These are the requirements for success on Track 2 that calls for an unrelenting focus on learning outcomes and little more needs to be said, except to observe that it is an image for teaching that can only be brought to realization with the support of a wide range of professional and para-professional staff, and also the availability of new technologies.

One is struck with the impressive array of hardware and software available to support the work of teachers in Britain, including the hand-held radio transmission computer that enables teachers to mark the roll and have the details of attendance sent immediately to the office for immediate transmittal to every hand-held computer around the school, so that every teacher knows who should be present at any particular time. Daily bulletins can be posted to these computers as well as to television monitors at points around the school, with updating throughout the day. Homes and workplaces can be connected to the same facility so that parents can be kept informed of matters concerning their children. The picture emerges of a paperless office and teachers freed of many tiresome tasks that take time and attention from their work. What is described here is just a sample of the seemingly endless possibilities for the technological support of teachers.

The final aspect of this element in the *gestalt* is the manner in which teachers, like students, can now access outstanding resources for teaching and learning from CD-ROM and an increasing array of web-sites. The images of lessons being written up from dog-eared lesson plans of the past and hastily scrambling together illustrations, assignment sheets, video-tapes and the like fades as a distant memory when one contemplates what is currently available but still not widely used. Material can be selected and then tailored precisely to the needs of particular students that may emerge with little notice. In this situation, materials cannot be ordered in advance from multiple sources, as was required in the past. Now they can be drawn almost immediately with the aid of information and communications technology.

Peter Ellyard (1997) coined the term Just-in-Time Learning in his description of the new learning culture, as set out later in the chapter for g7: Virtual schools. The equivalent is Just-in-Time Teaching and it parallels a style of operation now widely used in private enterprise. In the past, companies used to maintain large stocks of every part that might be required at any moment for the service of its products, but this proved inefficient in terms of space, production and personnel requirements.

Now, sophisticated networking and new design for parts enables almost immediately location, delivery or assembly of the exact part — 'just-in-time'.

This level of support for teachers will require other staff with high levels of expertise. Part of this vision is an expanded and richer role for the staff who were known formerly as teacher-librarians. They and their colleagues are highly skilled learning resource specialists in this vision and an increasing number are now bringing it to realization. Accessing the very best resources for Just-in-Time Teaching will call for ready access to all relevant sources and, understandably, instant billing arrangements to satisfy requirements of copyright. There will be outsourcing of many of these services, because the cost of maintaining them on a single site will be far too high. Schools or networks of schools will contract with various providers for this support. The issue of quality control will be critical in all of these matters.

### g5 Teams and pastoral care

*A capacity to work in teams is more evident in approaches to learning, given the primacy of the work team in every formulation of the workplace in the knowledge society. This, of course, will confound those who see electronic networking in an outdated stereotype of the loner with the laptop. The concept of 'pastoral care' of students is as important as ever for learning in this mode, and in schools that quite literally have no boundaries.*

Element g5 addresses two matters, one of which has already been described in several contexts. This concerns the emergence of teams as the preferred way of working in many aspects of schooling. It was shown in Chapter 8 how schools with high use of laptop computers have found that teamwork emerges as a matter of course in some aspects of learning, notably where large databases have been accessed and problem-solving is required. There is much to share, and working together is an exciting and effective way to solve the problem and synthesize learning.

Three instances have been cited of the way teachers work in teams. The first was in the study of Mackellar Primary School in Chapter 3, where a team of teachers was assembled to tackle the problems of literacy in the early years of primary school. Another was contained in the image of the 'new professional' in Chapter 6, and the example was given of teams of teachers of mathematics in Japanese secondary schools who work together to plan how to make effective for all students the particular approaches to learning and teaching they have adopted for each concept. The parallel is in medicine as teams of specialists share the outcomes of various approaches to the care of their patients. The third instance was cited in Chapter 5 in connection with school design for the middle years, spanning roughly Grades 5 to 8. The concern here is the flattened levels of achievement and motivation of students. An increasingly common design involves teams of teachers presenting as many subjects together to as small a number of students as possible.

The second aspect of this element is the concern for pastoral care of students and teachers. For students, this is evident in the care implied in the mission for

Track 2, namely, to focus unrelentingly on learning outcomes for students. It is evident in the school design known as the integrated services school and the adoption in schools of the case management approach. It will become increasingly important as the notion of a virtual school comes to realization, because some students will be working independently, either alone or in teams, on the school site or, increasingly, away from the site. The school has a duty of care to all students, and working out roles, responsibilities and accountabilities will be important.

Interestingly, the concept of pastoral care may apply most particularly to teachers and other professionals because of the major changes that are affecting their work. A change from the traditional role to that outlined in the specifications for the 'new professional' will be profound for many, and much support will be needed. Being a member of a team will assist in many instances, as in early literacy programs, so that all can learn and change together. The responsibility for providing this support will lie with several people, including the principal, the team leader, members of the team working together, and the individual. One aspect of pastoral care for teachers is professional development. System-wide and even national programs of support will be helpful in this regard, with an excellent example afforded in Britain's National Literacy Strategy and the National Year of Reading that commenced in September 1998. The pressure from government came with the focus on standards, to be increased from 57 per cent of 11-year-olds reaching standard in 1996 to 80 per cent reaching standard across the nation in 2002. The support comes in the form of three days training for all primary teachers, with access to 200 literacy consultants who will work with schools to update their skills. This is pastoral care through professional development in the journey on Track 2. The same needs and the same strategies are important for progress on Track 3, especially with universal adoption and expectations for utilization of communications and information technology. Schools will require cyber-policy on pastoral care.

### g6 Cyber-policy, access and equity

*Dale Spender's challenge in* Nattering on the Net *(Spender, 1995) to formulate 'cyber-policy of the future' is a priority. The issues of access and equity will drive public debate until such time as prices fall to make electronic networks as common as the telephone or radio, and that may soon be a reality, given trends in networked computers.*

The need for cyber-policy is self-evident, given the apparently widening gap between schools that are well endowed with the new technology, and have the capacity to move even further ahead, and those that do not have the resources and are lagging further behind, in relative terms. It is an educational parallel to the broader social concern raised by Jeremy Rifkin (1996), described in Chapter 7, in which the elite knowledge worker is empowered for success in the years ahead, while displaced industrial workers and their families are struggling to survive.

Even those who are doing well are sensitive to the disparities in this regard. Tony Hewitson, Headmaster of St Michael's Grammar School in Melbourne expressed his concern on the occasion of the announcement of a $3.75 million technology refit that might make his school the first in Australia to acquire a virtual capability: 'If Government schools don't have the same facilities we are going to have an incredible divide' (cited in Messina, 1997).

Progress is being made in addressing the issue in most nations that are referred to in this book, usually as part of a comprehensive strategy to achieve greater efficiency in the delivery of existing services and providing resources for new developments that will be an investment in the future. An example of this strategy may be found in Victoria which, since 1993, has closed or amalgamated about 350 of about 2000 schools. While the government had to respond to a major debt crisis and budget imbalance, the primary concern was to achieve greater efficiency in schooling, freeing scarce resources for other schools, taking account of the escalating costs of meeting community expectations, especially in respect to new learning technologies. Victoria has faced particular difficulties in these matters because of strategic decisions made decades ago. At the secondary level, a dual system of high schools and technical schools was created with the two kinds of schools often located nearby, in the same community. The dual system was abandoned in the early 1980s, and with rapidly declining populations of students in many communities, large numbers of very small schools remained. At the primary level, schools in metropolitan Melbourne were built an average of 1 kilometre apart whereas their counterparts in Sydney were built an average of 2 kilometres apart. Very small schools remained with declining enrolments in many communities (see Caldwell and Hayward, 1998, Chapter 3, for an account of the strategy to address these issues).

The strategy is illustrated in the case of two schools in inner Melbourne, Brunswick Primary and Brunswick East Primary. Enrolments in each case had fallen to levels that did not sustain a high quality program of a kind that would equip students for the knowledge society. Initially, government preferences for an amalgamation were not accepted by local communities who threatened militant action if this occurred. A year passed before acceptance of the inevitable, and there was agreement between the two schools that they should merge. Government then set about making the restructured school into a learning centre for the information age, with $350,000 for renovations and $100,000 for information technology, a further $30,000 for the latter provided by the school community. Principal Daryl Rogers observed that 'We are going to be extremely well off in terms of computer access for children and teachers' (cited by Elias, 1998).

An even broader strategy is addressed in a project known as VicOne. A $300 million broadband digital network will have 3100 access points that will include every school, hospital, public office and agency by 2001. Victoria's priorities in this matter were symbolized by it being the first government to appoint a Minister for Multi-Media. The initial appointee was also the Treasurer of the State, Allan Stockdale.

A similar strategy has been adopted in Singapore, which aims to become an 'intelligent island'. Chong and Leong describe it in the following terms:

A S$2 billion Masterplan for IT in Education has been launched for the purpose of developing IT-based learning, teaching and managing in schools. It aims at increasing curriculum time for IT-based learning and envisages a pupil–computer ratio of 2:1 in every school by the Year 2002. This is in line with the national IT plan to make Singapore an intelligent island. A S$1 billion package to change all double-session schools into single-session schools by the Year 2000 'will give [schools] greater flexibility in the use of the school day'. Schools are encouraged to be more client-oriented as part of the 'Public Service for the 21st Century' program; the new Teachers' Pledge ends with 'We will win the trust, support and cooperation of parents and the community so as to enable us to achieve our mission'. (Chong and Leong, 1997, p. 3)

An issue in many countries is the extent to which the support of the community, as contained in the Teachers' Pledge in Singapore, should extend to financial support. It certainly does in the case of private schools, and one of the reasons for the steady increase in fees for private schools in Australia in the late 1990s, at a time of low or zero inflation, was the escalating costs of providing and updating learning technologies. Government schools in Australia are not legally permitted to charge fees, but all set a so-called voluntary levy, the amount of which was steadily increasing, reflecting, as in private schools, the costs of new technology. There is, of course, disparity in the capacity of schools to raise funds from other sources, but it is noteworthy that Brunswick Primary School in inner Melbourne secured a $30,000 contribution from its community to bring its technology to an acceptable level.

Within schools, where a range of capacities to pay and support may be found, there is ample scope for issues of equity and access to be addressed. Zehr (1997) cites three instances of approaches in the United States that could be adapted in any setting. One, already cited in Chapter 7, involved students at Montgomery Blair High School in Maryland earning credit for creating learning centres in low-income apartments using donated computers. Cited in the next section of this chapter is the K–12 Foshay Learning Centre initiative in setting up eight learning centres in low-income apartment complexes across Los Angeles. In South Carolina, a foundation of community and business interests raised funds to help make laptop computers available for low-cost rent for students who do not have them. There was a sliding scale ranging from $15 per month to $60 per month.

Moving beyond the local community, governments are now working with the private sector to ensure that schools are included in the layout by companies in the information and communications technology field. In Britain, schools that won grants from government to become technology colleges were required to secure matching grants from the corporate sector and these were secured in large number.

A remarkable example is furnished in the United States in the NetDay initiative. NetDay was established in 1996 by Michael Kaufman, a senior director of digital learning for the Public Broadcasting System (PBS), and John Gage, a chief scientist for Sun Microsystems. It began as a one-off one-day event to wire schools in California for access to the internet. However, it was expanded at the urging of the White House and the US Department of Education. By mid-1997, more than

250,000 volunteers had helped wire 50,000 classrooms across the United States (Zehr, 1997, p. 38). This is a fine example of the how the third-sector can make a contribution to school education, in the style advocated by Rifkin (1996), as summarized in Chapter 7.

What is emerging is a set of strategies that are becoming more coherent and comprehensive as the years pass and are likely to 'close the gap', at the same time that the costs of technology are falling and every family will have a computer, even a laptop or hand-held computer, as a matter of course, just as occurred with television in the third quarter of the twentieth century and, more recently, with mobile or cellular telephones. Taking a longer historical view, the same occurred with books and the creation of libraries, first in the wider community as public libraries were created, and then in schools in public systems.

All students now have books. All students will have computers. Whether the time it takes for this to occur can be shortened by massive injections of funds is a contentious issue. Even if the funds were available, providing every student and every teacher with a laptop computer immediately would be pointless, given the several years it takes to prepare staff and the school to accommodate the new technology. Whether governments should significantly increase the taxes of companies in the information and communications technologies sector specifically to resource such a strategy is an option worth considering. It would be consistent with Rifkin's challenge in this matter:

> With profits expected to rise sharply in the years ahead from increased globalization of markets and automation of production and services, transnational companies ought to be encouraged to contribute more of their gains to help rebuild and sustain the many communities in which they do business around the world. Legislation should be introduced and enacted to provide more favourable deductions for companies willing to expand their corporate giving to the third sector. ( Rifkin, 1996, p. 273)

In general, governments, education departments, schools and other organizations and institutions with an interest in the future of schools should form clear strategic intentions and set high priorities for building the capacities of schools. Strategic plans should be made, with flexibility to take advantage of new opportunities as these come to hand.

### g7 Virtual schools

*The concept of the virtual organization or the learning network organization is a reality in the knowledge society. Schools take on many of the characteristics of such organizations, given that learning occurs in so many modes and from so many sources, all networked electronically.*

The term 'virtual school' is now widely used and rarely defined. Until now, school has been considered a place, and 'a place called school' captures the traditional meaning, as in the book of that title by John Goodlad (1984). What changes a place called school to a virtual school is that the learning does not necessarily occur at the place, nor at the time, nor in the style that traditionally characterized the place called school. Learning can occur anywhere. It need not occur between the hours of 9 and 4, it can occur at any time, 24 hours per day, 365 days per year, and not necessarily between the ages of 5 and 16, but any time from birth to death. The style will include that of the traditional classroom, with traditional roles for teachers and students, but the repertoire will be much wider. The notion of school is maintained because the learning is coherent and contractual.

There will still be a place called school if the full range of intelligences, such as those proposed by Gardner (1983) and Handy (1997) are addressed (see Chapter 5). Those who expect or advocate the disappearance of a place called school are foreclosing on some of these, including musical intelligence or emotional intelligence or interpersonal intelligence. Included in a place called school might be a home school, especially for young children, when the home becomes the source of coherence and some of the learning opportunities, networking with other homes or institutions, even other places called school in the traditional sense.

That schooling under these conditions can be anything other than self-managing schooling is very unlikely indeed. The concept of self-managing extends to smaller units, including classrooms, staff and students.

Two people who write about the future with great insight and sensitivity are Hedley Beare and Peter Ellyard. Their contributions to the 1997 Virtual Conference of the Australian Council for Educational Administration on the theme 'Beyond the Boundaries' are helpful in gaining an understanding of what is involved with virtual schooling (Beare, 1997; Ellyard, 1997).

### *Neighbourhood educational houses in a civil society*

Hedley Beare, Emeritus Professor at the University of Melbourne and co-author of *Education for the Twenty-First Century* (Beare and Slaughter, 1993), invited readers to consider the opportunity to create a school on a green field site at the dawn of the third millennium, as part of a plan to establish a new community in that location. The development company has invited contributions on the topic. The situation is not hypothetical, because the situation he described did occur in late 1996. Beare's view of a 'break-the-mould school for the future' had all of the characteristics described thus far in Chapters 8 and 9. There was no doubt about 'a place called school', the core of which he described as a 'central education barn', much along the lines of the 'educational shopping mall' described by Andrew Bunting and John Wood in Chapter 8. It is a virtual school in the way that learning is not bound by place, time and style. He made a notable contribution in his description of 'neighbourhood educational houses' for young children, enriching the view of the home school movement now gaining momentum around the world. He described the conception and the constraints in the following terms:

> At the very least, the very youngest learners — toddlers and children — need somewhere in their own (or the next) street where they can physically go to access

programs; to learn with other groups of learners; to interact physically with their 'teachers', 'tutors', counsellors, coordinating educators; to access richer learning materials than those they have online from their own home; and also to develop an identification with their neighbourhood 'storage house of learning'. The same holds true of learners of all ages. . . . The problem which educational authorities have always faced is that when neighbourhood buildings are put up and labelled 'primary school', their use becomes limited, they are reserved for only some learners, they become identified by age, territoriality sets in, and they are no longer considered a community or common resource. Furthermore, there is no guarantee in a mobile society that we can predict accurately how permanent they need to be or how many rooms or spaces need to be provided. (Beare, 1997, p. 6)

This account contains some important insights. First, that the neighbourhood educational house is not an isolated learning centre. There are several and they are networked, and the issues of access and equity can be partly resolved in this manner. Beare is explicit in his idea that children who may have limited resources in their house can find richer opportunities in others. Second, there is the constraining influence of an educational authority. His explanation may partly account for why the home school movement was resistant to plans in Western Australia to formally define home schooling as part of the public education system in the new Education Act proposed in 1997. Third, not referred to in this account, but implicit, concerns the transition to formal schooling. Imagine a child who has been part of a network of neighbourhood educational houses from a very early age then being required to attend the local primary school that is conducted on traditional lines. High levels of alienation can be expected if the school cannot accommodate the high level of learning across a range of intelligences, with extensive use of information technology, utilizing a style of learning that may have involved small teams.

Two further observations may be made about this account of neighbourhood learning houses. One is that their effectiveness is not necessarily restricted by the socio-economic status of the community in which they are found, assuming that within a very short time, most homes will have the basic technology. There need only be a few such homes to provide a network of learning centres in this style. The other is in some ways the most important of all. What Hedley Beare described was an outstanding example of the third-sector, the development of which holds the key to cohesion in the 'civil society' advocated by Jeremy Rifkin, as summarized in Chapter 7.

Neighbourhood educational houses can, however, be established at the direction and with the support of a school authority. An example is the Foshay Learning Centre, a K–12 public school in Los Angeles. Foshay set up eight satellite learning centres in low-income apartment complexes across the city so that, without leaving the building, students can obtain assistance with homework, gain knowledge and skill in technology and participate in enriched learning activities. Consistent with the concept of the virtual school, Cynthia Amos, program coordinator for Foshay's satellite project, observed that 'School is anywhere the equipment is . . . We're trying to show the kids that you can learn anywhere' (cited in Zehr, 1997, p. 36).

*Learning cultures for the virtual school*

Peter Ellyard is Executive Director of a Melbourne-based company, Preferred Futures. He is a former Executive Director of the Commission for the Future in Australia. He wrote a scenario for education in 2010 defined by a learning culture that contained eight elements (Ellyard, 1997). A 'virtual school' can be defined in terms of these eight elements.

- Life Long Learning that reflects a view that learning would have to become 'a pleasurable activity again' because 'We had grown up with the idea that most of our education occurred early in life during the period of compulsory education. Under these circumstances we could force-feed learning into often unwilling consumers. This was education as a factory'. (p. 1)

- Learner Driven Learning that applies to learning beyond the years of puberty, utilizing learning technologies with the aid of teachers and mentors.

- Just-in-Time Learning, explained earlier in connection with g4: great teaching and globalization, based on flexibility so that the best learning opportunities can be created when interest and motivation are at their peak.

- Customized Learning because 'modern technology enables us to package learning modules to suit people with different thinking and learning preferred styles . . . In this way the quality of learning has been dramatically improved for many people who were disadvantaged by the old system because their thinking and learning preferences were not fully catered for'. (p. 2)

- Transformative Learning, reflecting a commitment that transforms attitudes, values and beliefs, including higher aspirations and expectations for self and society.

- Collaborative Learning, utilizing learning technologies that shifted from highly individualistic modes in the 1980s to those that allowed teams at the same location or at different locations, indeed whole communities, to learn together.

- Contextual Learning, accepting that 'learning is most effective if it occurs in an environment which makes the learning relevant . . . to the experience and expectations of the learner'. (p. 3)

- Learning to Learn

Such a learning culture is evident in one program at Melbourne Grammar School. This program is titled the Virtual School for the Gifted and was established by Lynne Kelly, head of Information Technology. It was not designed to replace conventional schooling but to complement it by providing web-based learning for gifted students on topics as varied as humour, fractals, existentialism and quirky physics. Indeed, 10 such subjects were offered in 1997, each of which ran for 10 weeks for a maximum of 15–20 students. Student accounts of their experience highlighted the Customized Learning element in the Ellyard list above, for some had less than happy experiences in previous schools or preferred to learn in this mode with a like-minded group.

## Strategic Intention for Schools
### The Human Dimensions of Schooling for the Knowledge Society

1   Schools will establish a richer range of professionals to work with and support teachers, with many of these located on site but, increasingly in some respects, more will be located in other places as the best services are located and made available to meet the needs of all students.

2   Teachers will have access to the best resources to support their work, with many of these accessed from CD-ROM and the internet, being assisted by learning resource specialists who locate and advise on sources, and help with financial and other arrangements to protect intellectual capital.

3   Students, teachers and other professionals will increasingly work in teams, reflecting a pattern that is widely evident in workplace arrangements in other fields, with many parallels for professionals in education and medicine.

4   Schools will expand their policies and practices for the pastoral care of students, given the high expectations for all to succeed and, especially, as learning is dispersed, for schools will maintain their duty of care and will require cyber-policy on care in virtual schools.

5   Pastoral care for teachers will be important given the shift to the 'new professionalism' and major changes in roles, responsibilities and account-abilities, with professional development, individually and in teams, being one element in the strategy.

6   Issues of access and equity will be addressed in school cyber-policy, with a range of strategies including the sharing of resources among schools; partnerships with the private sector for donations and subsidies; and the creation of community-based learning centres.

7   A strategic approach will be taken to the adoption of new learning technology, taking account of the time required for training, encouraging creative approaches to utilizing and sharing such technology as it comes to hand, and setting targets for universal access.

8   Virtual schooling will be a reality at every stage of schooling, but there will still be a place called school, with approaches to virtual schooling including neighbourhood educational houses, especially for the very young.

9   Lifelong learning centres that include schools will be the symbolic if not the physical centre of some communities, being the outcome of comprehensive planning by a consortium of public and private interests.

10  New cultures for learning will take hold in schools for the knowledge society, complementing such widely accepted concepts as 'lifelong learning' with approaches such as 'just-in-time learning' that allows state-of-the-art approaches to learning and teaching to be designed and delivered at short notice in any setting for all learners.

# Chapter 10

# Leadership and Management for Schools of the Third Millennium

How shall leaders and managers of schools and school systems go about their work as change proceeds at the dawn of the third millennium?

In *The Self-Managing School* (Caldwell and Spinks, 1988) the focus was on management, with an annual cycle of goal-setting, policy-making, planning, budgeting, implementing (learning and teaching and the support of learning and teaching) and evaluation. Leadership was addressed to the extent that this management cycle was one means by which a shared vision for the school could be given expression, and the formation of that vision was seen as an important responsibility of leaders.

More attention was given to leadership in *Leading the Self-Managing School* (Caldwell and Spinks, 1992) because by this time, schools and school systems were in the midst of sweeping change and being able to set, articulate and build support for a vision was more important than ever, as was a capacity to energize members of the school community to make that change effective. Four dimensions of transformational leadership were proposed on the basis of observations in successful systems of self-managing schools: cultural leadership, strategic leadership, educational leadership, and responsive leadership. As for management, the annual cycle was as important as ever, but a capacity for strategic management became a high priority for those who sought senior positions in schools. A charter was proposed as a means of bringing coherence to system and school priorities. Multi-year development planning was also important to set and reset priorities in an increasingly turbulent time.

These approaches to leadership and management are as important as the decade draws to a close as they were at the time of publication. Chapter 10 is concerned with what is required to lead and manage 'beyond the self-managing school', in a period where the focus on learning outcomes is unrelenting and momentum is building for the creation of schools that are well suited to a knowledge society.

The first part of the chapter is devoted to strategy, but the perspective is much broader than strategic planning which is now just one choice in a repertoire of approaches to strategic management. Working strategically is seen as a continuous activity, rather than a periodic effort after which attention fades and people get on with things. The concepts of 'strategic thinking', 'strategic intention' and 'strategic conversation' are helpful. The final part of the chapter is devoted to leadership and, given the stresses and strains of the workplace, it is a more reflective, indeed emotional view of leadership than was provided in the first two books, consistent with David Loader's approach in *The Inner Principal* (Loader, 1997).

## Strategy Formation in Times of Turbulence

School leaders, like their counterparts in other fields of endeavour in the public and private sectors, have invested time and effort over the last decade in developing a capacity for strategic planning. Before that, doing a good job with annual planning, with perhaps a longer term for a major building program, was considered sufficient, and in the main it was. The rise of strategic planning coincided with appreciation of the manner in which external forces impacted organizations in education, and the now familiar SWOT analysis (of strengths, weaknesses, opportunities and threats) became routine. This capacity was enhanced with computer-based management information systems. Having a three-year strategic plan was a necessary achievement for management in the 1990s. Governments encouraged it, with triennial funding arrangements for some publicly funded enterprises.

As the decade draws to a close, it seems increasingly difficult to prepare a strategic plan, some might say any plan, given the turbulence and uncertainty in the external environment. In some instances, governments have retreated from a commitment to triennial funding. One senses that some leaders in education see little point in committing time and effort to strategic planning under these conditions. Others, having recently developed their capacities in this area, may experience a feeling of guilt that they cannot or have not produced a strategic plan for their organization.

In the midst of this turbulence, uncertainty, hesitation and guilt, leaders and managers must position their institutions for success in the future, for that is the essence of their work. Some core concepts are helpful in gaining an understanding of what is involved. In the pages that follow, strategic leadership is defined, with strategic thinking proposed as the underpinning generic skill. Then follows a model developed by Max Boisot that demonstrates a repertoire of responses that organizations may adopt in times of turbulence, these being the conditions that are likely to face schools in the foreseeable future. Strategic planning, seen as an important capacity in the late 1980s and early 1990s, is still important, but only under certain conditions. The pre-eminent capacity is strategic intent, viewed by Boisot as 'the distinguishing mark of the learning organization' (Boisot, 1995, p. 41).

### Strategic Leadership

De Pree (1990, p. 1) proposed that 'The first requirement of a leader is to define reality.' This suggests a pre-eminent capacity for strategic leadership in schools, defined in operational terms as:

- keeping abreast of trends and issues, threats and opportunities in the school environment and in society at large, nationally and internationally; discerning the 'megatrends' and anticipating their impact on education generally and on the school in particular;

- sharing their knowledge with others in the school's community and encouraging other school leaders to do the same in their areas of interest;

- establishing structures and processes which enable the school to set priorities and formulate strategies which take account of likely and/or preferred futures; being a key source of expertise as these occur;

- ensuring that the attention of the school community is focused on matters of strategic importance; and

- monitoring the implementation of strategies as well as emerging strategic issues in the wider environment; facilitating an ongoing process of review.

(Caldwell and Spinks, 1992, p. 92)

### Strategic Thinking

A capacity for strategic thinking is the essence of strategic leadership, defined by Garratt (1995, p. 2) in the following terms:

> 'Strategic thinking' is the process by which an organization's direction-givers can rise above the daily managerial processes and crises to gain different perspectives of the internal and external dynamics causing change in their environment and thereby giving more effective direction to their organization. Such perspectives should be both future-oriented *and* historically understood. Strategic thinkers must have the skills of looking both forwards and backwards while knowing where their organization is now, so that wise risks can be taken by the direction-givers to achieve their organization's purpose, or political will, while avoiding having to repeat the mistakes of the past.

 For Mintzberg (1995), 'strategic thinking' is 'seeing': seeing ahead, seeing behind, seeing above, seeing below, seeing beside, seeing beyond, and above all, seeing it through.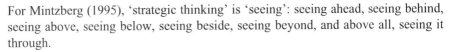

### Strategic Management

Max Boisot is Professor of Strategic Management at ESADE in Barcelona and Senior Associate at the Judge Institute of Management Studies at the University of Cambridge. He provided a helpful classification of management responses in the exercise of strategic leadership (Boisot, 1995). As illustrated in Figure 10.1, there are four, namely, emergent strategy, strategic planning, intrapreneurship and strategic intent. Which are possible and appropriate depends on the level of turbulence

Figure 10.1   A model for strategic management

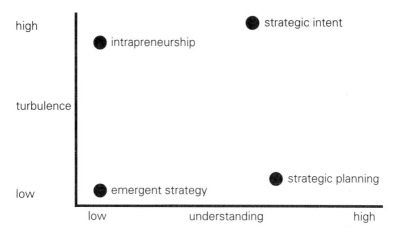

Source: Boisot, 1995

in an organization's environment ('turbulence') and the capacity of the organization to extract and process useful information from that environment ('understanding'). If used appropriately, these provide a repertoire of responses for strategic manage-ment in the learning organization.

- When turbulence and understanding are low, an *emergent strategy* is all that may be possible and hence is appropriate, being an 'incremental adjust-ment to environmental states that cannot be discerned or anticipated through a prior analysis of data' (Boisot, 1995, p. 34, based on Mintzberg). These are not the conditions that face schools at this time.

- When turbulence is low and understanding is high, *strategic planning* is possible and appropriate, being the setting of medium- to long-term plans on the basis of an environmental scan. These were the conditions that faced schools until about the mid-1990s but they are fast receding. ('The thinking that underpins strategic planning is a legacy of more stable times when the environment was changing sufficiently slowly for an effective corporate response to emerge from methodical organizational routines' (Boisot, 1995, p. 33).

- When turbulence is high and understanding is low, '*intrapreneurship*' may be appropriate (a similar concept to 'entrepreneurship' except that it is carried out within the organization). Intrapreneurship is an approach to management that encourages individual initiative when it is not possible to formulate a coherent and integrated organizational response. Some efforts may pay off and be incorporated later in an organization-wide strategy. For schools, intrapreneurship may be appropriate, for example, for some devel-opments in information technology.

- When turbulence is high and understanding is high, *strategic intent* is the desirable response, described and contrasted by Boisot in the following terms:

> Strategic intent describes a process of coping with turbulence through a direct, intuitive understanding, emanating from the top of a firm [school] and guiding its efforts. A turbulent environment cannot be tamed by rational analysis alone so that conventional strategic planning is deemed to be of little use. Yet it does not follow that a firm's [school's] adaptive response must be left to a random distribution of lone individuals acting opportunistically and often in isolation as in a regime of intrapreneurship. Strategic intent relies on an intuitively formed pattern or *gestalt* — some would call it a vision — to give it unity and coherence. (Boisot, 1995, p. 36)

In the opinion of Boisot (1995, p. 41) strategic intent is 'the distinguishing mark of the learning organization and, by implication, an essential component of its strategic repertoire'. This should be the case for schools in the third millennium, faced with a level of turbulence that is unprecedented. Leaders and managers ought to strive for a level of understanding of their environment, and develop a capacity for acquiring and processing information that will ensure a timely and effective response in any circumstance.

## Strategic Management in Action

The model in Figure 10.1 may be readily applied in the management of strategy for further change on Tracks 2 and 3. In the case of Track 2 in the area of literacy, for example, turbulence is now relatively low, since there is broad acceptance that something needs to be done, and there is a relatively high level of understanding of what is required. Schools have the means of measuring student achievement, and states and nations are setting targets, evidenced in 1998 in Britain, where each local education authority was given a target as part of a national strategy for having 80 per cent of 11-year-olds achieve standard by 2002. Schools were also required to set targets. More important, however, the level of knowledge about what needs to be done to raise levels of achievement is higher than it has ever been. This places schools and school systems in the bottom right quadrant of Figure 10.1, and it is possible to make strategic plans for the medium- to long-term to achieve targets. This was the expectation for all schools.

In the drive on Track 3 to create schools for the knowledge society that involve new learning technologies, it may not be possible to make strategic plans because the environment is highly turbulent and the level of understanding about what needs to be done at the school level is relatively low in many settings. This situation is defined by the top left quadrant in Figure 10.1, which calls for intrapreneurship. In this situation, leaders and managers ought to be encouraging many staff to try new approaches and to take risks. The outcomes are monitored, and always rewarded, with the aim being to settle on an approach that suits the school. With the knowledge gained from the effort, the context shifts from top left to top right, allowing the school to formulate strategic intentions, or if there is some measure of stability in the setting, it shifts to the bottom right, in which case strategic planning for implementation can proceed.

Given the level of turbulence associated with continuing change on all three tracks, the aim of those with responsibility at the school level is to gain as much knowledge as possible to formulate strategic intentions. It is hoped that this book has explored these tracks to a sufficient degree to guide the formation of such intents. The authors have suggested 10 strategic intentions at the end of each chapter as an indication of their strategic thinking on these matters.

### The Art of Strategic Conversation

The generic skill in these matters is strategic thinking, defined earlier in the chapter, with Mintzberg's (1995) refreshingly straightforward explanation: seeing ahead, seeing behind, seeing above, seeing below, seeing beside, seeing beyond, and above all, seeing it through. This suggests that strategic thinking should be a continuous activity on the part of leaders and managers and, for this reason, it should be given expression. The concept of 'strategic conversation' is helpful in this regard.

Larry Hirschhorn is wary of formalizing planning processes, at least in the early stages: 'High-stakes strategic issues stimulate executives to use more formal planning methods. These methods, in turn, create more superficial and less meaningful decisions' (Hirschhorn, 1997, p. 123). The alternative is strategic conversation:

> In this context, I believe that executives must learn to have what I call 'strategic conversations' with one another and with their subordinates. Such conversations, while supported by data and by rigorous thinking . . . should be as freewheeling as possible. (Hirschhorn, 1997, pp. 123–4)

Kees van der Heijden (1996) refers to scenario formulation, a key tool in strategic management, as strategic conversation and subtitled his book accordingly: *Scenarios: The Art of Strategic Conversation.* For van der Heijden, strategic planning is actually a tool in strategic conversation, with the aim of the latter being to create a shared view about the direction of the organization:

> If action is based on planning on the basis of a mental model, then institutional action must be based on a shared mental model. Only through a process of conversation can elements of observation and thought be structured and embedded in the accepted and shared organizational theories-in-use. Similarly new perceptions of opportunities and threats based on the reflection on experiences obtained in

the environment can only become institutional property through conversation. An effective strategic conversation must incorporate a wide range of initially unstructured thoughts and views, and out of this create shared interpretations of the world in which the majority of individual insights can find a logical place. (van der Heijden, 1996, pp. 41–2)

Professor Kwong Lee Dow, Dean of Education at the University of Melbourne from 1978 to 1998 modelled the art of leading a strategic conversation at his weekly senior management meetings with Heads of Departments and Associate Deans. There was rarely an agenda, but always a set of data about one trend or another, or a collection of newspaper or journal articles about a particular development. Most senior staff play key roles in various policy-related matters, either within the university or in the wider educational community. Several are consultants in major reform. The meeting was an opportunity for insights to be shared, common understandings to be reached, strategic intentions to be formed, debates to be conducted and progress to be monitored. It was freewheeling, just as Hirschhorn states that it should be, and it incorporated unstructured thoughts and views, out of which came shared interpretations, just as van der Heijden proposes.

This leadership style has served the Faculty of Education well, with several significant changes in direction along the way. There have been amalgamations and downsizing, major programs added and major programs wound out, innovations have been nurtured and scaled-up, or set aside if feasibility had not been established. Each of the approaches in Boisot's repertoire of strategic responses is evident in these changes in direction. Lee Dow has been a key person in setting strategic directions in school education and has led major inquiries for governments of all persuasion during his time as Dean. The challenge facing this Faculty of Education is not only to support schools and other enterprises in education and training, as they make the journey along the three tracks considered in this book, but also to succeed as it makes progress on parallel tracks in higher education.

Figure 10.2 suggests a relationship between some of the key concepts referred to thus far. For a school wishing to thrive in a climate of continuing change, it needs first a decision to act. It needs a capacity for strategic thinking that should be widely dispersed and utilized in a range of structures and processes in which various strategic conversations are conducted. The style of Kwong Lee Dow at the University of Melbourne is an example of how a strategic conversation can be conducted in one setting, namely, the structures and processes of a regular senior management meeting. An outcome of strategic conversation may be the selection of an appropriate response. The environment may be stable enough, and information of action may be understandable enough, for strategic plans to be formulated immediately. On the other hand, the level of turbulence may be so high that the school ought to form clear strategic intentions and proceed on that basis or, alternatively, some intrapreneurial effort might be encouraged (described as 'strategic creativity' in Figure 10.2). As suggested in the figure, there can be some interaction among the elements. Action will follow and outcomes will be secured, yielding data that can inform further strategic conversations in the future.

Figure 10.2    *Strategic conversation at the heart of strategic management*

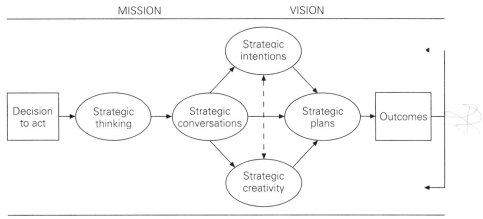

Figure 10.2 also illustrates how these events should be framed by the mission and vision of the school, with a cultural foundation in the values and philosophy of the school. There should also be a sense of 'time as a stream' in these activities, reflecting Garratt's view, cited earlier in the chapter, that strategic thinking 'should be both future-oriented and historically understood' (Garratt, 1995, p. 2).

Brian Caldwell employed the notion of strategic conversation when invited to contribute to a meeting of staff at Cabra Dominican College, a large and successful co-educational school in a suburb of Adelaide in South Australia. The event was part of a continuous process of considering the future of the college. The notion of strategic conversation seemed to suit the occasion. The Vision Statement provided a ready frame of reference to anchor that conversation in the past, present and future:

> Cabra Dominican College, as a Christian community in the Catholic tradition [past], strives to nurture and develop the unique gifts of individuals, to liberate them in the search for truth [present], and to empower them to create a better world [future].

The school also has a vision for learning that sits well with the needs of 'a civil society' (see Rifkin, 1996, in Chapter 7), and the learning culture suited to the knowledge society (see culture proposed by Ellyard, 1997, summarized in Chapter 9):

> As students move through Cabra Dominican College we believe their learning should be essentially four-fold.
>
> • They should learn to learn — to develop the motivation and resources to be learning for their own learning.

- They should learn to give — to develop a sense of responsibility, a concern for the welfare of others and a desire to give of their gifts.

- They should learn to stand — to build strong foundations for their behaviour and a code of ethics by which to live . . . a desire for discipline.

- They should learn to fly — to develop a spirit of inquiry and adventure, a desire to explore, have visions, reach out, take off . . . a desire for freedom.

The strategic conversation at Cabra lasted a morning, commencing with a presentation on the three tracks for change, followed by freewheeling conversations among groups of staff, who shared insights and laid the groundwork for the next stage in this continuous process.

Particularly engaging is the learning culture at Cabra that highlights empowerment and the view that students 'should learn to fly'. The challenge for staff at Cabra, as in all schools, is for staff to model this behaviour for their students. To do so will surely ensure success in the journey on Track 3.

### Leadership and the Heroic Quest 'Beyond the Self-Managing School'

There is much being written to help gain an understanding of what is occurring in society at the dawn of the third millennium, and why this understanding can empower the school leader. Some of these books proved helpful in Chapter 7 in establishing the role of schools in the knowledge society. They deal with the bigger picture in an external sense. They are concerned with major societal change and implications for the tasks of leadership.

There are other books that also deal with the larger picture, but dwell on the inner life of the leader. They give a sense of the scale of the heroic quest in leading 'beyond the self-managing school'.

The starting point is the notion of the psychic prison, choosing the allegory of shadows on the wall in Plato's cave. Attention is then given to the paradox that the more successful one is, the more one is in jeopardy. This is the Icarus paradox. Gareth Morgan's classic writing on *Images of Organizations* (Morgan, 1997) deals with the allegory and the paradox. The notion of 'the heroic quest' is then introduced with reference to Joseph Jaworski's eloquent account of a personal journey in *Synchronicity: The Inner Path of Leadership* (Jaworski, 1996). The same themes are given focus in David Loader's remarkable account of *The Inner Principal* (Loader, 1997), which places the emphasis four-square on the principalship in an era of change.

### *Plato's Cave*

Gareth Morgan uses the image of Plato's cave to describe the challenge faced by leaders in understanding the new realities (Morgan, 1997). He is referring here to Socrates' allegory in Plato's *The Republic* in which the reader is encouraged to imagine people chained to the wall of an underground cave. Outside the cave is a fire, behind which people go about their various activities, making sounds and moving objects. The cave dwellers can only see the shadows of these movements on the wall in front of them, and they try to make sense of their cause and their relationship to the sounds.

Morgan uses this allegory to suggest that organizations become 'psychic prisons', in which 'organizations and their members become trapped by constructions of reality that, at best, give an imperfect grasp of the world' (Morgan, 1997, p. 216). In school education, it is relatively easy to become trapped in this manner, leaving little opportunity to be directly involved in or gain a deep understanding of the wider work place locally, let alone globally. The forces shaping the transformation of society have led to the most dramatic change in the nature of work since the industrial revolution, developments which can, quite understandably, appear like the shadows on the wall of Plato's cave.

Another part of Socrates' allegory concerns what might occur if one of the prisoners in the cave manages to escape and leave the cave, to see and understand exactly what is happening out there. Should that person return to the cave, he or she could never live the same way again and, should they share what was discovered with fellow prisoners, it is likely that they would be ridiculed if not rejected for their efforts. Is this not the way some leaders have changed, and been received on return, when they have the opportunity to experience at first hand what is occurring outside the world of school education, or when they had the opportunity to travel widely and frequently, or when they had the good fortune to engage in an extended and challenging professional development program?

The implication for the school leader is to seek out ways to escape the 'psychic prison' and provide every opportunity for colleagues to do the same. Globalization, the knowledge society, the information revolution, the re-engineering of the public service, standards driven reform, and the new world of work will not be seen as shadows on the wall, opposite which one sits chained and powerless. All should be unchained and empowered to engage with the realities of the remarkable events that are taking place at the dawn of the third millennium.

### The Icarus Paradox

Morgan (1997, p. 217) draws on *The Icarus Paradox* (Miller, 1990) to show that, over time, the strengths of organizations may become weaknesses, leading eventually to their downfall. Icarus was the figure in Greek mythology whose artificial wax wings enabled him to fly so high as to come close to the sun. The wax melted and he plunged to his death.

The reader is challenged here to reflect on the extraordinary success of public schools that served so well over more than a century. In Australia, they enabled the nation to make its way in the world, even after advantages through the era of gold strikes and the ride on the sheep's back had run their course. This country is now exposed to the competition of a global economy and the need to restructure the world of work to keep pace. International comparisons of educational achievement and approaches to learning and teaching are becoming increasingly intense, as evidenced in the Third International Mathematics and Science Study. With the Icarus paradox, what served the nation so well with schools in the past may not stand the heat in the demands of the knowledge society and a global economy. The image provides no answers but, like Plato's cave, one is challenged to gain an understanding of the forces that are transforming society and their impact on schools.

### Synchronicity

Joseph Jaworski borrowed the concept of synchronicity from psychologist Carl Jung to describe a phenomenon of central importance in leadership. Synchronicity is 'a meaningful coincidence of two or more events, where something other than the probability of chance is involved' (cited by Jaworski, 1996, p. ix).

In the countries referred to in this book, there was a happy conjunction between the creation of systems of public schools and the developmental needs of each nation. In a sense, this is synchronicity on a grand scale, being the successful coincidence of organizational form and national need. Jaworski explored such possibilities for organizations and other collectivities but was concerned mainly with a personal journey for leaders. He sees this as the heroic quest, not in an exclusive or hierarchical sense, but more along the lines portrayed so well in Joseph Campbell's landmark book *The Hero with a Thousand Faces* (Campbell, 1988) and subsequent television series.

Campbell (1988, pp. 245–6) presented an archetype or template of the hero's journey to which Jaworski gives personal testimony in his own work in establishing the American Leadership Forum, and which can be a guide to all. In simple terms, this journey is characterized by a call to adventure, with perhaps an initial refusal of that call; the availability of a guide; crossing the threshold of adventure; the tests and trials that occur along the way; those who give support to the effort; perhaps a supreme ordeal leading to a sense of exultation or personal apotheosis; a return from that adventure; and finally, success and satisfaction, for self and others, being the gift of elixir (Jaworski, 1996, p. 89).

Dimmock and O'Donoghue (1997) provided accounts of life histories of successful school principals. Each had characteristics of the heroic quest, with success built around work that pervaded the new role of the principal (values, vision, goal setting, goal achievement).

Synchronicity occurs when in the course of the heroic quest one is presented with and accepts the opportunities that seem to appear with greater probability than chance alone. Every reader will readily identify instances where such events have occurred in their own journeys. They were evident in the life histories recounted by Dimmock and O'Donoghue.

Peter Senge has done more than any other to develop the notion of 'the learning organization' (Senge, 1990). He wrote the introduction to Jaworski's book and included these thoughts about leadership that appear to have direct application to the role of the school leader in the journey along the tracks for change in a new era for schools:

> Leadership exists when people are no longer victims of circumstances but participate in creating new circumstances . . . It's not about positional power; it's not about accomplishments; it's ultimately not even about what we do. Leadership is about creating a domain in which human beings continually deepen their understanding of reality and become more capable of participating in the unfolding of the world. Leadership is about creating new realities. (Senge, 1996, p. 3)

Senge believes that all are 'wrestling with the profound changes required in public and institutional leadership in the twenty-first century . . . [in which] . . . Our life-long experiences with hierarchy cast a long shadow, making it difficult for us to think outside the framework of hierarchical leadership' (Senge, 1996, p. 4). For leaders in schools in the public sector, this is the challenge of leadership in the self-managing school and beyond the self-managing school; for those who set out on an adventure in greater autonomy, outside the frameworks that have served so well in the past but may melt away in the heat of change ('the Icarus paradox'). This is the challenge of leadership that seeks to escape the 'psychic prison'. For principals of all schools, public and private, this is the challenge of leadership that seeks to create the new realities of schooling that will emerge in the third millennium.

### The Inner Principal

The inner path of leadership is described in engaging fashion by David Loader in *The Inner Principal* (Loader, 1997). David Loader is principal of Australia's largest private school, Wesley College in Melbourne, but is best known internationally as Principal of Methodist Ladies College, also in Melbourne, from 1978 to 1996. References have been made to MLC at several points in *Beyond the Self-Managing School*. It is possible that this school has accepted the challenge of information technology to a greater degree than any other school, nationally or internationally, with more than 2,000 of about 2,200 students having their own laptop computers. Virtually every aspect of schooling, for students and teachers, has been transformed. For his role in this transformation, David Loader is widely recognized as an outstanding strategic thinker in school education.

These are the external accomplishments in the leadership of David Loader. He has helped create the 'the new realities' of schooling for MLC, in the style of leadership set out by Senge (1996, p. 3, cited above). In *The Inner Principal*, he has written about his personal journey. His chapter on 'The Stumble Principal' harmonizes with Jaworski's concept of synchronicity, for Loader recounts the way he literally stumbled on opportunities that then became the new realities.

In one of the most insightful chapters, Loader draws on Coelho's modern fable to describe 'The Alchemist Principal' (based on Coelho, 1993). This fable concerns a boy named Santiago who travels the world seeking the treasure of his dreams. It is an adventure remarkably like the heroic quest described by Joseph Campbell.

There is the call to adventure, the guides along the way, the tests and trials, even a supreme ordeal where death seemed imminent, and a return, quite literally, to his home, where he finds the treasure beneath his feet. Santiago reflects on his heroic quest: 'It's true; life is generous to those who pursue their destiny' (Coelho, 1993, p. 176). The power of synchronicity prevailed, for 'Where you stumble, there your treasure lies' (Joseph Campbell cited by Jaworski, 1996, p. 119).

### Completing the Journey

A review of change in education around the world suggested that three different movements were under way. The image of a 'track' was invoked, because the three movements were occurring at the same time in most places, but schools, school systems and nations vary in the distance they have travelled down each track. Movement was viewed in this book as a 'journey'. Leadership is also a journey, as much internal as external, as illustrated in David Loader's book and the fable of Santiago.

The Chapter concludes with reflections on journeys undertaken by the authors. In an external sense, in respect to our work on self-managing schools, these journeys were recounted in Chapter 2. In an internal sense, in respect to our views about leadership, we decided to reflect on the most recent journeys we had undertaken, prior to completing the book in early 1998. We posed the question 'What did these experiences mean for us in our personal journeys to gain an understanding of leadership and learning in a new era for schools?' Brian Caldwell went to France. Jim Spinks went to Antarctica.

### *The Little Way (Brian Caldwell)*

In late 1997, I spent a week at the International Institute for Educational Planning in Paris, working with a cross-country team to write a book on needs-based formula-funding for self-managing schools. At the end of the week I spent a day in the country-side, visiting the little town of Lisieux near the Normandy coast, west of Paris.

Thérèse Martin was born in 1873, entered a Carmelite convent in Lisieux in 1888, aged 15, and died of tuberculosis in 1897, aged 24. She left a few letters and three exercise books containing reflections on her short life. Apart from a pilgrim-age to Rome to seek the permission of Pope Leo III to become a Carmelite at such a young age, she did not travel outside the towns and villages of Normandy.

Her journals were gathered together and published as a book in 1898 under the title *Story of A Soul.* By 1910, the first steps to canonization were taken. She became a saint in 1925. She is Patron Saint of Universal Missions, along with Saint Francis Xavier. She is Second Patron Saint of France and Second Patron Saint of Australia. In 1997, 100 years after her death, she was declared by Pope John Paul II to be a Doctor of the Church, joining 34 others, only two of whom were women (Saint Teresa of Avila and Saint Catherine of Siena).

This is an astonishing story of one who died so young and who had such a limited range of life experiences. How can this be explained? Gaucher (1997, p. 14) wrote that 'Her incomparable contribution to twentieth-century spirituality was a return to the Gospel in its purest form.' 'The little way' has often been used to describe her spirituality, as set out so simply and clearly in *Story of a Soul*, now translated into more than 60 languages and dialects.

In reflecting on 'the little way', the parallel in education lies in the importance of the most fundamental act of all, learning, and creating the conditions under which this can be nurtured for all. Every structure and every process exists to support this outcome. Schooling, like spirituality, has been made extraordinarily complex at times, and a multitude of rules and regulations often constrain rather than empower. If there is to be success for all in both domains, the journey must start on 'the little way'.

Saint Thérèse of Lisieux had an extraordinary capacity to understand the state of her own soul and, at the same time, discern the universal condition. She had high expectations for her own saintly role in these matters. The parallel for leaders in education is very much the principal theme in this chapter, namely, the importance of discovering self and discovering strategy in making the journey beyond the self-managing school.

### The Far Side (Jim Spinks)

In early 1998, I fulfilled a lifelong dream. I joined Antarctica Australis, an expedition to visit a series of bases and enjoy the wildlife of eastern Antarctica, aptly known as 'The Far Side'. Adventurers from all walks of life numbered 108, joining the captain and crew of the Russian icebreaker Kapitan Khlebnikov, with scientists from Australia and chefs from Austria. Expedition leader was Australian Greg Mortimer, one of the world's foremost mountaineers and Antarctic adventurers.

The goals of the expedition included new insights into the lives of whales, seals and birds, and understanding of glaciology, geology and the history of Antarctic exploration. There was also a focus on the future of Antarctica and preservation values.

Critical to our learning was gaining an understanding of the past, present and future of Antarctica. This was indelibly symbolized by the patron of Antarctica Australis, Dr Phillip Law, who was appointed the first director of the Australian Antarctic Division in 1947, continuing until 1966, during which time he made 28 visits to the Antarctic, established three stations on the Antarctic Continent and led expeditions that explored 3000 miles of Antarctic Coast. At 82, his physical and mental prowess continue to be extraordinary. He not only lent his name and reputation to our quest, but actually accompanied the expedition, and thrilled us with his knowledge, insights and reminiscences.

A journey to Antarctica remains one of the last great journeys on Earth. Departing from Fremantle in Western Australia, a course of 220° was set and maintained for 10 days before reaching Mawson Base on the Antarctic Continent. This involved crossing the 'roaring forties', 'furious fifties' and 'screaming sixties'.

All faced the prospect of violent storms with trepidation, most being well versed in journals from the past. Our fears were not realized due to advanced technology and strategic thinking on the part of the captain and crew. Satellite communications delivered exceedingly accurate weather charts. This enabled the captain to vary speed to allow storm centres to pass, either to South or North, with the ship always remaining in calm seas, a far cry from Cook's voyage in 1770 and Law's exploration in the 1950s.

Antarctica begins, ends, and is, ice. It is a totally foreign environment for humans. It was exciting to contemplate working in this environment, but also experiencing Greg Mortimer's leadership in pursuing our goals. By the time of arrival at the frozen continent, it was evident that the group consisted mostly of people who were leaders in their own everyday lives. Their capacities, aspirations, experiences and personalities differed widely, but they were all leaders who expected to fulfil a range of agendas. Add to this the potential hostility of the frozen environment and an exceptional leader was clearly required.

It was a pleasure to observe Greg Mortimer in action. All goals were achieved, both group and personal, many risks were taken, no one suffered any physical harm, and no egos were dented over a period of 25 days. Greg Mortimer's leadership was visionary, strategic, inspirational and expert. It was underpinned by attention to the basics: knowing everyone by their first names by the second day, extraordinary accuracy in judging the capacities of individuals, appropriately challenging each to excel, and sharing the wonder of discovery. It was a privilege to experience the last continent on Earth; it was equally a privilege to experience great leadership.

In reflecting on the experience, some parallels with the challenge of achieving success for all students from all backgrounds are striking. An alliance of international expertise was assembled. Past, present and future were linked in seamless fashion. A state-of-the-art ship and the latest information and communications technology ensured that ice floes were broken, storms were avoided, and calm waters were attained. In addition to being visionary and strategic, leadership focused on the needs and aspirations of each individual, with high expectations for all and celebration of the outcomes. What was a heroic quest for a few in the past is now success for all. Why not for leadership and learning in schools.

### Strategic Intentions for Schools
### Leadership, Management and the Heroic Quest in Learning

1 Leaders will create opportunities for themselves and their colleagues to gain knowledge and understanding of societal change and of the way schools will make a contribution to well-being in a civil society.

2 In all of these matters, the driving force and raison d'etre will be the provision of a quality education for every student, and every strategy and every intention will be weighed against this criterion.

3   Sound approaches to annual planning and longer-term strategic planning are prerequisites for successful school management but a wider range of approaches in matters related to strategy will be required to continue the journey 'beyond the self-managing school'.

4   A capacity for strategic thinking will be deeply embedded in a school, with a continuing strategic conversation the means by which shared understandings are developed as a prelude to formal planning.

5   There is a high level of turbulence in the environment for education and it will be difficult to make strategic plans in many matters so, under these circumstances, schools will form clear strategic intentions based on the best available information as the basis for action.

6   There will be recognition that sound strategy will take account of past, present and expected or preferred futures, so the effort will be framed by a commitment to take these into account in strategic management.

7   There will be a high level of harmony between learning, teaching and management cultures in the school, as illustrated by a commitment to empower the individual in all related matters, thus helping to create a better world.

8   Leaders will be aware that times of great success are also times of great risk, so they will work with all in the school community to search for, even stumble over, new opportunities to ensure high levels of performance in achieving the mission of the school.

9   There will be recognition that success in leadership in times of continuous and often turbulent change is as much a matter of discovering self as discovering strategy, so individually and collectively, there will be commitment to address the emotional well-being of the leadership team.

10  There will be commitment to leadership and management that views these as part of the heroic quest for learning in a civil society in which all in the school community are engaged and empowered.

*Strategic Intentions for Schools*

# Chapter 11

# Strategic Intentions for Schools

*The Self-Managing School* and *Leading the Self-Managing School* were intended to be guides to practice for leaders and managers in schools, as well as explorations of the theme of self-management on the basis of research and experience. Guides to practice in *Beyond the Self-Managing School* were presented in the form of 10 'strategic intentions' at the conclusion of each chapter.

The concept of 'strategic intention' is adapted from the work of Max Boisot, Professor of Strategic Management at ESADE in Barcelona, examined in more detail in Chapter 10.

> Strategic intention describes a process of coping with turbulence through a direct, intuitive understanding of what is occurring in an effort to guide the work of the school. A turbulent environment cannot be tamed by rational analysis alone so that conventional strategic planning is deemed to be of little use. Yet it does not follow that the school's response must be left to a random distribution of lone individuals acting opportunistically and often in isolation as in a regime of intrapreneurship. Strategic intention relies on an intuitively formed pattern or *gestalt* — some would call it a vision — to give it unity and coherence. (adapted from Boisot, 1995, p. 36)

Track 3 of change 'beyond the self-managing school' is organized in this book around the *gestalt*, described in an overview in Chapter 1 (Figure 1.1, p. 13) and explicated in Chapters 8 and 9. This *gestalt* helped the authors give 'unity and coherence' to their understanding of what is occurring.

Each chapter was intended as a contribution to the reader's efforts to gain an 'intuitive understanding' of what is occurring and its likely impact in their areas of interest. The 'strategic intentions' offered at the conclusion of each chapter are illustrative of the views of the authors as far as schools are concerned. Readers are invited to form their own.

The outcome is 100 'strategic intentions for schools' that are brought together in these final pages. It is hoped that they make a contribution to a successful journey 'beyond the self-managing school'.

### Track 1: Building Systems of Self-Managing Schools

*Tracks for Change (Chapter 1)*

1   Centrally determined frameworks of goals, policies, priorities, curriculum, standards and accountabilities will be strengthened.

2   More authority, responsibility and accountability will be decentralized to schools.

3   There will be unrelenting pressure to achieve high levels of learning outcomes for all students.

4   Schools will play an important role in the knowledge society and advances in technology will be central to this effort.

5   There will be a high level of coherence across areas of the curriculum, schools as workplaces will be transformed, the existing fabric of schools will be rendered obsolete, and globalization will be evident in learning and teaching.

6   A new concept of professionalism will emerge, based around necessary and unprecedentedly high levels of knowledge and skill.

7   A capacity to work in teams will be required in virtually every facet of professional practice.

8   Policies to address issues of access and equity will be required for the successful utilization of information and communications technology.

9   Virtual schooling will be a reality in every setting, but there will always be a place called school.

10  A continually updated 10 year time horizon will be necessary for every school to plan the journey along these tracks for change.

*Models for Self-Management (Chapter 2)*

11  Learning and teaching, and the support of learning and teaching, will be the starting point and the sole and continuing focus of effort in school leadership and management.

12  Schools will continue to need a basic model for self-management that shapes an annual cycle of goal-setting, policy-making, planning, budgeting, implementation (learning and teaching, and the support of learning and teaching), and program evaluation, with clearly defined roles for policy groups and program teams.

13  A basic model for self-management may be necessary but it is not sufficient, for success in times of continuing complexity and change will require a capacity for strategic management that includes priority setting and developmental planning within a multi-year timeframe.

14  Capacities for strategic leadership, cultural leadership, educational leadership and reflective leadership will be deeply embedded in the school.

15  The core task in strategic leadership will be to help build an understanding in the school community of the scale of social transformation now under way and its impact on the school.

16  The core task in cultural leadership will be to help build a school culture based around a commitment to excellence that values quality, effectiveness, equity and efficiency, and that recognizes and accepts the interdependence of these four elements.

17  The core task in educational leadership will be to help build the school as a learning community, in the fullest sense of that term, for all involved in learning and teaching, and the support of learning and teaching.

18  The core tasks in responsive leadership will be to build recognition that the 'right to know' about performance should be deeply embedded in the school and its community, and to develop a capacity to respond to needs and aspirations that arise from that knowledge.

19  Strategies based on a narrow reading of the need for school reform will be prone to failure.

20  There will be no 'one best way' as far as models for self-management are concerned; each school must design its own, based on situational factors that include mission and vision.

*Linking Self-Management to Learning Outcomes (Chapter 3)*

21  The primary purpose of self-management is to make a contribution to learning, so schools that aspire to success in this domain will make an unrelenting effort to utilize all of the capacities that accrue with self-management to achieve that end.

22  There will be clear, explicit and planned links, either direct or indirect, between each of the capacities that come with self-management and activities in the school that relate to learning and teaching and the support of learning and teaching.

23  There is a strong association between the mix and capacities of staff, and success in addressing needs and priorities in learning, so schools will develop a capacity to optimally select staff, taking account of these needs and priorities.

24  There is a strong association between the knowledge and skills of staff and learning outcomes for students, so schools will employ their capacity for self-management to design, select, implement or utilize professional development programs to help ensure these outcomes.

25  A feature of staff selection and professional development will be the building of high-performing teams whose work is needs-based and data-driven,

underpinned by a culture that values quality, effectiveness, equity and efficiency.

26  There is a strong association between social capital and learning outcomes, so schools will utilize their capacities for self-management to build an alliance of community interests to support a commitment to high achievement for all students.

27  Self-managing schools will not be distracted by claims and counter-claims for competition and the impact of market forces, but will nonetheless market their programs with integrity, building the strongest possible links between needs and aspirations of the community, program design, program implementation and program outcomes.

28  Schools will have a capacity for 'backward mapping' in the design and implementation of programs for learning, starting from goals, objectives, needs and desired outcomes, and working backwards to determine courses of action that will achieve success, utilizing where possible and appropriate the capacities that accrue with self-management.

29  Incentive, recognition and reward schemes will be designed that make explicit the links between effort and outcomes in the take-up of capacities for self-management and improvement in learning outcomes, acknowledging that as much if not more attention must be given to intrinsic as to extrinsic incentives and rewards.

30  A key task for principals and other school leaders is to help make effective the links between capacities for self-management and learning outcomes, and to ensure that support is available when these links break down or prove ineffective.

*Completing the Journey on Track 1 (Chapter 4)*

31  Schools seeking more autonomy will utilize every capacity that is made available under existing schemes of self-management, including where possible and feasible the outsourcing of services where there is a benefit to the school.

32  Schools will take the initiative in building strategic alliances with individuals and organizations possessing or supporting a higher level of self-management, including providers in the public and private sectors of education and training, and will provide support to students who are engaged in home schooling.

33  Schools will place a high priority on staff selection and professional development to ensure that knowledge and skills are consistent with professional capacities that will sustain as much autonomy as possible.

34  Schools will place a high priority on building their capacities in information and communications technology, including advanced cost accounting and management information systems, reducing as far as possible their dependence on the system in these matters.

35  Flexibilities in workplace arrangements will be utilized to the full, subject to the legal and industrial frameworks that apply, in order to secure an optimal mix and match to needs and priorities in programs for learning and the support of learning.

36  Schools will reduce their dependence on system support for learning and teaching, seeking other sources in the public and private sectors, consistent with school priorities, but without sacrificing what is needed to deliver programs of the highest quality.

37  Schools will resist through every means available to them any attempt on the part of the system to recentralize, especially in respect to matters that link to learning outcomes, including a capacity to select staff and deliver professional development programs that reflect school priorities.

38  Curriculum and standards schemes will be regarded as frameworks rather than prescriptions, and every attempt will be made to balance time and effort in key learning areas to reflect school needs and priorities, especially for, but not limited to, programs in literacy and numeracy.

39  Principals and other school leaders will be skilful in their dealings with teacher unions and other organizations representing the interests of their staff, creating alliances whose first priority is learning, and building high levels of trust.

40  Without sacrificing any source, schools will seek to reduce their dependence on funding from the public purse by seeking other substantial support, avoiding approaches that yield minimal resources from effort that diverts time and energy from the support of learning.

**Track 2: An Unrelenting Focus on Learning Outcomes**

*Setting the Agenda for Track 2 (Chapter 5)*

41  Primary (elementary) schools will select and develop teams of teachers that have state-of-the-art knowledge about strategies for success in literacy, and will ensure that these are effective and that all students learn to read well.

42  Teachers at all levels will critically examine approaches to learning and teaching in mathematics and science, guided by research, challenging assumptions and stereotypes where appropriate, and informed by the findings of

international comparative investigations such as the Third International Mathematics and Science Study.

43 Schools whose communities place students at a disadvantage and where achievement is lower than it ought to be, will work with other schools, and will secure resources from many sources, public and private, in efforts to achieve higher standards of achievement.

44 Learning outcomes for boys will be monitored and appropriate strategies will be developed to address low levels of achievement where these are evident, without sacrificing their effort in respect to learning by girls.

45 In addition to its place in the curriculum, communications and information technology will be harnessed to support learning and teaching across all learning areas.

46 Schools will seek and take up opportunities to obtain value-added data on student achievement, on a classroom-by-classroom and subject-by-subject basis, and will use the information so obtained in the design of learning for students whose achievement falls short of 'predicted' or 'expected'.

47 A range of symbols will be devised by schools to communicate and reinforce their intentions to focus on learning outcomes in unrelenting fashion, including the language of communication, public behaviour and ceremony, selection and appointment, and style of involvement of the community.

48 Schools will ensure a much broader agenda than is evident in much of public discourse, including literacy and numeracy, and without sacrificing attention to these, will build their capacity to address a range of 'intelligences'.

49 The notions of 'the learning organization' and 'the intelligent school' will be embraced, and strategies will be designed and implemented to ensure success.

50 A high priority will be placed on determining a school design that suits the setting and the needs, interests and aspirations of the school and its community, with participation in system-wide efforts to achieve scale-up of particular designs where these have proved effective.

*The New Professionalism in Action (Chapter 6)*

51 There will be planned and purposeful efforts to reach higher levels of professionalism in data-driven, outcomes-oriented, team-based approaches to raising levels of achievement for all students.

52    Substantial blocks of time will be scheduled for teams of teachers and other professionals to reflect on data, devise and adapt approaches to learning and teaching, and set standards and targets that are relevant to their students.

53    Teachers and other professionals will read widely and continuously in local, national and international literature in their fields, consistent with expectations and norms for medical practitioners.

54    Teachers and other professionals will become skilful in the use of a range of information and communications technology, employing it to support learning and teaching, and to gain access to current information that will inform their professional practice.

55    Schools will join networks of schools and other providers of professional services in the public and private sectors to ensure that the needs of all students will be diagnosed and met, especially among the disabled and disadvantaged, employing the techniques of case management to ensure success for every individual in need.

56    Professionals will work within curriculum and standards frameworks, as well as other protocols and standards of professional practice, with the same level of commitment and rigour as expected in medicine.

57    Schools will advocate, support and participate in programs of unions and professional associations that are consistent with the new professionalism in education.

58    Working within frameworks established for the profession, incentives, recognition and reward schemes will be developed at the school level that are consistent with the strategic needs of the workplace, with components that are skill-based and contain provision for collective rewards, gainsharing and team-based performance awards where these are possible and appropriate.

59    Staff will seek recognition of their work that meets or exceeds standards of professional practice, and will support and participate in the programs of professional bodies established for this purpose.

60    Schools will work with universities and other providers in a range of programs in teaching, research and development that support and reflect the new professionalism in education.


### Track 3: Creating Schools for the Knowledge Society

*Securing a Place for Schools in the Knowledge Society (Chapter 7)*

61    School leaders will help build an understanding among staff, students and others in the school community about the nature of the sweeping social

changes over the last century, and of the particular ways that transformation has affected and will continue to affect education in general and their school in particular.

62  Schools will understand that many problems of motivation and negative attitudes to work are a consequence of the major social dislocation that has followed the decline of industrial work.

63  School staff will understand that the changing nature of work and the decline in jobs in society at large will affect the school as they affect all places of work, with a higher proportion of part-time and contract appointments than in the past.

64  Portfolio work for some teachers and other professionals will be part of the employment scene, with the possibility of multiple appointments in several schools and in other organizations in the public and private sectors.

65  School leaders will be challenged to design incentive, recognition and reward schemes that will help secure loyalty and commitment among portfolio workers.

66  Student expectations will be more realistic in respect to the prospect of a job, as traditionally understood, with prospects for portfolio appointments and third sector contributions explained and illustrated in a constructive manner.

67  Curriculum offerings and approaches to learning and teaching will reflect the expectation that most workers will be knowledge workers.

68  Studies of society in schools will address the changing nature of the workplace, including an account of factors that are polarizing opportunities for knowledge workers and those displaced by the decline of industry.

69  School leaders will be advocates for a civil society and will actively seek ways of making a contribution.

70  Schools will change their employment arrangements to accommodate contract appointments and volunteer contributions from those with a capacity to add value to the school program, reflecting a commitment to the development of the third sector in a civil society.

*Transformation of Learning (Chapter 8)*

71  Approaches to learning and teaching will change to accommodate the reality that every student in every setting will have a laptop or hand-held computer, making the new learning technologies as much a part of the learning scene as books have been since the advent of systems of public education.

72  Subject boundaries will be broken and learning will be integrated across the curriculum as the new learning technologies become universal, challenging rigidity in curriculum and standards frameworks, without removing the need for learning in discrete areas as well in learning that spans the whole.

73  Schools will critically examine their approaches to the teaching of literacy and numeracy to ensure that the new learning technologies are incorporated, and every effort will be made to resource the latter without sacrificing targets for success in the basics for every student.

74  Rigidity in roles, relationships and approaches to school and classroom organization will be broken down, with multiple but rewarding roles for teachers and other professionals, more flexibility in the use of time, and abandonment of narrow specifications of class size that are rendered meaningless in the new workplace arrangements.

75  School buildings designed for the industrial age will be redesigned to suit the needs of the knowledge society.

76  Staff in self-managing schools will have critical roles to play in school design, sharing needs, aspirations and visions with architects who are tuned to the requirements of schooling for the knowledge society.

77  Information technology will pervade school design for the knowledge society.

78  Schools that serve the middle years in the Grade 5 to Grade 8 range, or thereabouts, will require major change in school design, reflecting what is known about the causes of flattened levels of achievement and motivation across the years of transition from the traditional primary to the traditional secondary.

79  School design will feature high levels of flexibility and adaptability, with the former referring to multiple uses of the same facilities in the short term, and the latter to a capacity for major redesign with minimal disruption in the medium to long term.

80  Schools will be adept at analyzing the relationship between function, form and culture in school design, helping to bring to realization a design that contributes to making schools exciting and uplifting places of work for staff and students.

*The Human Dimensions of Schooling for the Knowledge Society (Chapter 9)*

81  Schools will establish a richer range of professionals to work with and support teachers, with many of these located on site but, increasingly in

some respects, more will be located in other places as the best services are located and made available to meet the needs of all students.

82    Teachers will have access to the best resources to support their work, with many of these accessed from CD-ROM and the internet, being assisted by learning resource specialists who locate and advise on sources, and help with financial and other arrangements to protect intellectual capital.

83    Students, teachers and other professionals will increasingly work in teams, reflecting a pattern that is widely evident in workplace arrangements in other fields, with many parallels for professionals in education and medicine.

84    Schools will expand their policies and practices for the pastoral care of students, given the high expectations for all to succeed and, especially, as learning is dispersed, for schools will maintain their duty of care and will require cyber-policy on care in virtual schools.

85    Pastoral care for teachers will be important given the shift to the 'new professionalism' and major changes in roles, responsibilities and account-abilities, with professional development, individually and in teams, being one element in the strategy.

86    Issues of access and equity will be addressed in school cyber-policy, with a range of strategies including the sharing of resources among schools; partnerships with the private sector for donations and subsidies; and the creation of community-based learning centres.

87    A strategic approach will be taken to the adoption of new learning techno-logy, taking account of the time required for training, encouraging creative approaches to utilizing and sharing such technology as it comes to hand, and setting targets for universal access.

88    Virtual schooling will be a reality at every stage of schooling, but there will still be a place called school, with approaches to virtual schooling including neighbourhood educational houses, especially for the very young.

89    Lifelong learning centres that include schools will be the symbolic if not the physical centre of some communities, being the outcome of compre-hensive planning by a consortium of public and private interests.

90    New cultures for learning will take hold in schools for the knowledge society, complementing such widely accepted concepts as 'lifelong learn-ing' with approaches such as 'just-in-time learning' that allows state-of-the-art approaches to learning and teaching to be designed and delivered at short notice in any setting for all learners.

*Leadership, Management and the Heroic Quest in Learning
(Chapter 10)*

91   Leaders will create opportunities for themselves and their colleagues to gain knowledge and understanding of societal change and of the way schools will make a contribution to well-being in a civil society.

92   In all of these matters, the driving force and raison d'etre will be the provision of a quality education for every student, and every strategy and every intention will be weighed against this criterion.

93   Sound approaches to annual planning and longer-term strategic planning are prerequisites for successful school management but a wider range of approaches in matters related to strategy will be required to continue the journey 'beyond the self-managing school'.

94   A capacity for strategic thinking will be deeply embedded in a school, with a continuing strategic conversation the means by which shared understandings are developed as a prelude to formal planning.

95   There is a high level of turbulence in the environment for education and it will be difficult to make strategic plans in many matters so, under these circumstances, schools will form clear strategic intentions based on the best available information as the basis for action.

96   There will be recognition that sound strategy will take account of past, present and expected or preferred futures, so the effort will be framed by a commitment to take these into account in strategic management.

97   There will be a high level of harmony between learning, teaching and management cultures in the school, as illustrated by a commitment to empower the individual in all related matters, thus helping to create a better world.

98   Leaders will be aware that times of great success are also times of great risk, so they will work with all in the school community to search for, even stumble over, new opportunities to ensure high levels of performance in achieving the mission of the school.

99   There will be recognition that success in leadership in times of continuous and often turbulent change is as much a matter of discovering self as discovering strategy, so individually and collectively, there will be commitment to address the emotional well-being of the leadership team.

100  There will be commitment to leadership and management that views these as part of the heroic quest for learning in a civil society in which all in the school community are engaged and empowered.

# References

ANGUS, M. (1998) *The Rules of School Reform*, London: Falmer Press.

ARCHER, J. (1997) 'A different kind of union: What an innovative car company can teach educators about "new unionism"', *Education Week*, October 29, pp. 26–31.

ASSOCIATION OF INDEPENDENT SCHOOLS OF VICTORIA (AISV) (1997) *Funding Students' Learning in the Next Millennium*, South Yarra, Victoria: AISV.

AUSTRALIAN CURRICULUM STUDIES ASSOCIATION (ACSA) (1996) *From Alienation to Engagement: Opportunities for Reform in the Middle Years of Schooling*, Report of the National Project on Student Alienation during the Middle Years of Schooling, Canberra: ACSA.

BAKER, K. (1993) *The Turbulent Years*, London: Faber and Faber.

BARBER, M. (1996) *The Learning Game: Arguments for an Education Revolution*, London: Victor Gollancz.

BARBER, M. (1998) 'Creating a World Class Education Service', Presented at the North of England Education Conference, Bradford, January 6. Published by the Incorporated Association of Registered Teachers of Victoria as No. 71 in a seminar series, available from IARTV, Mercer House, 82 Jolimont Street, Jolimont, Australia 3002.

BARNARD, N. (1998) 'Reforms may spark a council jobs boom', *Times Educational Supplement*, January 9, p. 4.

BARNARD, N. and RAFFERTY, F. (1998) 'Labour set to tear up teachers' contract', *Times Educational Supplement*, January 23, p. 1.

BARRINGTON, J.M. (1994) 'New Zealand: System of Education' in HUSEN, T. and POSTLETHWAITE, N. (eds) *International Encyclopedia of Education*, 2nd edn, London: Pergamon Press, 7, pp. 4104–11.

BEARE, H. (1997) 'Designing a break-the-mould school for the future', Paper presented in a Virtual Conference of the Australian Council for Educational Administration on the theme 'Beyond the Boundaries', July.

BEARE, H. and BOYD, W.L. (eds) (1993) *Restructuring Schools: An International Perspective on the Movement to Transform the Control and Performance of Schools*, London: Falmer Press.

BEARE, H. and SLAUGHTER, R. (1993) *Education for the Twenty-First Century*, London: Routledge.

BELL, M. (1997) Presentation on 'Grant Maintained Schools' at the Successful Schools Conference organized by the Department of Education and University of Melbourne, Melbourne, June 3.

BIDDULPH, S. (1997) *Raising Boys*, Sydney: Finch Publishing.

BIERLEIN, L. and BATEMAN, M. (1996) 'Charter schools v. the status quo: Which will succeed?' *International Journal of Educational Reform*, **5**, 2, April, pp. 158–9.

BLACKMORE, J., BIGUM, C., HODGENS, J. and LASKEY, L. (1996) 'Managed change and self-management in Schools of the Future', *Leading and Managing*, **2**, 3, pp. 193–204.

BODILLY, S. (1996) 'Lessons learned: RAND's Formative Assessment of NAS's Phase 2 Demonstration Effort', in STRINGFIELD, S., ROSS, S.M. and SMITH, L. (eds) *Bold Plans for School Restructuring: The New American Schools Design*, Mahwah, NJ: Lawrence Erlbaum Associates, Publishers, Chapter 11, pp. 289–324.

BOISOT, M. (1995) 'Preparing for turbulence. The changing relationship between strategy and management development in the learning organization', in GARRATT, B. (ed.) *Developing Strategic Thought: Rediscovering the Art of Direction-Giving*, London: McGraw-Hill, Chapter 3.

BOLMAN, L.G. and DEAL, T.E. (1991) *Reframing Organizations: Artistry, Choice and Leadership*, San Francisco: Jossey-Bass.

BRADLEY, A. (1997) 'Accreditors shift toward performance: NCATE to stress candidate evaluation', *Education Week*, October 29, pp. 1, 10.

BRIDGES, W. (1995) *Jobshift: How to Prosper in a Workplace Without Jobs*, London: Nicholas Brearley.

BROWN, D. (1990) *Decentralization and School-based Management*, London: Falmer Press.

BROWN, D. (1998) *Schools with Heart: Voluntarism and Public Education*, Boulder, Colorado: Westview Press.

BRYK, A.S. (1998) 'Chicago school reform: Linkages between local control, educational supports and student achievement', Presentations with colleagues in the Consortium on Chicago School Research in a Symposium at the Annual Meeting of the American Educational Research Association, San Diego, April.

BULLOCK, A. and THOMAS, H. (1994) *The Impact of Local Management in Schools: Final Report*, Birmingham: University of Birmingham and National Association of Head Teachers.

BULLOCK, A. and THOMAS, H. (1997) *Schools at the Centre? A Study of Decentralization*, London and New York: Routledge.

BURNS, J.M. (1978) *Leadership*, New York: Harper and Row.

CAIN, J. (1995) *John Cain's Years: Power, Parties and Politics*, Carlton: Melbourne University Press.

CALDWELL, B.J. (1977) 'Decentralized school budgeting in Alberta: An analysis of objectives, adoption, operation and perceived outcomes in selected school systems', Unpublished doctoral dissertation, Department of Educational Administration, University of Alberta.

CALDWELL, B.J. (1986) *Effective Resource Allocation in Schools: A Summary of Studies in Tasmania and South Australia*, A Report of the Effective Resource Allocation in Schools Project, Centre for Education, University of Tasmania.

CALDWELL, B.J. (1991) 'Restructuring education in Tasmania: A turbulent end to a decade of tranquillity', in HARMAN, G., BEARE, H. and BERKELEY, G.F. (eds) *Restructuring School Management: Administrative Reorganization of Public School Governance in Australia*, Canberra: Australian College of Education, Chapter 10.

CALDWELL, B.J. (1993) *Decentralizing the Management of Australia's Schools*, Melbourne: National Industry Education Forum.

CALDWELL, B.J. (1994) 'School-based management', in HUSEN, T. and POSTLETHWAITE, N. (eds) *International Encyclopedia of Education*, 2nd edn, London: Pergamon Press, pp. 5302–8.

CALDWELL, B.J. (1997) 'Thinking in time: A gestalt for schools of the new millennium', in DAVIES, B. and ELLISON, L. (eds) *School Leadership for the 21st Century: A Competency and Knowledge Approach*, London: Routledge, Chapter 17, pp. 258–70.

CALDWELL, B.J. (1998) *Administrative and Regulatory Mechanisms affecting School Autonomy in Australia*, Paper prepared for the Commonwealth of Australia, Canberra: Department of Employment, Education and Youth Affairs.

# References

CALDWELL, B.J. and HAYWARD, D.K. (1998) *The Future of Schools: Lessons from the Reform of Public Education*, London: Falmer Press.

CALDWELL. B.J. and SPINKS, J.M. (1986) *Policy-making and Planning for School Effectiveness*, Tasmania: Education Department.

CALDWELL, B.J. and SPINKS, J.M. (1988) *The Self-Managing School*, London: Falmer Press.

CALDWELL, B.J. and SPINKS, J.M. (1992) *Leading the Self-Managing School*, London: Falmer Press.

CAMPBELL, J. (1988) *The Hero with a Thousand Faces*, London: Paladin Grafton.

CHASE, B. (1997) 'Paradigm lost: New schools challenge us to create new unions', *Education Week*, January 22, p. 7.

CHENG, Y.C. (1996) *School Effectiveness and School-Based Management: A Mechanism for Development*, London: Falmer Press.

CHEUNG, W.M. and CHENG, Y.C. (1996) 'A multi-level framework for self-management in schools', *International Journal of Educational Management*, **10**, 1, pp. 17–29.

CHEUNG, W.M. and CHENG, Y.C. (1997) 'Multi-level self management in school as related to school performance: A multi-level analysis', Paper presented at the International Congress of School Effectiveness and Improvement, Memphis, January 5–8.

CHONG, K.C. and LEONG, W.F. (1997) 'Singapore schooling in the 21st Century', Paper presented in a Virtual Conference of the Australian Council for Educational Administration on the theme Beyond the Boundaries, July.

COELHO, P. (1993) *The Alchemist*, San Francisco: HarperSanFrancisco.

COLEMAN, J.S. and HOFFER, T. (1987) *Public and Private High Schools: The Impact on Communities*, New York: Basic Books.

COLLARBONE, P. (1997) 'A journey of a thousand miles . . . the Haggerston journey' , in DAVIES, B. and WEST-BURNHAM, J. (eds) *Reengineering and Total Quality in Schools*, London: Pitman Publishing, Chapter 1.

COMMONWEALTH GRANTS COMMISSION (1993) *Report on General Revenue Grant Relativities*, Volume 1, Main Report, Canberra: Australian Government Publishing Service.

COMMONWEALTH OF AUSTRALIA (1996) *States Grants (Primary and Secondary Education Assistance) Bill 1996*, Parliament of the Commonwealth of Australia, House of Representatives, Canberra: Commonwealth Government Printer.

COOPER, B. (1990) 'Local school reform in Great Britain and the United States: Points of comparison — points of departure', *Educational Review*, **42**, 2, pp. 133–49.

COOPERATIVE RESEARCH PROJECT (1994) *Base-Line Survey*, Report of the Cooperative Research Project on 'Leading Victoria's Schools of the Future', Directorate of School Education, Victorian Association of State Secondary Principals, Victorian Primary Principals Association, The University of Melbourne (Fay Thomas, Chair) (available from Department of Education).

COOPERATIVE RESEARCH PROJECT (1995a) *One Year Later*, Report of the Cooperative Research Project on 'Leading Victoria's Schools of the Future', Directorate of School Education, Victorian Association of State Secondary Principals, Victorian Primary Principals Association, The University of Melbourne (Fay Thomas, Chair) (available from Department of Education).

COOPERATIVE RESEARCH PROJECT (1995b) *Taking Stock*, Report of the Cooperative Research Project on 'Leading Victoria's Schools of the Future', Directorate of School Education, Victorian Association of State Secondary Principals, Victorian Primary Principals Association, The University of Melbourne (Fay Thomas, Chair) (available from Department of Education).

COOPERATIVE RESEARCH PROJECT (1996) *Three Year Report Card*, Report of the Cooperative Research Project on 'Leading Victoria's Schools of the Future', Directorate of School Education, Victorian Association of State Secondary Principals, Victorian Primary Principals Association, The University of Melbourne (Fay Thomas, Chair) (available from Department of Education).

COOPERATIVE RESEARCH PROJECT (1997) *Still More Work to be Done But ... No Turning Back*, Report of the Cooperative Research Project on 'Leading Victoria's Schools of the Future', Department of Education, Victorian Association of State Secondary Principals, Victorian Primary Principals Association, The University of Melbourne (Fay Thomas, Chair) (available from Department of Education).

COOPERATIVE RESEARCH PROJECT (1998) *Assessing the Outcomes*, Report of the Cooperative Research Project on 'Leading Victorias' Schools of the Future', Department of Education, Victorian Association of State Secondary Principals, Victorian Primary Principals Association, The University of Melbourne (Fay Thomas, Chair) (available from Department of Education).

CORSON, D. (1990) 'Applying the stages of social epistemology to school policy making', *British Journal of Educational Studies*, **28**, 3, pp. 259–76.

CREVOLA, C.A. and HILL, P.W. (1997) 'The Early Literacy Research Project: *Success for All* in Victoria, Australia', Paper presented in a symposium on International Adaptations of *Success for All* at the Annual Meeting of the American Educational Research Association, Chicago, March.

CURTIS, K. (1986) *The Development of Funding and Resource Management in South Australian Government Schools*, Part 3 of the Report of the Effective Resource Allocation in Schools Project, Centre for Education, University of Tasmania.

DE PREE, M. (1990) *Leadership is an Art*, New York: Currency Doubleday.

DEAN, C. (1997) 'Class size pledge risks parent anger', *Times Educational Supplement*, August 15, p. 3.

DEMAINE, J. (1993) 'The New Right and the self-managing school', in SMYTH, J. (ed.) *A Socially-Critical Review of the Self-Managing School*, London: Falmer Press.

DEPARTMENT FOR EDUCATION AND EMPLOYMENT (1998) *Fair Funding Improved Delegation for Schools*, Consultation Paper, London: DfEE (May).

DEPARTMENT OF EDUCATION, SOUTH AUSTRALIA (1970) *Freedom and Authority in the Schools*, Memorandum to Principals from the Director-General of Education (Alby Jones), Adelaide: Department of Education.

DEPARTMENT OF EDUCATION SERVICES, WESTERN AUSTRALIA (1997) *School Education Bill 1997*, Materials prepared for community consultation as part of the Education Act Review Project, Department of Education Services, PO Box 7533, Cloisters Square 6850, WA.

DEPARTMENT OF EDUCATION, QUEENSLAND (1997a) *Partners for Excellence*, The Strategic Plan 1997–2001 for the Department of Education, Brisbane: Department of Education.

DEPARTMENT OF EDUCATION, QUEENSLAND (1997b) *Leading Schools: Partnerships for Excellence — The Pilot Program 1997*, Brisbane: Department of Education.

DEPARTMENT OF EDUCATION, VICTORIA (1997) *Full Staffing Flexibility: A Guide for Principals'*, Melbourne: Department of Education.

DEVEREAUX, J., EDSALL, S. and MARTIN, R. (eds) (1996) *Privatization, Competition and Schools and Colleges*, Southbank: Australian Education Union.

DIMMOCK, C. (1995) 'School leadership: Securing quality teaching and learning' in EVERS, C.W. and CHAPMAN, J.D. (eds) *Educational Administration: An Australian Perspective*, St Leonards, NSW: Allen and Unwin, Chapter 16.

DIMMOCK, C. and O'DONOGHUE (1997) *Innovative School Principals and Restructuring: Life History Portraits of Successful Managers of Change*, London: Routledge.

DIXON, R.G.D. (1994) 'Future schools: How to get there from here', *Phi Delta Kappan*, **75**, 5, pp. 360–5.

DOE, B. (1998) 'Tory competition fails to raise standards', *Times Educational Supplement*, January 9, p. 1.

DRUCKER, P.F. (1993) *Post-Capitalist Society*, New York: HarperBusiness.

DRUCKER, P.F. (1995) *Managing in a Time of Great Change*, Oxford: Butterworth Heineman.

DRYFOOS, J.G. (1994) *Full-Service Schools: A Revolution in Health and Social Services for Children, Youth and Families*, San Francisco: Jossey-Bass.

DYE, T. (1975) *Understanding Public Policy*, Englewood Cliffs, N.J.: Prentice Hall.

EDUCATION COMMISSION, HONG KONG (1996) *Quality School Education*, Consultation Document for Education Commission Report No. 7, Hong Kong: Education Commission.

EDUCATION COMMITTEE (1994) *The School Global Budget in Victoria: Matching Resources to Student Learning Needs*, Report of the Education Committee (Brian Caldwell, Chair): Directorate of School Education.

EDUCATION COMMITTEE (1995) *The School Global Budget in Victoria: Matching Resources to Student Learning Needs*, Interim Report of the Education Committee (Brian Caldwell, Chair): Directorate of School Education.

EDUCATION COMMITTEE (1996) *The School Global Budget in Victoria: Best Practice in Matching Resources to Student Learning Needs*, Final Report of the Education Committee (Brian Caldwell, Chair): Department of Education.

EDUCATIONAL PLANNING BRANCH, TASMANIA (1997) *Directions for Education*, Hobart, Department of Education, Community and Cultural Development.

EDUCATION REVIEW (1997) 'Middle school challenge', *At The Chalkface*, An Education Review Lift-out published by the Australian College of Education, North Sydney, November, pp. 13–16.

EDUCATION WEEK (1997) *Technology Counts: Schools and Reform in the Information Age*, Special Report, November 10.

ELIAS, D. (1998) 'School squeeze', *The Age*, January 31, News Extra, p. 3.

ELLYARD, P. (1997) 'Developing a learning culture', Paper presented in a Virtual Conference of the Australian Council for Education Administration on the theme 'Beyond the Boundaries', July.

ELMORE, R.F. (1979–80) 'Backward mapping: Implementation research and policy decisions', *Political Science Quarterly*, **94**, 4, pp. 601–16.

ELMORE, R.F., PETERSON, P.L. and MCCARTHEY, S.J. (1996) *Restructuring in the Classroom: Teaching, Learning and School Organization*, San Francisco, Jossey-Bass Publishers.

EVANS, B. (1993) *Leaders and their Learning*, Report for the National Project on Leadership and Management Training for Principals, Canberra: Australian Government Publishing Service.

FANTINI, M.J. (1986) *Regaining Excellence in Education*, Columbus: Merrill Publishing.

FITZ-GIBBON, C.T. (1995) *Issues to be Considered in the Design of a National Value-Added System*, General Report No. 1, London: School Curriculum and Assessment Board.

FITZ-GIBBON, C.T. (1996) *Feasibility Studies for a National System of Value-Added Indicators*, General Report No. 2, London: School Curriculum and Assessment Board.

FUKUYAMA, F. (1995) *Trust: The Social Virtues and the Creation of Prosperity*, London: Penguin Books.

GANNICOTT, K. (1997) *Taking Education Seriously: A Reform Program for Australia's Schools*, St Leonards, NSW: The Centre for Independent Studies.

GARRATT, B. (ed.) (1995) *Developing Strategic Thought: Rediscovering the Art of Direction-Giving*, London: McGraw-Hill.

GARDNER, H. (1983) *Frames of Mind*, London: Heinemann.

GAUCHER, G. (1997) *Saint Thérèse of Lisieux*, Strasbourg: Éditions du Signe.

GEORGE, P.S. and ALEXANDER, W.M. (1993) *The Exemplary Middle School (second edition)*, New York: Holt, Rinehart and Winston.

GERSTNER, L.V., SEMERAD, R.D., DOYLE, D.P. and JOHNSTON, W.B. (1994) *Reinventing Education: America's Public Schools*, New York: Dutton.

GLATTER, R. (1990) 'Review of the self-managing school', *Journal of Educational Administration and History*, January.

GMSAC (1997) 'An OFSTED view of GM performance', Excerpt from a publication of GMSAC, an organization representing governors and headteachers in grant maintained schools, available from GMSAC, Maidenhayne House, Musbury, Axminster, Devon, UK EX13 6AG.

GOLEMAN, D. (1996) *Emotional Intelligence: Why It Matters More Than IQ*, London: Bloomsbury Paperbacks.

GOODLAD, J.I. (1984) *A Place Called School*, New York, McGraw-Hill.

GOODSON, I. (1997) ' "Trendy theory" and teacher professionalism', in HARGREAVES, A. and EVANS, R. (eds) *Beyond Educational Reform: Bringing Teachers Back In*, Buckingham: Open University Press, Chapter 3.

GOVERNMENT OF VICTORIA (1986) *The Government Decision on the Report of the Ministry Structures Project Team*, Ministry of Education, Melbourne: Government Printer.

GREEN, A. (1997) *Education, Globalization and the Nation State*, Basingstoke: Macmillan.

GROSSKOPF, S., HAYES, K., TAYLOR, L. and WEBER, W. (1995) 'On competition and school efficiency', Paper presented at the 70th Annual Western Economic Association Meeting, San Diego, June 7.

GUNTER, H. (1997) *Rethinking Education: The Consequences of Jurassic Management*, London: Cassell.

GURR, D. (1996a) 'The Leadership Role of Principals in Selected "Schools of the Future": Principal and Teacher Perspectives', Unpublished doctoral thesis, Faculty of Education, University of Melbourne.

GURR, D. (1996b) 'On conceptualising school leadership: Time to abandon transformational leadership?' *Leading & Managing*, **2**, 1, pp. 221–39.

GURR, D. (1996c) 'Reply to Gronn and Lakomski', *Leading & Managing*, **2**, 1, pp. 246–8.

GUTHRIE, J.W. and KOPPICH, J.E. (1993) 'Ready, A.I.M., reform: Building a model of education reform and "high politics" ', in BEARE, H. and BOYD, W.L. (eds) (1993) *Restructuring Schools: An International Perspective on the Movement to Transform the Control and Performance of Schools*, London: Falmer Press, Chapter 2, pp. 12–28.

GUTHRIE, J. and PIERCE, L. (1990) 'The international economy and national education reform: A comparison of education reforms in the United States and Great Britain', *Oxford Review of Education*, **XVI**, 2, pp. 179–205.

HALLINGER, P. and HECK, R.H. (1996) 'Reassessing the principal's role in school effectiveness: A review of empirical research, 1980–1995', *Educational Administration Quarterly*, **32**, 1, pp. 5–44.

HALLS, W.D. (1994) 'United Kingdom: System of Education' in HUSEN, T. and POSTLETHWAITE, N. (eds) *International Encyclopedia of Education*, 2nd ed., London: Pergamon Press, **11**, pp. 6513–23.

HANDY, C. (1994) *The Empty Raincoat*, London: Hutchinson.

HANDY, C. (1995) *Beyond Certainty*, London: Hutchinson.

HANDY, C. (1997) *The Hungry Spirit*, London: Hutchinson.

HANNAN, E. (1997) 'Industrial discord', *The Australian*, August 30, p. A24.

HANUSHEK, E.A. (1996) 'Outcomes, costs and incentives in schools', in HANUSHEK, E.A. and JORGENSON, D.W. (eds) *Improving America's Schools: The Role of Incentives*, Washington, D.C.: National Academy Press, Chapter 3, pp. 29–52.

HANUSHEK, E.A. (1997) 'Assessing the effects of school resources on student performance: An update', *Educational Evaluation and Policy Analysis*, **19**, 2, pp. 141–64.

HARGREAVES, A. (1997) 'From reform to renewal: A new deal for a new age', in HARGREAVES, A. and EVANS, R. (eds) *Beyond Educational Reform: Bringing Teachers Back In*, Buckingham: Open University Press, Chapter 8.

HARGREAVES, D. (1994) *The Mosaic of Learning: Schools and Teachers for the New Century*, London: Demos.

HARGREAVES, D. (1997) 'A road to the learning society', *School Leadership and Management*, **17**, 4, pp. 9–21.

HARMAN, G., BEARE, H. and BERKELEY, G.F. (eds) (1991) *Restructuring School Management: Administrative Reorganization of Public School Governance in Australia*, Curtin, ACT: Australian College of Education.

HAYWARD, D. (1993) *Schools of the Future: Preliminary Paper*, Melbourne: Directorate of School Education.

HENDERSON, B. (1997) 'Action builds negotiations falter', *The News*, Australian Education Union, Victorian Branch, September 11, p. 1.

HENDRIE, C. (1997) 'Hornbeck trumpets improved test scores in Philadelphia', *Education Week*, September 17, p. 9.

HILL, P.T., PIERCE, L.C. and GUTHRIE, J.W. (1997) *Reinventing Public Education: How Contracting can Transform America's Schools*, Chicago and London: University of Chicago Press.

HIRSCHHORN, L. (1997) *Re-Working Authority: Leading and Authority in the Post-Modern Organization*, Cambridge, MA: MIT Press.

JACOBSON, L. (1997) 'New alliance endeavours to put schools first', *Education Week*, October 1, p. 21.

JAWORSKI, J. (1996) *Synchronicity: The Inner Path of Leadership*, San Francisco: Berrett-Koehler Publishers.

JOHN, M. (1998) 'A new forum for a new ICT [Information and Communications Technology] era', Editorial in *TES Online Education, Times Educational Supplement*, January 9, p. 3.

JOHNSTON, C. (1997) 'Leadership and learning organization in self-managing schools', Unpublished thesis for the degree of Doctor of Education, Faculty of Education, University of Melbourne.

JONES, B. (1995) *Sleepers, Wake!: Technology and the Future of Work*, (Fourth Edition), Oxford: Oxford University Press.

JÖRESKOG, K.G. and SÖRBOM, D. (1993) *LISREL 8: User's Reference Guide*, Chicago: Scientific Software, Inc.

KEARNS, D.T. and ANDERSON, J.L. (1996) 'Sharing the vision: Creating New American Schools', in STRINGFIELD, S., ROSS, S.M. and SMITH, L. (eds) *Bold Plans for School Restructuring: The New American Schools Design*, Mahwah, NJ: Lawrence Erlbaum Associates Publishers, Chapter 1, pp. 9–23.

LAWTON, M. (1997a) 'New images of teaching', *Education Week*, April 9, pp. 20–3.

LAWTON, M. (1997b) 'Chicago study credits school-based reforms', *Education Week*, November 5, p. 3.

LEPKOWSKA, D. (1998a) 'Minister promises to act on boys' failure', *Times Educational Supplement*, January 9, p. 8.

LEPKOWSKA, D. (1998b) 'Whatever happened to likely lads?' *Times Educational Supplement*, January 9, p. 9.

LEPKOWSKA, D. (1998c) 'Gap closed in a year', *Times Educational Supplement*, January 9, p. 9.

LEVACIC, R. (1995) *Local Management of Schools: Analysis and Practice*, Buckingham: Open University Press.

LEVACIC, R., HARDMAN, J. and WOODS, P. (1998) 'Competition as a spur to improvement? Differential improvement in GCSE examination results', Paper presented at the International Congress for School Effectiveness and Improvement, Manchester, January.

LEVIN, H.M. (1997) 'Raising school productivity: An X-efficiency approach', *Economics of Education Review*, **16**, 3, pp. 303–11.

LOADER, D. (1997) *The Inner Principal*, London: Falmer Press.

LOKAN, J., FORD, P. and GREENWOOD, L. (1996) *Maths and Science on the Line: Australian Junior Secondary Students' Performance in the Third International Mathematics and Science Study*, Monograph No. 1, Camberwell, Victoria: Australian Council for Educational Administration.

LOKAN, J., FORD, P. and GREENWOOD, L. (1997) *Maths and Science on the Line: Australian Middle Primary Students' Performance in the Third International Mathematics and Science Study*, Monograph No. 2, Camberwell, Victoria: Australian Council for Educational Administration.

LUEBBERS, J. (1977) 'Redundancy Award retained: But varied', *The News*, Australian Education Union, Victorian Branch, September 11, p. 3.

LYNN, R. (1988) *Educational Achievement in Japan: Lessons for the West*, London: Macmillan.

MACFARLANE, J. (1998) 'When those old certainties disappear', *Times Educational Supplement*, January 30, p. 27.

MACGILCHRIST, B., MYERS, K. and REED, J. (1997) *The Intelligent School*, London: Paul Chapman.

MADEN, M. and HILLMAN, J. (1996) 'Lessons in success' in NATIONAL COMMISSION ON EDUCATION *Success Against the Odds*, London: Routledge, pp. 312–63.

MALEN, B., OGAWA, R.T. and KRANZ, J. (1990) 'What do we know about site-based management: A case study of the literature — A call for research', in CLUNE, W. and WITTE, J. (eds) *Choice and Control in American Education Volume 2: The Practice of Choice, Decentralization and School Restructuring*, London: Falmer Press, pp. 289–342.

MARSH, C. (1988) *Spotlight on School Improvement*, Sydney: Allen and Unwin.

MARSH, C.J. (1997) *Planning, Management and Ideology: Key Concepts for Understanding Curriculum 2*, London: Falmer Press.

MARTIN, R. (1996) *Commonwealth and State / Territory Relations and Schools: Past and Future*, Southbank: Australian Education Union.

MARTIN, R., MCCOLLOW, J., MCFARLANE, L., MCMURDO, G., GRAHAM, J. and HULL, R. (eds) (1994) *Devolution, Decentralization and Recentralization: The Structure of Australian Schooling*, South Melbourne: Australian Education Union.

MESSINA, A. (1997) 'Mouse in, books out in tomorrow's classroom', *The Age*, August 11, p. A6.

MEURAT, D. and SCHEERENS, J. (1995) 'An international comparison of functional and territorial decentralization of public educational systems', Paper presented at the Annual Meeting of the American Educational Research Association, San Francisco.

MILES, M. (1987) 'Practical guidelines for school administrators: How to get there', Paper presented in a symposium on Effective Schools Programs and the Urban High School, Annual Meeting of the American Educational Research Association, Washington, D.C., April.

MILLER, D. (1990) *The Icarus Paradox*, New York: HarperBusiness.

MINTZBERG, H. (1995) 'Strategic thinking as "seeing"', in GARRATT, B. (ed.) *Developing Strategic Thought: Rediscovering the Art of Direction-Giving*, London: McGraw-Hill, Chapter 5.

MISICH, T. (1996) *Options for Self Managing Schools in Western Australia: A Discussion Paper for WA School Leaders*, A report of experiences and recommendations of Australian and New Zealand principals as reported by Tony Misich, President of the Western Australia Primary Principals Association, as recipient of the Australian Primary Principals Association 1995–96 Telstra Research Award, Perth, WAPPA.

MISKO, J. (1986a) *Effective Resource Allocation in Government Schools in Tasmania and South Australia*, Part 1 of the Report of the Effective Resource Allocation in Schools Project, Centre for Education, University of Tasmania.

MISKO, J. (1986b) *Case Studies of Effective Resource Allocation in Government Schools in Tasmania and South Australia,* Part 2 of the Report of the Effective Resource Allocation in Schools Project, Centre for Education, University of Tasmania.

MOREHEAD, A., STEELE, M., ALEXANDER, M., STEPHEN, K. and DUFFIN, L. (1997) *Changes at Work: The 1995 Australian Workplace Industrial Relations Survey*, South Melbourne: Longman.

MORGAN, G. (1997) *Images of Organization*, Thousand Oaks: Sage.

MURNANE, R.J. (1996) 'Staffing the nation's schools with skilled teachers', in HANUSHEK, E.A. and JORGENSON, D.W. (eds) *Improving America's Schools: The Role of Incentives*, Washington, D.C.: National Academy Press, Chapter 12, pp. 241–58.

NAISBITT, J. (1982) *Megatrends*, London: Future Press.

NAISBITT, J. (1995) *Megatrends: Asia*, London: Nicholas Brealey.

NAISBITT, J. and ABURDENE, P. (1990) *Megatrends 2000*, London: Pan.

NATIONAL COMMISSION ON EDUCATION (1996) *Success Against the Odds*, London: Routledge.

NATIONAL COMPETITION COUNCIL (1997) *Legislation Review Compendium*, Canberra: Australian Government Publishing Service.

NATIONAL OFFICE OF OVERSEAS SKILLS RECOGNITION (NOOSR) (1997) *Recognition of Teaching in Australia*, Canberra: NOOSR (web-site document).

ODDEN, A. and ODDEN, E. (1996) *The Victoria, Australia Approach to School-Site Management*, A Report of research sponsored by the Consortium for Policy Research in Education (CPRE) under a grant from the Carnegie Corporation and the Office of Educational Research and Improvement, US Department of Education, University of Wisconsin, Madison, CPRE, September.

ODDEN, A. and KELLEY, C. (1997) *Paying Teachers for What They Know and Do: New and Smarter Compensation Strategies to Improve Schools*, Thousand Oaks, CA: Corwin Press.

OECD, DIRECTORATE OF EDUCATION, EMPLOYMENT, LABOR AND SOCIAL AFFAIRS, EDUCATION COMMITTEE (1994) *Effectiveness of Schooling and of Educational Resource Management: Synthesis of Country Studies*, Points 22 and 23, Paris: OECD.

OLSON, L. (1997) 'Shaking things up', *Education Week*, September 10, pp. 29–31.

OLSON, L. (1998) 'Memphis study tracks gains in whole-school designs', *Education Week*, May 27, p. 9.

OSBORNE, D. and GAEBLER, T. (1993) *Reinventing Government*, London: Macmillan.

PAPERT, S. (1993) *The Children's Machine: Rethinking School in the Age of the Computer*, New York: Basic Books.

PHELAN, M. (1998) 'Ghosts by machines', *The Tablet*, January 10, pp. 40–1.

PHILLIPS, V. (1997) 'The role of accountability in student achievement', Paper presented to the Doctor of Education in Educational Leadership and Management, School of Management, Lincoln University Campus, University of Lincolnshire and Humberside, September 26–27 (available from the International Centre for Educational Leadership and Management, Lincoln University Campus, Brayford Pool, Lincoln, UK LN6 7TS).

PYKE, N. (1997) '£1 m heals reading blight', *Times Educational Supplement*, 31 January, p. 1.

PYLE, A. (1997) 'Riordan ally Ouchi is new LEARN chief', *Los Angeles Times*, March 20, pp. B1, B6.

RAFFERTY, F. (1998a) 'Minister sets tough targets for literacy', *Times Educational Supplement*, January 9, p. 4.

RAFFERTY, F. (1998b) 'Action zone news is broken in lions' den', *Times Educational Supplement*, January 9, p. 5.

REPORT OF THE COMMITTEE OF ENQUIRY INTO EDUCATION IN SOUTH AUSTRALIA 1969–1970 (1971) Peter Karmel (Chair), Adelaide: Government Printer.

REPORT OF THE INTERIM COMMITTEE OF THE AUSTRALIAN SCHOOLS COMMISSION (1973) Peter Karmel (Chair), Canberra: Australian Government Printing Service.

REYNOLDS, D. (1988) 'Foreword', in CALDWELL, B.J. AND SPINKS, J.M. *The Self-Managing School*, London: Falmer Press.

RIFKIN, J. (1996) *The End of Work: The Decline of the Global Labor Force and the Dawn of the Post-Market Era*, New York: Putnam.

SALVARIS, M. (1995) *Public Education, Citizenship and Constitutional Reform: Constitutional Guarantees for Public Education*, Discussion Paper 2 commissioned for the Australian Education Union, South Melbourne: Australian Education Union.

SCHEERENS, J. and BOSKER, R. (1997) *The Foundations of Educational Effectiveness*, Oxford: Pergamon.

SCHNAIBERG, L. (1997) 'Michigan tests show charter schools lagging behind', *Education Week*, September 24, p. 5.

SEARS, N. (1997) 'Like bees around a honeypot', *Times Educational Supplement*, December 19, pp. 6–7.

SECRETARY OF STATE FOR EDUCATION AND EMPLOYMENT (UK) (1997) *Excellence in Schools*, White Paper presented to Parliament, London: The Stationery Office.

SENATE ECONOMICS REFERENCES COMMITTEE (1996) *Report on Consideration of the Workplace Relations and Other Legislation Amendment Bill 1996*, Parliament of the Commonwealth of Australia, Canberra: Senate Printing Unit.

SENATE EMPLOYMENT, EDUCATION AND TRAINING REFERENCES COMMITTEE (1998) *A Class Act*, Report of the Inquiry into the Status of the Teaching Profession, Parliament of the Commonwealth of Australia, Canberra.

SENGE, P. (1990) *The Fifth Discipline*, New York: Doubleday.

SENGE, P. (1996) 'Introduction', in JAWORSKI, J. *Synchronicity: The Inner Path of Leadership*, San Francisco: Berrett-Koehler Publishers.

SERGIOVANNI, T. and STARRATT, R. (1988) *Supervision: Human Perspectives*, 4th edn, New York: McGraw-Hill Book Company.

SIZER, T. (1984) *Horace's Compromise*, Boston: Houghton Mifflin.

SMITH, C. (1986) *Effective Resource Allocation in Non-Government Schools in Tasmania and South Australia*, Part 4 of the Report of the Effective Resource Allocation in Schools Project, Centre for Education, University of Tasmania.

SMITH, M.S., SCOLL, B.W. and LINK, J. (1996) 'Research-based school reform: The Clinton Administration's Agenda', in HANUSHEK, E.A. and JORGENSON, D.W. (eds) *Improving America's Schools: The Role of Incentives*, Washington, D.C.: National Academy Press, Chapter 2, pp. 9–27.

SMYTH, J. (ed.) (1989) *Critical Perspectives on Education Leadership*, London: Falmer Press.

SMYTH, J. (ed.) (1993) *A Socially-Critical Review of the Self-Managing School*, London: Falmer Press.

SALOVEY, P. and MAYER, J.D. (1990) 'Emotional Intelligences', *Imagination, Cognition and Personality*, **9**, pp. 185–211.

SPENDER, D. (1995) *Nattering on the Net: Women, Power and Cyberspace*, North Melbourne: Spinifex.

SPENDER, D. (1997) 'From the factory system to portfolio living: Access, equity and self-promotion', Paper presented to the Annual Conference of the Australian Council for Educational Administration on the theme 'Beyond the Boundaries', Canberra, ACT, July.

STRINGFIELD, S., ROSS, S.M. and SMITH, L. (eds) (1996) *Bold Plans for School Restructuring: The New American Schools Design*, Mahwah, NJ: Lawrence Erlbaum Associates, Publishers.

SUMMERS, A.A. and JOHNSON, A.W. (1996) 'The effects of school-based management plans', in HANUSHEK, E.A. and JORGENSON, D.W. (eds) *Improving America's Schools: The Role of Incentives*, Washington, D.C.: National Academy Press, Chapter 5, pp. 75–96.

SWANN, R. (1998) 'Compassionate leadership in schools', Unpublished thesis for the degree of Doctor of Education, Faculty of Education, University of Melbourne.

TASK FORCE TO REVIEW EDUCATIONAL ADMINISTRATION (1988) *Administering for Excellence*, Report of the Task Force to Review Educational Administration, B. Picot (Chair), Wellington: New Zealand Government Printer.

TAYLOR, S. and McKENZIE, I. (1997) 'The team solution', in DAVIES, B. and WEST-BURNHAM, J. (eds) *Reengineering and Total Quality in Schools*, London: Pitman Publishing, Chapter 9.

TELFORD, H. (1996) *Transforming Schools through Collaborative Leadership*, London: Falmer Press.

THOMAS, H. and MARTIN, J. (1996) *Managing Resources for School Improvement: Creating a Cost-Effective School*, London and New York: Routledge.

TIMES EDUCATIONAL SUPPLEMENT (1998) *TES Online Education*, London: Times Educational Supplement, January 9.

TOWNSEND, T. (1996) 'The self-managing school: Miracle or myth?' *Leading and Managing*, **2**, 3, pp. 171–94.

TOWNSEND, T. (ed.) (1997) *Restructuring and Quality: Issues for Tomorrow's Schools*, London and New York: Routledge.

VAN DER HEIJDEN, K. (1997) *Scenarios: The Art of Strategic Conversation*, New York: John Wiley & Sons.

VIADERO, D. (1997a) 'A tool for learning', *Education Week: Technology Counts: Schools and Reform in the Information Age*, Special Report, November 10, pp. 12–13, 15, 17–18.

VIADERO, D. (1997b) 'Special assistance: Technology is revolutionalizing instruction for disabled students', *Education Week: Technology Counts: Schools and Reform in the Information Age*, Special Report, November 10, p. 14.

VICTORIA, *Education Act 1958*, Melbourne: Government Printer.

VUYK, E.J. (1994) 'Netherlands: System of Education', in HUSEN, T. and POSTLETHWAITE, N. (eds) *International Encyclopedia of Education*, 2nd edn, London: The Pergamon Press, 7, pp. 4067–77.

WATTS, J. (1998) 'High-pressure cramming class grooms young Japanese', *The Age*, January 30, p. A9 (reprinted from *The Guardian*).

WHITTY, G., POWER, S. and HALPIN, D. (1998) *Devolution and Choice in Education: The School, the State and the Market*, Buckingham: Open University Press.

WIRT, F.M. (1991) 'Policy origins and policy games: Site-based management in the United States and the United Kingdom', in HARMAN, G., BEARE, H. and BERKELEY, G.F. (eds) *Restructuring School Management: Administrative Reorganisation of Public School Governance in Australia*, Curtin, ACT: Australian College of Education, Chapter 2.

WITTE, J.F., THORN, C.A., PRITCHARD, K.M. and CLAIBOURN, M. (1994) *Fourth-Year Report: Milwaukee Parental Choice Program*, Department of Political Science and the Robert La Follette Institute of Public Affairs, University of Wisconsin, Madison, WI.

ZEIIR, M.A. (1997) 'Partnering with the public', *Education Week* Technology Counts: Schools and Reform in the Information Age*, Special Report, November 10, pp. 36–8.

# Index